Karmic Cycle

Can You Be What You Want To Be?

by

Pritam L. Ahuja, Ph.D.

authorHOUSE™

1663 LIBERTY DRIVE, SUITE 200
BLOOMINGTON, INDIANA 47403
(800) 839-8640
WWW.AUTHORHOUSE.COM

First published by AuthorHouse 07/21/05

ISBN: 1-4208-5554-9 (sc)

Printed in the United States of America
Bloomington, Indiana

This book is printed on acid-free paper.

TABLE OF CONTENTS

Dedicated
To my father who taught me that to understand
the purpose of life, there is something which goes
beyond the realms of modern science:

J ñ ā n a
(Self-knowledge)

PROLOGUE

It was my first job interview in America after emigration from India. The interviewer, while browsing through my resume, learnt that I had left as an executive and was now starting all over again in the United States. He ventured to know the reason. However, sensing hesitation in my response, he interjected, "After all, you have one life to live." That statement has stuck with me ever since. Is it true that we have one life to live, and, can we be what we want to be? Or is it that we are all, in some mysterious way, carrying on with our assigned mission in life, knowingly or not, which is predestined for us?

After years of search for the answer, and studying all available material on the subject, I came to the realization that to find a meaning in life, we need to understand first who we are, and then to seek out for ourselves how far we can go to reach our goals.

This book is a compilation of all possible human traits that should make us the best we can be, while appreciating the marvel of universal wisdom.

ACKNOWLEDGEMENT

The writing of this book would not have been possible without the untiring support of my dear wife, Saroj, who occasionally grimaced about my long indulgence with a seemingly unrewarding endeavor.

My special thanks are due to my son-in-law, Mark, who initiated me into the computer technology for script-writing, and provided constant support in the execution of this project.

I am deeply indebted to my daughter-in-law, Summi, who despite a heavy load of personal responsibilities, took on the task of formatting the final script, editing it, and seeing it through the publishing process.

To my entire family, including Mona, Mickey, Neil, Priya, Shaan and Taj, I owe this book to you.

OVERVIEW

Can you be what you want to be? Yes, if the quest is simply to survive. On the other hand, if you want to be guided by some set goals and give your own directions to life, to be the very best you can be, then delays, frustrations and defeats will inevitably occur, and these give rise to the issue of who controls our destiny? If you want to be someone who desires for a measure of immortality, a drive fueled by some spirit within individuals, the outcome depends on a number of factors, some of them beyond the control of individuals.

Why is it that some people, in spite of not showing promise of brilliance early on in life rise to be the role models or superstars, while others, despite being endowed with all the qualities of leadership, end up being run of the mill? There are many factors responsible in grooming a person to be someone distinguishable. Right from birth, the influence of parenthood, social environment, schooling, geographic location, all determine the final outcome of one's efforts. A combination of basic personal skills, drive, mentors, genetic code, and, of course, destiny play important role in what makes a person successful or accomplish what he has set out to be.

It is not by accident that we are born to those parents and placed in that environment. There are soul connections. Our setting is given to us according to what is best for our evolution. It is the past which links it to its present condition and surroundings. Tenzin Gyatso, the Dalai Lama of Tibet, was identified at the age of two as the fourteenth reincarnation of the Buddha of compassion. He was taken to Lhasa and brought up by doting monks, who tutored him in philosophy, medicine, and metaphysics. In 1950, he became the spiritual and secular leader in exile of the Tibetan people. Despite not having a power base, he is recognized as a world statesman on the sheer force of his moral authority. No human being could be more predisposed by his upbringing and by the role he has been thrust into to have pure and noble thoughts.

Dennis Quaid, a movie actor and star of such films as *Any Given Sunday, The Parent Trap, The Big Easy,* and *The Right Stuff,* is positive that fate pushed him into acting. While in college, an acting teacher inspired him to want to do this. "I believe in predetermination, I don't believe in free-will," he says. "I think things are destined to occur, and there's nothing we can actually, really do about it, the things that happen in our lives. We have the illusion that we can do something about it, but we really can't. That's not fatalistic, that's just the way it is. We are programmed. We are born with our genes—-what we are going to look like and the way we are going to be, to a certain extent. We have our chemical make-up and we have our conditioning, which is our parents." He was being interviewed about his movie *Frequency,* in which a young man and his dead father are able to transcend time and space and, may be, change the course of history.

No matter what you plan ahead, there are some karmic forces which draw you in a direction which is predestined. You have to deal with that environment whether it is people, place or personal circumstances. Karma takes us where we have to go, not necessarily where we want to go. We have to take care of unfinished business first. You carry your karma around with you. No matter what situation or circumstances you are in, same problems—-your pattern of seeing, thinking, and behaving—- catch up with you. The fact that we were born in certain circumstances indicates that our lives are molded in a particular pattern right at the outset. Our present existence has not sprung from nothing. We have brought our ideas, our instincts, and our obstacles with us. Our former lives contain the seeds of our new life. How do then people change with time from rags to riches or turn into angels or outlaws has again to do with the encounters with those situations as preordained from our past lives. It is during this course of interaction that we settle our scores with people who we have to deal with, and then, we move on from one step to the other. Where each one of us ends up to be is a cumulative effect of the past lives and the present one. There are times when we are not able to see why certain things happen to us in this life. Perhaps the cause lies in a past life. The concept of reincarnation and karma may seem rather questionable to those who assume the existence of only a single earth life. However, such an approach cannot lead to an understanding of why a person's life takes an altogether different course despite best laid plans and concerted actions.

We see that the power of acquiring knowledge varies in each individual, and this shows that each one of us has come to this earth with our own fund of knowledge. If we have not experienced it in this life, we must have experienced it in other times. It is only by believing in this approach to life that one can live in peace with oneself. There is no escape from this law of nature. It is not surprising, therefore, that two-third of the world's population believe in reincarnation, rebirth of a life force or soul in a new physical body. Reincarnation may mean that our energy or consciousness lives on after death, not that we as specific individuals are born repeatedly. A survey reported on ABC/20-20 TV program dated December 5, 2003, shows that about sixty million Americans now believe in the reincarnation of soul. Janis Amatazio, M.D., author of the 2004 book 'Forever Ours: Real Stories of Immortality' writes that after more than 25 years of work performing autopsies on the deceased and sharing experiences of their loved ones, she found that the most grieved people get vision, synchronicities, and other connections. In one instance, she talks of a woman who was awakened at home by her husband who had died moments before in a car accident. He told her where his body was located, allowing his wife to quickly direct police to the scene. We live in many dimensions at once; the appearance of being trapped in space and time is an illusion. Many invisible levels are enveloped by the physical world. The current superstring theories use at least eleven dimensions to explain the physical world. Many of the leading physicists suspect that there may be an abundance of parallel universes where time travel may be possible. There may be a nonphysical process out there that we are not yet aware of. Thus, the concept of we, as multi-dimensional beings, is not just mystical. No matter how much the medical science revolutionizes genetic understanding of the mind and body functions, or, computer technology sharpens our skills in decoding brain neuro system, the final outcome cannot be changed. We will continue to have the mysteries of life that surround us on a daily basis.

Many books have been written about the qualities of leadership, what makes a chief executive of a multi-billion dollar corporation and how these people are different from those who did not make it to the top. But, there is no emphasis laid on those who had all the skills and qualifications but remained dormant for some reason or another. That is where I shall endeavor to focus the attention. Could they have succeeded by charting a different course? The answer is no, because you have no control on what you want to be. Each person plays his role according to his karma. That which is not destined will not happen despite every effort. What is destined is bound to happen. All the activities which the body has to go through are determined when it first comes into existence. It does not rest with you to accept or reject them. The only freedom you have is to turn your mind inward and renounce activities there. When you free yourself from hate, desire, disillusionment, and all the negative emotions, you have freed yourself from the law of cause and effect. That's freedom from karma. It is an issue that needs to be addressed from a karmic point of view. Karma affects everything, there are no chance occurrences. Everything happens only when its time comes. No matter what plan you may have with all the world's expertise put into it, it can go awry for some excuse or the other. There is some one else's hand on it. That's what we need to recognize.

This subject is becoming more significant with increasing downsizing of corporate America. During these turbulent economic times our mental outlook is undergoing a change. More and more people are realizing that it is important to do what they want. They want to find their special place and fill it. They are searching for a meaning in life instead of the erstwhile life-style of a guaranteed job until retirement, even if it involves risk and a possible drop in income. They think they're entitled to a job that is emotionally rewarding and lets them discover who they are. "Blessed is he who has found his work," are the famous lines from the nineteenth century English essayist, Thomas Carlyle. For more than one hundred years, this familiar sentence has emphasized the dignity of a life's work and a life's purpose. There is now a growing awareness of the desire to profit from one's own talent in this era of self-fulfillment. Therefore, it is better to reconcile with yourself early on in life and go with the flow. Strive to achieve what you can, but don't make any claims if you succeed, or don't fret if you meet with disappointment. It is not in your hands. In the following pages, I shall show you why.

This book contains quotations from famous authors, scholars and pioneers who have made significant contributions toward the advancement of our knowledge on this subject. As you go through each chapter, you will notice contradictory statements pertaining to a particular issue. That is because of the personal opinion or experience of each individual or source. We need to draw inferences from these based upon our own level of comprehension and understanding. There is a gradual evolution of thought process as time goes by. Eventually, we learn from our personal experience and reach our own conclusions what life is all about. It is said that great innovators and proponents of new ideas are seldom entirely original; what they do is to collect together and coherently present new ideas at a time when they are just about presentable. I hope this book is a modest attempt to present ideas whose time has come.

*"Life is a sruggle to be what we are not
and to do what we cannot"* —*William Hazlitt*

Some people struggle against nature to make themselves something they were never intended to be. Yet struggle most of us do.

PART I:

BASIC TRAITS OF SUCCESSFUL PEOPLE

INTRODUCTION

*"A man is a success if he gets up in the morning and goes to
bed at night, and in between, does what he wants to do."*
—Bob Dylan

Within each one of us, there is the impulse to be the very best we can possibly be. Greatness is the real goal of every person's life. All worthwhile goals require commitment and hard work to reach. Life has no rational purpose beyond mere survival if all we do is react to whatever the world throws at us. Goals are more likely to be met if they have personal meaning and reflect your own preferences and capabilities than if they are imposed upon you by others. We need to have a purpose of our own to give direction to life. Having purpose acknowledges that you are named to be something that only you can be. Your challenge is to find it, discover it, and do whatever is necessary to realize it. Realizing one's calling is to look out to the world for signs as well as back to the seed or gift with which we were born. It also takes our gaze back into our personal histories to search for clues. It is never too late to hear your call; now is always the right time. The primary reason for our existence is to find answer to "Why am I here?" You discover the meaning of your life through knowledge, facts and feelings in your mind, body and soul. The drive for achieving greatness is fundamentally fueled by some spirit within individuals. People progress according to what they are ready for. You have a mission in your life. Believe it, with all your heart and mind. You came when and where you did because it was your destiny. Fame, fortune and power are ephemeral. They do not constitute a mission. They are tools for implementing a mission. If they are not seen as tools to implement a mission, then they exist only to satisfy ego.

Most men and women who achieve great success in any field do it by developing their natural talents and abilities to a very high degree in some special area of interest. They set big exciting goals for themselves, and then persist indomitably, sometimes for many years, before realizing them. Success comes through self-reliance, risk-taking, hard work and the courage to believe in yourself. Most truly successful people are not overburdened by stress. Nor do they achieve success at the expense of their physical and emotional health. In fact, many individuals in high-demand situations actually thrive on stress.

Success is not something you're born into. Success strategies aren't genetic qualities that some people have and others don't. Michael Jackson wasn't born with the ability to dance. Robin Williams, a stand-up comic and actor, wasn't born a creative genius. He started performing as a young kid for his mother, going, "Love me!" What drives him to perform now is the need for that primal connection. Somewhere in childhood, housed in memory, are the fears and longings that drove him to achieve extraordinary early success. Ray Kroc, the brain behind the McDonald's corporation, wasn't born into riches. It takes drive, desire, discipline and dedication. We can go through life listless and not do much with our abilities or we can pour our lives at stake and go for more. When we put our lives at risk we will be forced to live out of our comfort zone, which will create a need for us to accomplish more in life. Your success in life will be in direct proportion to your ability to embrace stress. See your problems as challenges, puzzles that have a solution.[1]

More than half of all CEOs of fortune 500 companies in America come from poor or lower-middle-class backgrounds. And eighty percent millionaires have not inherited their wealth but earned their millions themselves, taking advantage of the opportunities and believing in themselves. A 2001 national survey conducted by Caliper, a human resources consulting firm based at Princeton, NJ, found that the top executives are born with 40 percent of their leadership ability and develop the remaining 60 percent through experience. "I have always known this – instinctively – I have always believed that someday I would be very successful. I am a recent convert to the power of an optimist, self-reliant outlook," says Rush Limbaugh, Radio & TV talk show host.[2] Courage is behaving in a way that conjures up fear. Entrepreneurs recognize the fear in what they do, but they deal with it. They overcome their fears. That's why they are successful. Certainly, Ray Kroc, who was an ambulance driver in World War I, had enormous courage to think he could market food to the world by creating the McDonald's fast food chain. He pictured his empire long before it existed, and he saw how to get there. He invented the company motto – "Quality, service, cleanliness, and value" – and kept repeating it to employees for the rest of his life. For things to change in your life, it requires that you take a new and sometimes scary action. If we don't explore new paths, we'll never make new discoveries. That requires a firm and unquestioning belief in something for which there is little or no proof. Find faith in yourself and discover what makes you passionate about life. Faith is proceeding in the face of adversity with merely the slightest amount of validation. Your greatest rewards are always preceded by your greatest stresses. The stress of an action diminishes rapidly after that action is performed. The power of faith is suspending judgment long enough to gain the rewards available.

Nolan Bushnell, who cofounded Atari, the electronic game company, forerunner of today's giant computer game industry, with $500 and sold it to Warner four years later for $28 millions has the following to say: "Success boils down to just one critical action step: getting off your ass and doing something."

There is one quality which one must possess to win, and that is "definiteness of purpose", the knowledge of what one wants, and a burning desire to possess it. Pundit Jawahar Lal Nehru, in his presidential address to the Congress in 1929 for attaining total sovereignty from British rule for India said, "Success often comes to those who dare and act; it seldom goes to the timid who are ever afraid of the consequences. We play for high stakes, and if we seek to achieve, it can only be through great dangers."
[3] Winning is a war fought by visionaries and risk-takers, whose weapons are genius, determination and courage. Visionary is a man who would not be deterred. Someone who knows exactly where he is going. Vision goes beyond the present realities. It is designed to close the discrepancy between present conditions and ideal conditions. It means a projection of what your organization can become. Craig McCaw, who sold the firm he

founded (McCaw Cellular Communications) to AT&T, created a vision of the cellular technology as the growth engine of the telecom industry. Later, he conceived an entirely new way to deliver the internet by creating a constellation of 840 satellites. The system would be able to transmit signals from any point on the planet to any other with the speed and capacity of fiber-optic cable. A key part of this vision was that the internet would be possible without being dependent on wires.

Phil Knight was a mediocre in college. He was trained under the watchful eye of Bill Bowerman, the renowned university of Oregon track coach. In an effort to improve the time of his athletes, he toyed with running shoes. Their improvement became his silent passion. The innovative coach had theorized that slicing even an ounce off a runner's cleats might just prove the critical difference between winning and losing. After completing an MBA from Stanford University, Phil Knight and Bowerman formed the Blue Ribbon Sports Company in 1964 to distribute Japanese athletic shoes. But, Bill Knight's dream rested on a larger goal. He knew he was a big fish in a small pond. The sport shoe market was new, wide open, and seemingly inexhaustible. In 1971, Knight and Bowerman decided to go after a larger share of the American market by developing their own shoe. Bowerman, ever the tinkerer, fashioned a waffle iron and urethane rubber together to produce a more durable, cushioned sole. The new "Waffle Sole" proved popular and exceeded expectations. They adopted a "Swoosh" logo, and called their product Nike, after the Greek goddess of victory. In 1980, Nike went public, shooting Knight's networth to $300 million. Phil Knight and Bill Bowerman saw what those of a lesser vision didn't see and rode the crest of a booming industry.

Time magazine selected Jeff Bezos, the CEO of Amazon.com, as the cover-person of the year 1999. One of the richest men in the world, Bezos owns forty percent of the stock in his company worth thirty billion dollars today. When Bezos read a report projecting annual growth rate of Web sales at 2,300 percent in 1994, the Princeton graduate conjured up the notion of a new company in a new industry. Quitting his job as senior vice president at D.E. Shaw, a hedge-fund firm, Bezos, along with his wife MacKenzie and their golden retriever, drove West. On the way to Seattle, he wrote the business plan for what was to become Amazon. com. Five days later in the their rented house in Bellevue, Washington, they opened their new business in the garage. Jeff Bezos created a clear vision of speeding up consumer access to products that "inspire, educate, and entertain." On-line shopping is the wave of the future. Starting with books, Amazon now covers anything that one can buy on-line.

4

Success is the story of people with the courage to risk, the ability to create, and the determination to achieve. Confidence is the product not of experienced success, but of will and preparation. Some people have to work at it harder than others. If you want to succeed, you will have to learn to be confident. Donald Trump, the real estate tycoon, has a gift for recognizing opportunity before most other people do, and acting immediately. He sticks to what he knows. The only thing that makes one distinct is uniqueness. We all have to take chances in life. And mankind would be vastly poorer if it had not been for men who were willing to take risks against the largest odds. In setting out to discover a new route to India, Columbus was taking a chance that few men of his time were willing to hazard. Again, when Henry Ford started to make the first Model T, he was embarking on one of the most gigantic speculations of all times. It requires a single mindedness of approach to seek out and support or create the new fields. Courage is present at birth for many people. Some children explore more, climb higher, and show less avoidance of things that have hurt or startled them. Others develop their courage later as a result of their experiences and environment. Courage can develop in an environment where risk taking, competition and determination were emphasized, modeled, required and rewarded. Thoughts of danger and the pursuit of safety may have been discouraged or, at least, not encouraged.

Successful people, as a group, are the most persistent failures on the planet. Each failure taught them something – gave them feedback. They succeeded because of their failures. Failure can teach us what we are good at and what we are not; what we enjoy and what we hate. Once we know that, we can plan our lives better. Start thinking of failure as the first step you take on your way to success. You are what you think. Winners and losers aren't born; they are the product of how they think. Lee Iacocca was not sure he could pull Chrysler Corporation back from the brink, but he was willing to jump when challenged. He rose to the opportunity and was not afraid of failure. See good in every set back. Be prepared to fail your way to success. "A vital ingredient of sustained success is occasional failure. Decision making is a prime responsibility of those in top positions, and their batting average between right ones and wrong ones must be high," according to Malcolm S. Forbes. Great leaders must always exude self-confidence. They are never petty. They are never buck-passers. They pick themselves up after defeat. Good leaders are decisive. They have infectious optimism, and the determination to persevere in the face of difficulties. They also radiate confidence, even when they are not too certain of the outcome. Successful people are non-conformists, except in their adherence to their own ideals and beliefs. A truly successful person is essentially a dissenter, a rebel who is seldom, if ever, satisfied with the status quo. He creates his success and wealth by constantly seeking, and often finding, new and better ways to do and make things. These men rely on their own imagination, originality, individualism and initiative. Success depends greatly on self-improvement and independent thinking. Success does not come by chance. It is an opportunity that has been well rehearsed and organized.

Successful individuals are people with ideas, values, energy and guts to do what needs to be done. They have a desire to win that overrides their attachment to the past, and they have the courage to face reality even when it means eating their pride. Bill Gates proved himself the master of abandonment in 1995 when Microsoft, after disdaining the internet, virtually dropped dozens of projects and embraced the internet. It cost Microsoft millions to make the about-face. Instead of asking if Microsoft will be killed by the internet, people are now wondering if the company will dominate it.

According to Wharton School of Business report,[4] few general traits that most successful people seem to share relate one way or another to an ability to keep going in the face of failure or rebuff. They have the ability to overcome the fear of failure and inspire confidence. They remain inwardly optimistic and don't get shattered by frequent turn downs. They possess inner strength to roar back after suffering frequent defeats. They have vision. They are risk takers, not gamblers. They coolly evaluate the level of risk and are not afraid to go ahead with it. "Success is going from one failure to the next without a loss of enthusiasm," said Winston Churchill.

Rupert Murdoch, the news media and TV magnate, has a deep-seated affinity for taking risks. His great strength lies in his genius in understanding – instinctively – exactly what must be done to turn a losing property into a successful one. Like most successful people, he makes his own luck through hard work and effort, by having the right people to do a job and replacing them quickly when they fail. Murdoch is driven by forces he himself doesn't understand. He simply does what he does because he has to; it is his nature to work and plan and strive and achieve. "I am my own man," said Murdoch."[5]

William Wrigley Jr. (Spearmint gum) attributed his success to lack of fear. He said, "I have been broke three times since I started business, and it didn't cause me a minute's loss of sleep." Successful people are committed to doing their job right, no matter how long it takes or what it entails. They look on failure as a part of the process, and learn something from each one. They are the people who never stop pushing and pressuring until they get what they want. "Toughness is a quality made up of equal parts of strength, intelligence and self-respect."[6] What separates the winner and the loser is how a person reacts to each twist of fate. View any and all obstacles as lessons, not indications of failure.

It needs a diamond-hard will-power to be what you want to be. Enzo Ferrari, at the age of 20, as a post-world war I army surplus, was denied a job at Fiat. This slight by Fiat festered in his brain, creating an anger that blossomed with the passage of time. It was a debt he swore to fulfill no matter how many years it might take. He believed that Fiat's refusal to hire him in 1918 was fully repaid after half a century when he set up his own company bearing his name and took away the racing title from Fiat. Ferrari died in 1988 at the age of 90. If there was an essential quality about the man, it was his iron-bound tenacity, his fierce devotion to a single cause - winning automobile races with cars bearing his name.[7]

Some of the successful people are dreamers who see their dreams come true. Others are meticulous planners who master every detail. Some are dogged inventors, persisting despite ridicule. Others are brilliant scientists whose minds roam freely. Still others are organizers who understand that motivating teams of people is the first step on the celestial path. But all reach the expert level through skill and perseverance. All great enterprises succeed because of a combination of skills, application and luck. According to Dennis Waitely's theory, if we took all the money in the world and distributed it evenly, it would be back in the hands of the people who had it before.

You can't be what you want to be without help from less visible partners whose contributions are, at least collectively, as indispensable. Get others to do the work for you. Use the wisdom, knowledge, and the legwork of other people to further your own cause. Not only such assistance will save you valuable time and energy, it will give you an aura of efficiency and speed. Sir Isaac Newton once remarked, "If I have seen so far, it's because I stood on the shoulders of giants." Steve Jobs would not have made his mark in personal computers without the cofounder of Apple, Steve Wozniak, the technical wizard. Second, two young Steves were able to move out of the garage because Mike Markkula Jr., who had made a small fortune from Intel, helped arrange for $600,000 in venture capital financing. Third, sudden business success owes much to chance, the happenstance of stumbling at the right place at the right time.[8] Jobs's resurgence as a pioneer in digital entertainment after a dozen years of being dubbed as a washed-up former CEO of Apple is full of lessons in redemption. Joe Montana, the legendary quarter back, and his mentor, San Francisco Hall of Fame coach Bill Walsh together created something that neither could imagine. Walsh took full advantage of Montana's unique strength and his managerial ability to make each other greater than either one alone could have been. They stretched each other beyond what is imaginable. Same exhibition of excellence was the outcome of a team work of director Martin Scorsese and actor Robert De Niro in the movie Raging Bull. Steven Spielberg has set almost "impossible" goals in nearly every project he has ever attempted since he began his film career. Goals that were impossible to achieve by himself became achievable through his brilliant direction and his ability to recruit best available resources he needed to convert his dream into reality. I am personally touched by a story narrated by Zig Ziglar in his book, Something to Smile About. Nathaniel Hawthorn was heart-broken when he went home to tell his wife, Sophia, that he was a failure because he had been fired from his job in the customhouse. Upon hearing the news, she startled him with an exuberant exclamation of joy. "Now", she said triumphantly, "You can write your book!" To that, Hawthorn responded with the question, "What are we going to live on while I am writing this book?" To his surprise and delight, she opened a drawer and drew out a substantial sum of money. "When did you get that?" he asked. "I've always known you're a man of genius," she told him, "And I knew that someday you would write a masterpiece, so every week, out of the money you gave me for housekeeping, I saved part of it. Here is enough of it to last for a whole year." From his wife's trust, confidence, thrift, and careful planning came one of the classics of American literature-*The Scarlet Letter*. Talking about the role played by presidential marriages that shaped American history, Katie Marton writes in Hidden Power that many of the men for whom 'Hail to the Chief' has been played probably would have ended up as peanut merchants, obscure lawyers or morose ranchers without support from their ladies. As an example, she claims that Lady Bird made the Lyndon Johnson presidency possible by coaxing him into running on his own in 1964, when he was in the final months of John Kennedy's unfinished term. Lady Bird wrote, "Beloved, you are as brave a man as Henry Truman, FDR, or Lincoln. To step out now would be wrong for your country, and I can see nothing but a lonely wasteland for your future."

In order to get ahead, it is important to have a mentor. You need people to help you stay out of trouble, because there are others who will try to get you into trouble. You are never too big or too smart to learn from anyone. Buckminster Fuller, the brilliant and eccentric futurist philosopher, designer, engineer and architect once admitted that his passionate pursuit of the daring aspects of life on the edge was greatly facilitated by his knowledge that no matter what he might do, his wife, Anne, would always be there to support him morally and financially, which she did throughout her life. On the other aspects of success, however, he came to the conclusion after numerous jobs with large corporations that his temperament was simply not suited to working for someone else and that he was far more successful when he was self-employed and in total control of his time and endeavor. He came to believe that a single human being is far more powerful than any bureaucracy, government or industry because bureaucracies and organizations cannot think. He didn't need anyone else's approval to think or act. Also, after a series of business failures, at age thirty-two, he decided not to worry about how things worked out any longer for himself personally. Instead, he asked himself continuously for the rest of his life, "What is it on this planet that I know something about that probably wouldn't happen unless I take responsibility for it?" He also professed that if humanity is to pass safely through its present crisis on earth, it will be because a majority of individuals are now doing their own thinking.

Ally yourself with as many people as you may need for the creation and carrying out of your plan. To get what you want you must communicate with others in a way that inspires them to want to give it to you. The most powerful people on this planet are communicators and public speakers. Your success in life will be largely determined by your ability to communicate both with yourself and with other people. Self-communication is the ability to inspire yourself to take action. People who don't have the ability to bond are always judging others harshly and not accepting the other person as they are. Networking is absolutely essential for any successful venture. Choose people who inspire you, share mind-power with you, reflect and magnify your own faith.[9] Eighty-five percent of your success in life is going to be determined by your social skills, by your ability to interact positively and effectively with others and to get them to cooperate with you in helping you to achieve your goals. This, however, may not be true for a person like Einstein who said, "I am a horse for single harness, not cut out for tandem or team work."

Good timing is lot more than luck. It grows out of experience, doing your home work, and learning to trust your intuition. You have to be at the right place at the right time and be prepared to act. Perhaps, William Shakespeare said it best:

> *"There is a tide in the affairs of men,*
> *which, taken at the flood, leads on to fortune;*
> *omitted, all the voyage of their life*
> *is bound in shallows and in miseries.*
> *On such a full sea are we now afloat,*

and we must take the current when it serves,
or lose our ventures."

People who succeed learn that self understanding and inventiveness come only with time and courage. Those who can't tolerate frustration, who can't wait for answers, who become anxious when immediate direction is not forthcoming, can feel betrayed.

Facing fear head-on is one of the great qualities of successful people. Hugh Downs, former co-host of TV show, 20/20, says, "Fear or at least facing and conquering of it, is to a large extent what drives me. It is something I have had to deal with all my life. I was always full of fear. First, I was a terribly timid child. I discovered that there is only one way to handle fear: 'Go out and scare yourself'."[10] It is the desire to conquer fear that drives him to undertake difficult and dangerous tasks - to prove himself. In both, his professional and private life, Downs has resisted easy choices. "Everything I have done has been terribly chancy," he says. By facing and overcoming fears, we mature and fulfill our deepest human potential. Fear is the everyday reality of one of the most human emotions. Our growing understanding of the brain's fear circuitry gives us the tools to intelligently manage our fears. We now have the tools to transcend the destructive, irrational fears.

It is important to want to be "the best" at something. It does not really matter very much what. Success in business means sticking to what you do best. In other words, looking for opportunities that will either improve existing line of business or interact with what is already there to create synergism. Excellence means determination, working smarter and doing something different to break out of the crowd. It requires understanding of what is going on inside yourself, what you stand for, knowing what is important in terms of fundamental beliefs and basic values, having a strong faith spiritually, coupled with courage to rely on that faith, and exercising self discipline to live your convictions. It takes courage to embrace the idea that what you make of your life is up to you and to actually do what you need to do; doing what inspire you to action. Regardless of what your connection is to the divine source, cultivate it well, for you will need it to call upon it in those moments when you require courage.

If you are determined to succeed, you can find a way around any obstacle, even money. Companies that have risen to global leadership over the last twenty years invariably began with ambitions that were out of all proportions to their resources and capabilities. But they created an obsession with winning at all levels of the organization. For example, Komatsu's obsession was summed up in the slogan, "Encircle Caterpillar."

Years ago, Komatsu's available resources at the time were so meager that Caterpillar did not find much to worry about. Komatsu and many other companies defied conventional wisdom, but they did not do so blindly. What they set out to achieve was within the realm of the possible. Goal-setting, backed by will, determination and sheer desire to succeed is what it takes. Make a game of your endeavors, a game that you enjoy, but are determined to win. Look at your goals. Do they inspire you? Do they wake you up in the morning? Are these goals worthy of your talent and your effort? If they are not, change them.[11] Every person fired by an idea and free to pursue his or her dream can make history. Trust your instincts and discover unique talent that you were created for.

Some years ago, Tom Clancy was a full-time insurance salesman, specializing in selling policies on cars and boats. But, during his rare moments of idleness, he began to ponder on what he had achieved in his life. He realized that he was caught in a middle-class trap of his own making, and that there was no easy way out of it. He would have to remain where he was in order to earn enough to maintain the payments and meet all his other commitments. It was during this time, while he was in his early thirties, that his schoolboy dream of writing books surfaced. Nowadays, his insurance career is behind him, for he is a full-time adventure-story writer with nine best-sellers to his credit. His lifelong love of military hardware provided the impetus for his new career as an adventure story-teller. He had a vivid imagination, and a proven ability in English. His first book The Hunt for Red October got published in 1984 and has sold more than 4 million copies by now. In 1986, while addressing college graduates, Tom focused his mind in an effort to account for his sudden change in life. He told them: "There is a defense against the trap into which you are all about to embark, and the defense is within yourselves- Nothing is as real as a dream. The world can change around you, but your dream will not. Your life may change, but your dream doesn't have to. Responsibilities need not erase it, duties need not obscure it. Your spouse and children need not get in its way, because the dream is within you. None can take your dream away."

Walk, talk and look like the person you want to be. Our body language, facial expressions, and the energy we give off are constantly sending out messages. Recent studies show that 86 percent of our communications are nonverbal. You create impression on the first meeting mostly by the way you look and sound. When we use our voice, people acquire a great deal of information about us. We are judged by the way we sound. Careers can be damaged by an unpleasant voice. Our voice is automatically influenced by our feelings. For example, anxiety heightens breathing and raises vocal

11

pitch. Voice quality influences personality judgments. Talking assertively, calmly, confidently stimulates the production of a whole range of neuro-transmitters or brain-hormones, which affect everything from alertness and concentration to depression. Moreover, controlling your facial muscles and posture as well as your voice will eventually result in a feeling of confidence.[12] If your voice is lifeless, a real monotone, that reflects a sense of powerlessness over your problems. Confidence is an expression of an inner strength which allows us to speak out, secure in the knowledge that it is the world that is confused and not they. This confidence is not the obstinacy of the fool, but the surety of him who knows what he knows, and knows also that he can convey it to others in a meaningful way. Richard Burton, who had perhaps the most mesmerizing voice of all time, said that each morning while showering he sang a number of songs to keep his vocal cords strong and supple. You are not stuck with the speaking voice you have now. By practice, you can create the voice you would like to have. It is said about the world-renowned tenor, Luciano Pavarotti, that he trained his voice to be the expression of his soul. Peter Drucker, the management guru, was once asked why he talked so much. His answer was, "Because I learn so much when I speak. Talking helps you bring out what's inside you – to recognize every issue's many sides – and it allows you to rationalize your actions." Also, you must train yourself to always be on "high receive." When someone is speaking, stop what you are doing, look at the person, and listen. A common barrier to effective listening is the habit of mentally preparing an answer while another person is speaking. Hold your fire and patiently wait your turn to speak. Good listeners are considered great conversationalists. Listening is equated with wisdom and intelligence. The way you carry yourself will often determine how you are treated. By acting regally and confident of your powers, you make yourself seem destined to wear crown. Downplay your failures and ignore the limitations. If we believe we are destined for great things, our belief will radiate outward. This outward radiance will infect the people around us, who will think we must have reasons to feel so confident. You have to demonstrate your distinction from others by acting with dignity, no matter the circumstance. Dignity, in fact, is invariably the mask to assume under difficult circumstances. It is as if nothing can affect you, and you have all the time in the world to respond. This is an extremely powerful pose.

No body gives you power. You just take it. Those who succeed are usually the ones who go for it. Powerlessness is a state of mind. If you think you are powerless, you are. "Ready, fire, aim," that was the winning strategy what Ross Perot claims was his secret to taking EDS to the top.

The urge to achieve success and recognition also comes from a powerful awareness of personal incompleteness in early life. This feeling leads one to become a seeker fascinated with adventure and the exploration of realms beyond – new places, new experiences – as an expression of the desire to get away and seek personal fulfillment. People who may have been intrigued early in life by what lies on the other side of their natures may express this through the feeling that they are somehow destined to do something great and magnificent. It was this feeling of personal incompleteness in early childhood that led Charles Lindeburgh to his first ever trans-Atlantic flight. He wanted to prove to his stronger father that he could accomplish great feats on his own.[13] Bill Clinton, former president of the USA, like many successful people who escaped from traumatic childhood, became very ambitious and productive in the effort to overcome past injuries. Abandoned by his natural father, who died before his birth, left by his mother for his first four years while she chose to pursue a nursing degree out of state, then living with an alcoholic abusive step-father, Clinton had to assume the role of grown-up in a chaotic family situation.

> *"Lives of great men all remind us we can make our lives sublime,and departing leave behind us footprints on the sands of time." — Henry Wadsworth Longfellow*

> *"Ride on over all obstacles, and win the race." — Charles Dickens*

> *"Fortune favors the prepared mind."— Louis Pasteur*

> *"Life is a big canvas and you should throw all the paints on it you can." — Danny Kaye*

> *"You may be disappointed if you fail, but you're doomed if you don't try." — Beverly Sills*

> *"Success is 99 percent failure." — Soichiro Honda, Founder, Honda Motor Co.*

"The person interested in success has to learn to view failure as a healthy, inevitable part of the process of getting to the top."— Dr. Joyce Brothers

"God gives us a gift. But to perfect it, you have to work. You miss out on so much. You can't go to parties, to discos, stay up late. It's hard to keep playing at the same level. You suffer a lot. I think I was one of the few players who played more than 20 years at the same level- that's why I am Pele. We have only one Frank Sinatra, only one Beethoven, only one Pele."— Pele, Soccer Legend,retired at age 34 in 1974 after winning the 1970 World Cup for the third time with Brazil

"I want to bridge the gap between life and death. To me, the only success is immortality."—James Dean

Part 1 deals with some basic skills which need to be developed in order to achieve a certain measure of success. In this section, I have divided success ingredients into four categories:

1. *Passion*
2. *Persistence*
3. *Attitude*
4. *Decisiveness*

CHAPTER ONE - PASSION

"Whenever you find something getting done, anywhere, you will find a monomaniac with a mission."— Peter Drucker

There is only one success – to be able to spend your life in your own way – with an infinite passion of life. When you are passionate about a cause, a feeling of faith rises up in your heart; faith that you will do whatever it takes to make that which you care about a success. It is said that any desire that you plant deeply in your subconscious will eventually seek expression through the physical world. Concentration, a tremendous desire to make something happen, to keep moving forward, to stay true to your course and fight for your dreams is the secret of success for all superachievers. They have an unshakable belief in their ability to overcome obstacles. This mindset seemed to offer them powers unavailable to ordinary individuals. They set high standards and achieve lofty goals, often in the face of overwhelming odds and in defiance of the projections of those around them. "A man becomes what he thinks about most of the time," said Ralph Waldo Emerson.

In order to make a true impact on the world, discover your passion for what you believe in. Your passions are signs of your purpose. What gets you really excited is something of great meaning to you. You have a sense of purpose in front of you. Whatever lights your fire and propels you to action is a sign of your purpose. Give passion the credit for average people whose accomplishments exceed their abilities. In 1963, over after one year on the job, a young assistant football coach at the University of South Carolina was fired by the head coach. The head coach told him that he was not cut out for coaching and advised him to find another profession. However, the young man was committed to coaching.. He loved it and had set what, to most people, seemed an impossible goal:- Head coach at the University of Notre Dame. In all probability, the man who had just fired him would have considered that goal to be just out of reach for him. It was during this period of turmoil in his life that, while reading a book by David Schwartz, Holtz drew up his original list of 107 goals, anything from meeting the Pope to becoming the head football coach at the University of Notre Dame. Today, Holtz has achieved 99 of those goals, including that of becoming headcoach at Notre-Dame. In his biographical book, *Winning Every Day,*[1] Lou Holtz writes, "Everything that happens to us is the result of the choices we make. You choose to act or procrastinate, believe or doubt, succeed or fail, lead or follow. Find something to engage your passions. Start living your dreams. Whatever you choose, it should propel you out of bed every morning hungry to accomplish something." When a man gets into his head to do something, and when he exclusively occupies himself in that design, he must succeed, whatever the difficulties. Concentrate on a single goal, a single task, and beat it into submission.

Shortly after she had made her acting debut in *The Color Purple,* and while her daily talk-show was starting to be syndicated nationally, Oprah Winfrey appeared in her first interview with Barbara Walters. In response to a question as to what was it like growing up in the deep South with terrible feeling of discrimination, she said, "I discovered very early in life that there is no discrimination against excellence." Her phenomenal success as a TV talk-show host is due to her passion for her work and for excellence. In an interview for her role in a movie version of Toni Morrison's book *Beloved,* she said, "I have always had faith that my life will be fine. God can dream a bigger dream for you than you can dream for yourself, and your role on earth is to attach yourself to that divine force and let yourself be released to it."

You need real passion. It is the essential driver for whatever you do. The risks are far greater, but the rewards outweigh any sacrifices. You need a personal vision and mission to identify what you can do better than anyone else. Maintaining this vision is the hard part for most people. For many it is too easy to give it up when the struggle and discomforts of the current reality set in. But successful creative people are capable of adhering to their vision and resolve the tension by dealing with the obstacles. Kris Kristofferson, a Rhodes scholar, golden gloves boxer, song writer and actor, was born and reared in Texas. He was the only son of Air Force major general and it was assumed that he would follow his father into the military. After school he joined the army and became a pilot.

He loved to fly but his chaotic spirit was constrained by military ways. Finally he quit the military. He was discovering what life would teach him repeatedly: that there was a crucial difference between who he was and who he thought he should be. When he was a boy, music reached him with a force that was non-negotiable. "It felt like something I needed," he says. In it he discovered what he calls "honest emotion." So, leaving his family, he headed for Nashville, where he got a job as a janitor at a recording studio. By day, he mopped floors. At night, he hung out at traverns and swapped songs. "It was enough to keep me alive and in touch with the world I was trying to enter," he remembers. As time passed, he fell in love with the music and the musician's life, which he construed as his salvation. Eventually, he landed a gig on "The Johnny Cash Show". That was the beginning of his passion come true. At the age of 62, Kris rekindled his acting career with roles in two movies *Blade,* and, *Dance With Me.*

At 21, Salma Hayek became one of Mexico's most popular soap opera stars on Teresa. But after just eighteen months, she decided to leave for Hollywood. "I was famous, but it wasn't what I wanted," Hayek recalled. "I wanted to make movies. When I decided to move to the U.S., I didn't know if it would happen. I only knew I was giving up what I didn't want." In 1995, she got a break in *Desparado* with Antonio Banderas, which made her a star overnight. Comedian Jerry Seinfeld had been driven for years by fame and fortune until those drives withered through satisfaction. In a New York Times interview, he acknowledged that he has kind of graduated from show business (TV Series). "I have no further need of this business. It's not about money any more, and it's not about fame. Now, it's just about maintaining a creative arc (standup comedy)." People committed to their creative passion are usually happier and more active. Their values give them energy, direction, meaning, and goals.

James Wood, the veteran film actor known for his role as a rebel and misfit in movies like *Salvador* and *Citizen Cohn,* was a scholastic student and won a scholarship to MIT. While performing in school's drama workshop, he found that he was not only naturally good at acting but also enjoyed it immensely. He left MIT without completing his degree in pursuit of his love for theater and acting. Most of his friends thought he was insane. His mother was an exception. She supported his decision to go for his passion, but asked him to promise that he will do his very best he can be and make her proud. She told him, "Whenever you follow your heart, the best things happen." He kept his promise. Today, James Wood is busy performing memorable roles which he is well known for.

In 49B.C., Roman General, Caesar made a crucial decision to cross the river Rubicon with his army, thereby effectively declaring civil war against Pompey, who held power in Rome. It was illegal for a General to bring his troops out of the boundary of his command, and the boundary between Caesar's command and Italy was the Rubicon. Once he crossed the Rubicon and ventured into Roman heartland, he knew there was no turning back. Either he and his soldiers would take the city, or Pompey would destroy them. Caesar's decision changed the course of history. The proverbial saying 'crossing the Rubicon' defines that critical moment in which a person moves from a motivated state, waffling about intentions, to a volitional state, acting with willpower toward solid objective. Pop singer, Jewel Kilcher, now an international star, loved the arts – literature, drawing, dance, music – as a child. But she could not pursue any of these demanding careers due to financial constraints. Her parents were divorced and mother Nedra could barely provide for their survival. As she grew, Jewel decided that singing and song writing meant the most to her. Still, she couldn't help feeling a flicker of fear. "May be I should have a fallback plan," she suggested to her mother. "If you have a fallback plan, you will fall back. You are young. Be brave. Have faith in yourself," mother responded. So the decision was made. After facing a lot of rough shods, her breakthrough came in 1996 when *Pieces of You* went gold more than a year after its release. By the time her second CD *Spirit* was released in 1998, Jewel had an international following. If her mother had encouraged her to have a fallback plan, she would have made one. "I was scared, but being safe didn't mean being happy." Happiness came instead from following her passion and realizing there could be no turning back. Early on, while performing in bars and taverns, she observed first hand what happens to people who lose their passion for life and end up merely existing. And she vowed it would never happen to her. Another popular country music singer, Faith Hill says, "I was fourteen when I consciously decided to become a singer. I had an image of myself performing in front of people. I believe you have to envision things to make them happen." She was chosen to perform National Anthem at superbowl 2000.

As you pursue your vision, you will discover an unfolding of an unpredictable process. You get flashes of insight to best accomplish the task. Your body chemistry changes and you get new surges of motivation and energy. If you stay on course and hold on to your dream, it will come true. All of us need to do something that we know is the next step in the journey of our soul's unfoldment, and most of us know deep in our heart what that is. There is only one thing that no one can give you, motivation and determination. You will have to get this from within. Your own ability and insight will often show you new paths which may even be better suited for you. Success comes from your ability to respond, incorporate and act upon information from within and without. Follow your dream, may be the rest will fall into place. Leaders can born and they can be developed. While skill in diplomacy can be a great asset, the most important requirements are the ability to carry a vision and to have courage.

Robert H. Schuller, the world-renowned evangelist, proclaims in his book *My Journey* that as long as you have a burning desire and a dream, you can go anywhere from nowhere. He coined the term 'Possibility Thinking' while trying to raise funds for the $15 million Crystal Cathedral in Garden Grove, California in 1975. He preaches that you change your outlook from impossibility to possibility. With faith, hope, optimism and energy, you can transform a seemingly impossible concept into a reality. "Invest all you have in your dream. Visualize miracles. Expect to experience success. Believe it. If you can dream it, you can do it," is his sermon. His dream came true on September 14, 1980, when organ music filled the space of the world's largest all-glass auditorium. From his boyhood on a poor Iowa farm, Robert Sculler became a counselor to Presidents and an inspiring vioce to millions.

When you are doing something you love to do, you transform your energy level, you experience a sense of freedom. You feel liberated, creative, unaware of time, and in harmony with yourself. Living a fulfilled, exciting, adventurous life is what keeps energy and enthusiasm up. The key to choose a course in life is doing what you enjoy the most, and then pursue it with all your strength and vigor. The opportunities are there all the time. It's our burning desire that enables us to see them. When the desire to fulfill a mental picture is strong enough, the opportunity will appear. Be sure your objectives excite you so much that they give you a driving desire to accomplish. Start concentrating on doing what it is you could do better than anyone else in the world. Fill your day with an activity you enjoy doing so much that you would do it even if you were not getting paid for it. Then figure out a way to get paid for it, and work to become the best in the world at doing it.

Successful entrepreneurs start and build a business with much the same attitude as a recreational runner takes toward a marathon. They do it simply for the joy of doing it. Once they have given birth to it, they will move on or use it to accomplish some other purpose. Success is making a fortune doing something you'd choose to do even if you were not getting paid for it. Align your talents with your desires. When you do that, everything drops into place for you. Michael Jordan is genuine excellence. No one has ever played the game the way he does. He's taken it to a new level. He has reinvented basket ball. Those who really make a difference create a whole new way of doing business in their part of the market. According to Virginia Postrel, author of *The Hidden Power Of Play,* while there are many spurs to creativity, one of the most important is the power of play – the things we do for their own sake, for fun, for the pleasure of overcoming the challenges they present. Innovation requires a different spirit. The spirit of play leads us to experiment, to try new combinations and to take risks – sometimes with spectacular results, she says. But first you have to have ideas and then indulge in play. The work of renaissance artists like Leonardo Da Vinci and Michelangelo came out of the mental attitude of play. The founders of the internet directory Yahoo! were graduate students just fooling around to index all the information on the web, just for fun. Without knowing it, they had created a vast market through their play.

If you want to get lucky, then spread confusion in your wake. Don't let the ruts get deeper than they already are. Break with the past and recreate your future. And don't back away from passion. When you see your future, it will start to happen. A fierce determination to succeed is characteristic of those who survive and thrive in all arenas of life. "I have always thought of problems as challenges," said Sam Walton, founder of Walmart. Excellence is an attitude and a way of life. Learn to play when the game gets tough and you'll be able to play the game when it's easy. The moment that you make a decision to proceed forward, providence has a funny way of taking over. The universe has a way of aligning and allowing you to accomplish what you set out to do. The phenomenal success of Apple Computer had more to do with its founder Steven Job's ability to get people excited than it did with technology. Many people were involved with the computer industry at the time and yet one of the major reasons that Apple did so well is that Jobs was able to make the ride so much fun. When you are specific about where you're going, and you are so passionate that the trip looks fun, then it is easy to invite and inspire others to come along.

An extraordinary will to succeed and an intense desire to be different is the hallmark of all successful people. You just have to believe in what you are doing so strongly that it becomes a reality. The principal forces which motivate a person are an incredibly high need for personal achievement and a different vision of the world. Have an extraordinary level of optimism and believe that you can do anything. Believe that your dream is worthwhile and you deserve to have what you want. Also, understand that we don't always see immediate results. Sometimes there are lags or setbacks, yet everything happens for a reason, whether we understand it or not. See setbacks and defeats as temporary challenges that can be overcome by will and courage. By defying the verdict, constantly exhibiting courage, and actively tackling the work required – all while maintaining the sense of humor – one can triumph over adversity. Changing the strategy or aiming for another target is not defeatism. Defeat or disappointment can be used to revisit and reformulate aspects of your dream. If something is not working or if the current methods are not effective, then assess the situation and find new ways to reach the goals. Sometimes, if not always, struggles and sufferings are necessary to achieve greatness.[2]

A creative individual builds a company for the same reason a mountain climber climbs, a painter captures a flower arrangement, or a landscaper creates a lovely garden. It happens because of complete dominance of the mind with one idea. "Put your ass into the ball," said Sam Snead while helping president Eisenhower to improve his golf swing.

"Once a necessity arose within him and was expressed, it happened – all hindrances were surmountable," someone said about the famous Hindu mystic, J. Krishnamurti. It takes great self-discipline and faith to keep passion burning in your heart when all the circumstances of fate seem to work against you. You must welcome the obstacles you face as you pursue your dream recognizing that they are the very tools you need to build a foundation strong and stable enough to support the realization of your ultimate purpose. By following your inner voice, you have designated yourself for greatness. You are not yet ready to reap the reward, but that is only because where you are truly going is far greater than any future you have anticipated for yourself. Anything less – as dazzling as it may seem to you at the time – is an illusion. You owe it to yourself and to the world to do something fresh, new, unexpected, daring. So take a risk. If you hope to make the transition from lowliness to the heights, there is only one way. You must be willing to lose it all.[3] It is the spirit that counts. The time may be long, the vehicle may be strange or unexpected, but, if the dream is held close to the heart, and imagination is applied to what there is close at hand, everything is still possible.

You must learn to first trust what you want, allowing it to take root and grow inside you, and then take it out to the world. Trust your vision and stay open to it. Devotion of any kind produces a zealousness in a person, a kind of fervency. Commit yourself to what you believe in, more than anybody else. Sam Walton, founder of nation's number one retail store, said, "I think I overcame every single one of my personal shortcoming by the sheer passion I brought to my work. I don't know if you are born with this kind of passion, or if you can learn it. But I do know you need it. If you love your work you will be out there every day trying to do it the best you possibly can, and pretty soon everybody around will catch the passion from you – like a fever."

Power of the mind can, in fact, draw the things, people and circumstances necessary to convert desires into results. The more certain you are about your purpose in life, the more focused you will be in the present, and the more enthusiastic you will be in your day to day work. Thus, you set in motion a self perpetuating cycle of enthusiasm and success.[4] Fulfillment comes from dedication and service to a worthy cause, whether as a foot soldier or as the commander-in-chief. Henry Ford was a chief engineer with Thomas Edison's light company in 1895 when he drove his own model car on the streets of Detroit. Thomas Edison believed that electrical power was the fuel of the future, scoffed at the combustion engine and discouraged Ford's work in developing cars as a public transport. Regardless, Ford left Edison in 1899 to pursue his dream, and founded the Ford Motor Company in 1903. Ford's fundamental business decision to make "a car for the great multitude" drove his success. It led to the development of the economical Model T in 1908. Within a few years of building his revolutionary factory, Ford Motor Company was producing half of the cars in the world. He was a man without formal education, but a person of single-minded will. Although few researchers in science or medicine work alone anymore, the greatest breakthroughs come from brilliant individuals with a passion for understanding the world and the ability to concentrate obsessively on a problem until they have solved it.

All success springs from thinking. Not only success but everything else first comes into being as a thought in mind. If we can get it firmly into our head, and eternally keep it at the forefront of our mind, that thinking is the material of which success is made. The billion dollar steel corporation, U.S. Steel, was a thought in the mind of one individual, Charles M. Schwab.

Wernher Von Braun, pioneer of the rocketry, as a 19 year old engineering student dedicated much of his vacation time to the pursuit of "scientific hobby." He was obsessed with the notion that one day he would soar through the heavens and explore the mysterious universe. His imaginative solutions to technical problems were hailed and accepted by the inner circle. He said, "One day huge rockets would carry me into space." At age 19, he propounded 'rocket theories' and exchanged mathematical equations and proposed solutions in rocket design and propulsion with such luminaries as Albert Einstein. In June 1945, after World War II, he was brought to the USA from Germany. Hitler, recognizing Von Braun when he was only 31 years old, for A-4 rocket successful launching in 1942 said of him:- "Most people waste the best years of their lives on accomplishments of no consequence. But rarely, very rarely, a great talent accomplishes much at young age."[5]

Our vision links us to a journey. We "hear" the decisive message from within ourselves, or find it in dreams, myths, literature etc. – examples of values, expressions or energies that inspire, touch us deeply, help us reveal our true self. Spiritual life helps us define our directions.[6] "Follow your dreams or stick to your conscience, even if you are the only one in a sea of doubters," said Ronald Reagan. When you feel passionate enough about something to spend a lot of your time at it, you acquire an intuitive feel for it that can be instrumental in the unearthing of opportunity. Intense familiarity with a subject develops intuition and hunches that tip us off to things before other people know it.

To overpower all forms of resistance to achieving our goals is called will-power. Will-power is so common among highly successful people that many see its characteristics as synonymous with success: a maniacal focus on goals, willingness to 'pay the price,' ability to defeat any opposition and surmount any obstacles. However, psychologists are virtually unanimous that fundamental belief in "powerlessness" (Karmic function) cannot be changed readily. They are developed early in life. For most of us, beliefs change gradually as we accumulate new experiences – as we develop our personal mastery.[7]

The key to the doorway to happiness is honoring your passion. It is the intense emotional and spiritual connection with your deepest interest. A recent case is narrated in the Reader's Digest of a fire-fighter in the Bronx's Engine Company, Dennis Smith, who discovered his passion by writing in four short paragraphs a letter to the editor of The New York Times in protest against an article he had read in their book review. It narrated that William Butler Yeats, the Nobel Prize-winning light of the Irish Literary Renaissance, had transcended his Irishness and was forever to be known as a universal poet. This hurt the pride of Dennis's Irish ancestry in that Irishness was not something to be transcended. He just knew that he had to write that letter to the Times, in the same way a priest has to pray, or a musician has to play an instrument. He had never written anything before of much substance. The editor of Times was impressed with his sentiments and decided to publish the letter. This led to a series of interviews and requests to him from publishers to write a book about his life. And so, he wrote "Report From Engine 82," which went on to sell two million copies and got translated into twelve languages. This was followed by three more best sellers. Dennis Smith started searching his mind as to how did all that happen? The clearest explanation he found was that he felt so strongly about the subjects he was writing for that something burnt within him as he wrote. He felt a fire deep down in the pit of his stomach. That's why he stood up for Ireland's greatest poet.

"People who don't invest their words with the passion they feel rarely get the response they were hoping for."
— unknown

"Part of setting a goal is finding a way to reach it."
— Charles Schwab

"Nothing great was ever achieved without enthusiasm."
— Ralph Waldo Emerson

"To gain that which is worth having, it may be necessary to lose everything else."— Irish Political Activist Bernadette Devlin

"You cannot discover new oceans unless you have the courage to lose sight of the shore." — unknown

"When you believe in something, believe in it passionately." — unknown

"When you are inspired by some great purpose, some extraordinary project, all your thoughts break their bonds: your mind transcends limitations, your consciousness expands in every direction and you find yourself in a new, great, and wonderful world. Dormant forces, faculties, and talents become alive, and you discover yourself to be a greater person by far than you ever dreamed yourself to be."— Patanjali

"I wouldn't mind being in jail if I had three cellmates who were decent bridge players."

— Warren Buffett, billionaire investment czar, chairman, Berkshire Hathaway Inc.

"Point of life is to make sure that we do not die with our music still inside us." — *unknown*

"If you keep on going and put your mind to anything, you can achieve it." — *Madonna; on the eve of her HBO special concert August 26, 2001, after more than 20 years of sustained limelight*

"Being a musician is who I am and what I love doing. I am what I always dreamed of doing. When I go on stage, something lights up. It's spontaneous and it's natural. It's a sense of power. When it clicks, it's the best feeling in the world – at times, probably better than sex."— *Enrique Iglesias, pop singer, writer, actor*

Getting started, getting finished – both ends of a journey require a demonstration of passion. It took nineteen years for Christopher Columbus to find a sponsor for his trip. All this long, he endured the agony of public humiliation for his conviction that he can establish a new trading route by sailing West. "I've found that it's better to be alone and acting upon the truth in my heart than to follow a gaggle of silly goose doomed to mediocrity," he wrote.

CHAPTER TWO - PERSISTENCE

"History shows that if you hold on long enough,
something always happens."—Winston Churchill

Persistence is a measure of belief in yourself and your ability to succeed when the going gets tough, It is the ability to endure when you have no assurance of success. All our experience has meaning. Each development was necessary for our growth. Nature has its own rhythm and time cycle. You accept all your experience and give it a meaning. In most of life's endeavors, characteristics like persistence and self-discipline are much more important than the kind of talent measured by standardized tests. Success in high school has little or nothing to do with success in life.

To win you have to make sacrifices. The hardest part of sacrificing to get what we want is that there is no guarantee that we will get it. Winning is not only abnormal, it is unpredictable. You can have all the talent and all the opportunities in the world, but if you cannot bring an exalted level of feeling to what you do, if you cannot enjoy the process as well as the outcome, then the journey is not worth the effort. Patience and perseverance are two cardinal virtues to extract meaning and purpose from events occurring in our life. Herman Hesse won the Nobel prize in literature in 1946, but earlier in his life he seriously considered suicide, so deep was his conviction that there was no point to living. His talent as a writer blossomed later in life and his books explored problems of personal identity, inner meaning and hidden purposes of life. The difficulty of his own road illuminated his writing, which in turn inspired a generation.

Rethink your ideas about goals, persistence, success and failure. Focus on testing your ideas and look for that which is easiest for you to do, that can take you in the direction you want to go. Mark Victor Hansen failed miserably in construction business. He went bankrupt. He quit the entire industry, turned his back on everything he knew and had studied for, on all his experience, and decided to try an entirely different field. He quickly discovered he had a special knack and love for inspirational speaking. Presently, his book, *Chicken Soup For The Soul,* and sequences have climbed onto and stayed put for months on the New York Times bestseller list. On the other hand, his co-author, Jack Canfield had $48,000 in the credit card debt when he invested time and money in attempting to sell this book. Although this would seem to be an outlandishly high risk to the outsider, the entrepreneur feels sufficiently in control to proceed. The successful people vary their rhythms and patterns, change course, adapt to circumstance, and learn to improvise. They step back and look where they are going. They recreate themselves by forging a new identity. Incongruity means the end of the known road, an abrupt terminus, a place where you have to jump. "It is a place that is so dangerous and threatening that it has the power, for a few, to change the way they see things and demand from them not an incremental improvements, but the exceptional, unorthodox work that creates revolutions," says James Gleick in his book, *Chaos: Making a New Science.*

There are virtues to having tunnel vision, especially when it inspires you to keep going where lesser mortals would have quit —- but not if it comes at the expense of good judgment. William Boeing had a legacy of integrity and rock hard ethics. His never-say-die attitude epitomized as a motto for the world-renowned airplane manufacturing company. Nolan Ryan, the legendary baseball pitcher, when interviewed at the age of 45, while still playing the game, said, "I have the attitude that if you are going to do something, you have to be committed and make the sacrifices it demands." You may feel quite overwhelmed many times. But, somewhere deep in your body there is a voice to remind you, "Don't give up, hang on." That is if you remain persistent.

Few general traits that most successful entrepreneurs seem to share relate in one way or another to an ability to keep going in the face of failure or rebuff. They have ability to overcome the fear of failure and inspire confidence. They remain inwardly optimistic and don't get shattered by frequent turn downs. They have the inner strength to roar back after suffering defeats. They have vision, are responsible for their action and not afraid of taking calculated risks. [1] Joe Liemandt was a 30-year old chairman and chief executive officer of an Austin, Texas-based company called Trilogy Software Inc., he started in 1990 after dropping out of Stanford University. In building Trilogy to more than $100 million in revenue, he learned that taking risk and suffering the consequences are a crucial part of the business and he wanted new hires to understand the experience first-hand. A month into her job at Trilogy, Lauren Arbitter, a 21-year old college fresh-out stood at a roulette wheel at a Los Vegas casino along with 35 other new recruits and, egged on by her coworkers and bosses, put down a $2,000 bet. Until she joined Trilogy, she never thought of herself as a gambler. If you really want something, don't let anything get in the way. Have the guts to go for it. Don't miss the chances life gives you, you might not get anymore. Take a risk.

Of twenty venture capital funded start-ups in Silicon Valley, four go bankrupt, six lose money, six do okay, three do well and one hits the jackpot. Success is the byproduct of an exceptional number of failures – vigorous tries that don't amount to anything. On the other hand, by creating an innovation that leapfrogs what's already there, can put big companies out of business. For example, AT&T is stuck with billions of dollars in copper wire buried in the ground in the age of fiber optics and wireless. It does not need a huge amount of capital to start a company and to get its products or services into the hands of the customers. *Inc.* magazine publishes an annual list of the 500 fastest growing companies in the United States. In one list, it states that about a third of these companies came to life with less than $10,000, over the half with less than $50,000, and three-quarters for less than $100,000. However, to eventually roll out a company's product or services across the globe may take millions and the help of venture capitalists and kindly bankers.

Success, statistically speaking, is merely the by-product of the far more numerous failures. Lots of tries, lots of time spent, lots of possibilities explored, and may be a hit or two will ensue. A common thread that ran through all famous men and women is that they all seemed to have, or to develop, an unshakeable belief in their ability to overcome all obstacles and reach some great heights. Fortune magazine ran an article on products rejected by customers at the first go. The list included Chrysler minivan, Post-its, VCRs, fax machines, FedEx, CNN, Cellular phones and even heart-assist pumps. It took 12 years for Post-it note's inventor Art Fry to transform his notion into a market place success. (Now 3M is booking in the neighborhood of $1 billion from Post-its and ancillaries). Products that invent/reinvent a market are rejected at the start by customers, a painful process that can take years to work out. The lesson is that those who survive the agony of early rejection or continuing rejection end up being only ones who transform the world. New York Times best seller book, *Chicken Soup for the Soul,* was turned down by 33 publishers before Health Communications Inc. agreed to publish it. All the major New York publishers said, "Nobody wants to read a book of short little stories." Since then, over 7 million copies of this series have been sold worldwide, with the books translated into 20 languages. "One of the secrets of success is to refuse to let temporary setbacks defeat us," said Mary Kay, the cosmetic queen.

Succeeding takes courage and initiative. It takes the willingness to ask the questions, to make the phone calls, to write the letters. All too often we can think of a possible answer to our dilemma, or a way to maximize an opportunity, but we shy away from it because we hesitate to make an investment, we fear rejection, or we simply think that the odds are too long. You have to take action. Within each setback is contained the seed of triumph. One should be fully prepared to take any risk or pay any price in order to accomplish something that he really believes in. When a man is in the right path, he must persevere. It is a go-aheadedness, this determination not to let the horrors or the blues take possession of you, so as to make you relax your energies in the struggle for independence, which you must cultivate. Nine out of ten rich men in USA started out in life as poor boys, with determined wills, industry, perseverance, economy and good habits. Bill Gates, founder of the Microsoft company, and the richest man in America, says in his book, *Business @ the Speed of Thought,* that ignoring bad news is a formula for decline. Business must stay alert to change. Once you embrace unpleasant news not as a negative but as evidence of a need for change, you aren't defeated by it. You're learning from it. It's all in how you approach failures. "The weight of all the failures at Microsoft could make me too depressed to come in to work. Instead I am excited about the challenges and by how we can use today's bad news to help solve tomorrow's problems," he says.

Mental toughness means developing self-esteem, being in physical shape, focusing on important issues. Ken Rosewall, the great tennis player from Australia, was masterful in ruling out the past and focusing on the present. Brain does not change its software quickly. It takes about two months of concentrated struggle, and that's why many players never correct fundamental mistakes in their game. They don't have the patience and determination. They desire quick fixes. But the brain does not work that way. Be willing to take risks in order to learn. The capacity for pleasure in learning is one of life's great gifts. Try not merely to play, but win. Change your mind and attitude toward the match. Give yourself the license to win.[2] Former NBA star and US senator Bill Bradley, in his book *Values of the Game,* shares some insights he learnt in the world of basketball. He says adversity offers a richness of experience all its own, and even victory itself has pitfalls. "Victory is the more subtle impostor. When you begin to expect it as a continuum instead of seeing it as a reward that has to be fought for, you are in trouble." Julius Erving, the great Hall of Famer basketball player once said that sustaining focus after a failure isn't a problem—indeed, it might even sharpen your alertness—because you would be intent on making up for the mistake. It's after you've pulled off a great play that focus is difficult, because there is strong temptation to dwell on what you just did. By the time you finish congratulating yourself, the opponent has scored three baskets.

Studies have shown that people who hoped (and strived) for success were happier and accomplished more than those who feared (and expected) failure. If you are willing to accept the initial failures on your way to success, you will find the energy you need to keep digging until you hit pay dirt. What may seem defeating at first is really constructive, you are building bridges that will eventually take you to where you really want to be. So don't let failure stop you from trying. You can make much progress toward realizing your everyday and life goals if you keep digging.[3]

Follow realistic goals, and you will feel better about yourself. Tolerate frustration and stay with the project. Every step of the way, you will see improvement, and from that, experience great pleasure. During this uncomfortable time, if you understand and enjoy the learning process and the sense of growth it brings, you will feel tremendous gratification. But, it wouldn't be immediate and it will be mixed with frustration: being mentally tough matters. Being able to perform under stress, you make your own luck. Stress is an inevitable part of life. While it is true that we can learn, by making intelligent choices, not to make things worse for ourselves in certain ways, there are many things in life over which we have little or no control. Stress is part of life, part of being human, intrinsic to the human condition itself. But we can learn to find meaning in it and grow in wisdom and compassion. If we do not achieve our goals according to our time table, we assume the negative and tend to give up on the whole process. In truth, a dead-end usually points out that we are still short of our preparation or we need to go in a different direction. It is those who have developed the resilience to absorb life's shocks and conflicts – without passivity, blaming, bitterness, or self-destructive behaviors – who are best able to enjoy their life. Resilience is the ability to roll with the punches; it is faith, even in the bleakest and loneliest of times, that you can be stronger than life's perversities. It is the people who bank their inner resources to survive setbacks again and again. When faced with emotional crises, they have learnt to sleep on major decisions and wait until they can respond in a calm, measured way. Setting goals and planning for the future is a stronger factor in dealing with adversity.

Believing in oneself and recognizing one's strength is important. Changes, even the most pleasant of them, always produce stress and anger.

Anger is the strong energy of not wanting things to be the way they are and blaming someone (often yourself) or something for it. But people who learn how to turn stress in their professional life to productive or creative use seem to thrive and feel more alive. If the turmoil caused by our emotions tends to make time move faster, it follows that once we control our emotional responses to events, time will move much more slowly. This altered way of dealing with things tends to lengthen our perception of future time, opens up possibilities that fear and anger close off, and allows us the patience that is the principal requirement in the art of timing. Keep a tight rein on your emotions. Adopt a detached, philosophical attitude. Be patient. Don't be overwhelmed and feel as though you have to do everything in a day. Many of the important endeavors take time. But, when we find the right moment to act, the plan must be executed with speed and force to bring things to a swift and definitive conclusion.

Formula for success is focused persistence. People who concentrate their time and energies on relentlessly pursuing one or a very few goals achieve the highest levels of success. Success favors those who are determined to make their own luck. If you make it a regular practice to keep your eye on the ball and your mind on the task at hand, wondrous things can sometimes happen. There is a Japanese proverb, "Fall seven times, stand up eight." And, "Keep going and you will win." "A man who takes chances also risks a fall." It was once said about Albert Einstein, "He does not wear socks and forgets to cut his hair, could be retarded." After Fred Astair's first screen test in 1933, the memo from the MGM testing director said, "Can't act, slightly bald, and can dance a little!" Successful people are persistent and take immediate action. When they decide on an idea and a plan, they will do whatever it takes to accomplish their objective.

Age is not a factor in holding on to your dreams. Your are not old until you have lost all your marvels. Your best and most productive years are in front of you. Successful people constantly find new ways to challenge themselves, new ways to invigorate themselves, especially when they reach middle age. They avoid burnout. General Mac Arthur said, "In the central place of your heart, there is a recording chamber. So long as it receives messages of beauty, hope, cheer and courage, so long are you young." If you continually introduce new learning situations and put yourself at some risk, even an older, developed brain can sprout new foliage and make new neural connections. Neuroscientists are now fully coming to appreciate that in contrast to the digital, hard-wired switchboard, there is extraordinary flexibility in the brain. They mean the brain is flexible, that it can be reshaped and structured by experience. By altering the activity and the structure of the connections between neurons, experience directly shapes the circuits responsible for such processes as memory, emotion, and self-awareness. Lack of experience can lead to cell death in a process called "pruning". This is sometimes called a "use-it-or-lose-it" principle of brain development. In other words, you're not necessarily stuck with the brain you were born with. Arguments continue, though, over how much of mental ability is fixed at birth by biology, and whether nature or nurture is more important in shaping perceptual powers and behavior.

America rejoiced senator John Glenn's return to glory with the shuttle *Discovery's* launch in October 1998. He turned 77 on July 18th. He is tenacious yet patient in the pursuit of his mission, and those traits have served him well. That's why he broke the coast-to-coast flight record in 1957. Why, in 1962, he became the first American in orbit. And that is why, on October 29, he was the oldest human to fly in space. In response to a question as to why he ventured to undertake that risky space mission in 1962, he responded, " While I was not rushing to leave this life any more than anyone else, I have always felt that it is more important how you live your life than how long you live." There are many painful effects of normal human aging. Muscle atrophy and cardiovascular shifts, sleeplessness and weakening of the immune system, in addition to the brittling of the bones and partial impairment of memory. There are similar changes to the body that astronauts endure in weightlessness before recovering fully soon after returning to the gentle pull of earth's gravity. What he saw in these two situations was a mission, a legitimate scientific research to explore the new human frontiers, as well as an inspiration to older people to be more active and productive. It is not just living longer that matters; it's what one chooses to do to make something more meaningful and rewarding out of those years. Ralph Waldo Emerson said, "We don't count a man's years until he has nothing else left to count."

It is often said about highly successful people that they are individuals who got up one more time than they fell down. Perseverance is a great element of success. A person who fails, fails because he is not willing to shoot for the moon, to give his dreams all that he has. It is just a matter of time until the offsetting positive to any negative occurrence makes its appearance. Law of averages plays an integral part in the individual's ultimate triumph. Colonel Sanders supposedly approached over one thousand restaurants before he finally succeeded in getting one to carry his chicken recipe on its menu. Keep asking and you are almost sure to get results. For eight years, the struggling young writer wrote incredible number of short stories and articles for publication, and for eight long years they were rejected. Fortunately, he did not give up. Finally, after many years of effort, he wrote a book that has deeply affected the entire world and helped him to become one of the most influential writers of the '70s. His name is Alex Healey, and the book *Roots*, which was made into one of the most watched television miniseries of all times. Another Afro-American who has become the best-selling author of a number of books recently, represents a remarkable example of perseverance, sacrifice, and faith. Her name is Iyanla Vanzant, the author, a radio and television talk-show host, and an inspirational speaker. She was reportedly raped when barely nine years old. She had a child at age sixteen and a nervous break-down at age twenty-two. She spent eleven years on welfare. She earned a law degree and became a criminal defense attorney. Iyanla is a living proof that it is not where you start or even what happens to you along the way that's important. What is important is that you persevere and never give up on yourself.[4]

Perseverance grows out of inner confidence in ourselves and our abilities. A steadfast belief in ourselves and, by extension, our goals, makes us tenacious. To give in is to give up on ourselves and our dreams. Walt Disney went bankrupt several times and had a nervous breakdown before he finally met with success. Albert Einstein failed math. And Scottie Pippin, a guard for the Chicago Bulls, was equipment manager for his high school basket ball team before he actually played on the team. The talent in all these individuals was there, but so was perseverance.

The life story of late Orville Redenbacher is a classic example of persistence. He is America's popcorn king. By the age of sixty-three he had spent a decade and many thousands of dollars crisscrossing the country, pursuing what nearly everyone thought to be a foolish dream: selling hybrid specialty popcorn at nearly two and a half times the regular price. Buyers at supermarkets all had the same reaction. No one would be willing to pay more than the going rate. Yet, Radenbacher persisted. "Anything worth having is worth striving for with all your might. Be persistent. That's all there is to it. There are no magic formulas," he was fond of saying. Today, Orville Redenbach's Gourmet Popcorn is the world's leader in a market that sells in excess of one billion pounds of popping corn each year.

Quality of persistence sets up in one's mind some form of spiritual, mental or chemical activity which gives one access to supernatural forces. De Gaulle returned to power after thirteen years, on his own terms. In spite of his efforts to hasten that time, the call did not come for thirteen years, and when it did, he gave France his greatest legacy - a new constitution providing for a strong presidency which produced stability in the country.

After eight years of wandering in the wilderness – at the age of sixty-five – Winston Churchill was called back into office to lead Britain in the darkest hour. Until then, he stuck to his guns. Donald Trump, in his book, *Surviving At The Top* says, "If the story of my deals proves anything, it is the value of perseverance in the face of adversity."

Hang in there, even when no one seems to believe you. Wendy's assailed the unassailable by starting a third hamburger chain when McDonald's and Burger King had the market sewn up. Wendy's took two attributes, "hot and juicy" and based their entire marketing campaign around that theme line. The company prospered.[5]

Thomas Paine wrote, "I love the man that can smile in trouble, that can gather strength from distress, and grow brave by reflection. It's the business of little minds to shrink, but he whose heart is firm, and whose conscience approves his conduct, will pursue his principles unto death."

"If I were asked to give what I consider the single most useful bit of advice for all humanity it would be this: Expect trouble as an inevitable part of life and when it comes, hold your head high, look it squarely in the eye and say, I will be bigger than you. You can't defeat me."— Ann Landers

"I know instinctively that my unyielding drive was my most important asset. Perseverance will always be just as important as talent."— Joan Rivers

"Be patient. You'll know when its time for you to wake up and move ahead."— Ram Dass

"If you are satisfied just to get by, then step aside for the man or woman who isn't."

— Arthur G. Gaston, the dean of black entrepreneurs

"Press on. Nothing in the world can take the place of persistence. Talent will not; nothing is more common than unsuccessful men with talent. Genius will not; unrewarded genius is almost a proverb.Education alone will not; the world is full of educated derelicts.

*Persistence and determination alone are omnipotent."—
Calvin Coolidge*

*"Persevere without hope of success or fear of failure."—
Gandhi*

*"Certainly, at times you lose confidence, but I always
believed I was going to make it. I just thought it may
take a while. It's a matter of perseverance, luck, and
being ready when opportunity does arrive."— Tony
award-winning actor, Nathan Lane, talked about
hanging in there. It took him a long time, against heavy
odds, to realize his dream.*

Human limits, sometimes, force us to get pessimistic about our goals, but, in the long run, persistent seeking enables people to achieve great things, almost giving semblance to the execise of free-will.

CHAPTER THREE - ATTITUDE

*"Relate to every circumstance in your life as something
that has happened for the best." — Napoleon Hill*

Your attitude is under the direct control of your will. You can decide what is going to be every minute of every day. A positive mental Attitude is a generally optimistic and cheerful way of greeting the people, problems and events that you encounter throughout your day. James Ballard, in his book *What's the Rush?,* says that many people wake up each morning with a vague sense of dread, anxiety associated with their inability to predict or control their futures. They feel powerless; they worry about their future, about money, about their health. It seems they can do nothing to change things. But they can do something – they can change their mind. You are not the doer in life, but the instrument of action of a larger plan. "We are not in control anyway; it is acting as if we are that exhausts us," says Deepak Chopra.

Positive self-image allows you to 'over believe' on goals when the "facts" as you see them may not justify your pursuit of them. It enables you to persevere even when circumstances are difficult. It helps you use a crisis as an opportunity, not a defeat. It shows you the way to keep yourself pointed in a positive direction.[1] Go ahead and feel proud. Let your mind linger for several minutes on the success you already are. Your positive qualities are just as real as the negative ones. Mind moves in the direction of its dominant thoughts. When you are expecting opportunity to occur and you are preparing for it, not only will you be ready when it does pop up, you will also find it in more places since that is what you are looking for. Opportunity is when preparation and circumstances meet. "When the student is ready the teacher appears," says an ancient Buddhist expression. Despite the circumstances, try to maintain a subjective attitude of optimism and reasonable control. A perception of control involves the freedom you feel to shift your attention and activity to those things you believe are important. Many doctors have begun to realize that cultivating an optimistic outlook is just as important as maintaining a healthy diet and getting a moderate amount of exercise.

Henry David Thoreau, the famous scholar, writer said, "If one advances confidently in the direction of his dreams and endeavors to live the life which he has imagined, he will meet with a success unexpected in common hours." It is said about Indira Gandhi, "She had the confidence of one who sees her destiny fulfilled."

The greatest discovery of our generation is that a human being can alter his life by altering his attitude of mind. By maintaining a playful attitude toward life, one tends to be more creative. John F. Welch Jr., former CEO of the General Electric Company, gives the credit to his mother for molding his character. "Whenever I got out of line, she would whack me one. But always positive. Always uplifting. Always constructive. Control your own destiny – she always had that idea." According to Jack Welch, the real test of leadership is to deal with new things, to find yourself regenerating, create a new environment and come up with a fundamentally different approach. "When you flunk those tests, you leave," he affirms. Today, General Electric is the most admired company even though it's not the best performer in financial terms. The reason is admiration for Jack Welch, who has rewritten the book on management while keeping *GE* huge, nimble and immensely profitable. Welch's vision is "how to anticipate change, how to cope with change, and how to change a very big company that does many things well." In his biography called, *Jack: Straight From the Gut,* published in September 2001, he makes the following comments: "Throughout my 40 years at GE, I've been called by many names. Truth is, down deep, I've never really changed from the boy my mother raised in Salem, Mass."

Art Williams, an award winning high school football coach, and a successful businessman, wrote in his book *Pushing-up People*, "I made up my mind a few years ago that I was going to be as happy as possible, no matter what happened. I decided that my life was going to be a great experience."

Energies from outside a person, and changes brought about from within through physical, mental, emotional, or spiritual activities, all leave an impression on an individual's energy pattern. Thoughts attract energies similar in structure to themselves, so that blocks are quickly built-up. When we feel depressed, our thoughts attract similar patterns of energy in the vicinity so that we may quickly find ourselves sinking deeper into negativity. If we exert our will in time to attract a positive-thought block, it will immediately change the situation for the better. While science has recently revealed that one's genetic predisposition clearly plays a role in an individual's characteristic way of responding to the world, most social scientists and psychologists feel that the large measure of the way we behave, think, and feel is determined by learning and conditioning.

Positive thinker is one who assumes success before it becomes a reality, in order to make it happen. The individual is largely responsible for his own life, achievements and success. It is not the positive thinking itself that does it. It merely energizes the system that you set up to make positive things happen in your life. You must set goals. Positive thinking gives it power to achieve them. Henry Ford, a great visionary, recognized the power of optimism when he said, " Whether you believe you will succeed or fail, you are right." He understood, perhaps better, than most of us how one's outlook on life has a lot to do with what one does with that life. Optimism is more of an attitude or a decision to view the world in a certain way. And the decision is ours; it is not a character trait that people are born with. Our outlook plays a large role in how things go in our lives. Positive thinking is useless in the hands of people with no goals, no dreams, no hopes.[2]

What counts the most in life is not so much what happens to us or what does not, but rather how we make meaning out of what life presents us. The happiest, most well-adjusted people share this magical trait— the ability to make meaning from life's experiences in a way that truly serves them. Each emotional state we experience results in the brain producing neuropeptides and neurotransmitters. As an example, when we feel powerful and invincible, our brain produces a substance similar to interleukin 2, one of the most powerful substances known to destroy cancer cells. When we feel depressed, the brain produces substances that inhibit the immune system. When we feel calm and settled, we produce a natural tranquilizer similar to valium. A fascinating characteristic of such states is that it is not only the brain that experiences the state, but the whole body. Each cell in the body has neuroreceptors for receiving the chemical signal put out by the brain. From a biochemical perspective, then, the whole body experiences the emotional state. Master your emotions. The roots of emotions (anger, fear, shame) take hold in childhood. When emotional reflexes steer our actions, we are not acting in our best interest. An emotional response to a situation is the single greatest barrier to a successful outcome. Emotions cloud reason; if you cannot see the situation clearly, you cannot prepare for and respond to it with any degree of control.

Anger and emotion are strategically counter-productive. You must always stay calm and objective. Be as fluid and formless as water; never bet on stability or lasting order. Everything changes. Success comes from the rapidity with which you can change.

"I never think of the negative," Donald Trump said, summing up his philosophy of life. "All obstacles can be overcome." If things don't work out as you had hoped, there might be a good reason. Be grateful, surviving all the screwy things is what life is all about. Your attitude toward defeat is crucial to mastering it. You can see it only as a loss or as a chance for gain. If you accept defeat as an inspiration to try again with renewed confidence and determination, attaining success will be only a matter of time. The secret to this is your positive mental attitude. Believe in fate, but stalk your goals. Take responsibility for how you view and respond to life in general and your circumstances in particular, by taking the initiative rather than being complacent, and responding to circumstances rather than reacting to them.

The word crisis has two roots, danger and opportunity. We tend to forget or overlook the important opportunity often locked up in crisis. If Ford Motor Company had not learned from the Japanese and had not made "quality" its' top priority, it would not be today the country's most profitable automaker. Revlon company has come up with a tiny, disposable, make-up samples of lipstick and eye-shadows, with the paranoia about sharing make-up samples triggered by the AIDS epidemic, the system is guaranteed to be a success, and is another example of a positive response to a crisis.[3] James Barksdale, the charismatic CEO of *Netscape*, is a world class example of coolness under crisis. In his days at *Federal Express,* he worked his way through the tough times of doing battle against the giant *UPS* (then known as United Parcel Service). Later he became a key figure at *McCaw Communication* when the company fought valiantly against *AT&T.* In the mid-1990s he was instrumental in navigating *Netscape* through the near-crisis caused by *Microsoft corporation.* Bill Gates and *Microsoft* decided to challenge *Netscape's* Navigator's dominance in providing internet devices. Even during the times when the competitive threat was most intense, Barksdale had a calming and reassuring effect on his employees. There are no such things as problems, there are opportunities. Learn to see your stresses and struggles as challenges and opportunities, not liabilities or handicaps. Very seldom do opportunities stand up and wave a flag at you; they more likely come disguised as problems or failures.

Opportunities for adventure await us at every turn of life's road, but will appear only when we learn to drive fear of the unknown from our minds. We must be courageous and open-minded enough to move beyond what is comfortable to us. It doesn't matter how many times you fail, you are never a failure until you start to blame other people. Blaming other people is an escape mechanism. To overcome the fear of failure, you must have a sincere motivation to do what you want to do. Then you just do the best you can, and you don't have to worry about it. Sincere motivation removes fear and gives you self-confidence. In July 1978, Lee Iacocca was on top of the world. From his huge presidential site in Dearborn, Michigan, he had just led Ford through two record years during which the company had earned over three and a half billion dollars. He had been president for eight years and a Ford employee for 32 years, ever since he left college. One day Henry Ford called him to his office and fired him. When Iacocca pressed him to ask for the reason, Ford responded, "Well, sometimes you don't like someone." The next day Iacocca was working out of a tiny transition office in a warehouse. Lee Iacocca didn't stay defeated very long by the ruthless way Henry Ford fired him. He understood that neither Ford, nor anybody else, was running his life. Within two weeks he got control of Chrysler and turned his greatest misfortune into his greatest opportunity. Nobody can make you inferior without your consent. To some people, life is like the weather——it just happens to them, and they have no control. To others, it is an exciting adventure that they totally orchestrate and direct.

George Burns, who began a solo career near the age of 80 after the death of his wife, Gracie Allen, liked to tell the story of how NBC-TV came to him when he was 90 years old and asked him to sign up with them for a five-year contract. The comedian said, "Five years! How do I know you'll be around for five years?" Two years later, NBC's parent, RCA, was bought up by General Electric. George Burns stayed around until his one-hundredth year.

For things to change in your life, you have to change. You develop an attitude of positive expectancy, formulate objectives that will lead you to what you want in life, and then intensify your belief that you will succeed. Successful people appear to be lucky because, in some mysterious way, they know how to control their circumstances. It is said that Bill Clinton has always followed a pattern of waiting until luck comes his way, which seems to happen quite often. It's not blind luck, but an instinctive sense of timing combined with manipulated design. In politics, at several critical points when his career seemed threatened, he had been lucky about who his adversaries were and skillful at forcing them to overplay their hands against him. It is self-defeating when you no longer feel responsible for your own future and therefore your success. It is destructive to think that

41

anyone or anything else can be responsible for our life because it simply isn't so.

All growth and progress requires you to move out of your comfort zone in the direction of something bigger and better. Greater success and happiness are only possible when you are willing to feel awkward and uncomfortable during the process of creating a new comfort zone at a higher level of effectiveness.[4] You have to take a risk in pursuit of happiness. Like it or not, change, instability and insecurity are a fundamental part of our world. If insecurity is a given, why not make ourselves happier by taking the risk of doing what we love? You always need to maintain a sense of personal control, high self-esteem and an optimistic attitude against all odds. Helplessness is the enemy of happiness and the ally of fear. Our low self-esteem stems in large part from our thinking, colored by past experiences. Perhaps we get stuck in the often deep and still bleeding wounds of childhood. When you lower your expectations, your self-esteem and productivity are enhanced. Try to be more naturally sensitive to the needs of other people, and avoid making constant comparisons between yourself and others. Develop inner strength to feel comfortable in different situations and value yourself.

Having positive attitude is the thing. Under all circumstances, walk, talk and look like a winner. "When you are down, stay calm and have a positive attitude. Just play it well, no matter whether you win or lose," says Chris Everett, the veteran tennis star. A remarkable example of this attitude was displayed on July 9, 2000 at the Wimbledon grand slam final tennis match between Pete Sampras of the United States and Patrick Rafter of Australia. Patrick was leading by one set and was 4-1 in the second set tie-breaker when nerves took control of him. He went down and eventually lost the match. Sports columnists commenting on Pete's record breaking thirteen grand-slams and seventh Wimbledon victory said that Sampras prevailed against Rafter not because of his punishing serve, or his workman-like volley, or his laser-like forehand, but because of sheer will. Empty your mind of fears, insecurities, hates, regrets and guilt feelings. Immediately start filling your mind with creative and healthy thoughts. Think your way to success and happiness. Never ask from weakness, even if you are down and out. Asking should be done of equals, by equals and for equals. Instead of saying "It is a problem," say "That sounds like a challenging opportunity." Consciously change the images you are holding about yourself. Soon your mood will change as well, along with your sense of life's possibilities. We can either face the music of our lives or shrink from the encounters during difficult times and live a diminished existence. In the moment of crises, see your sufferings as a hand coming from the higher power to pull you into a new story, a tale in which the wounding occurs in the middle, the ending of which is the birth of a new grace. Personal wounding opens us to the large reality that we contain. You have forces within yourself that will allow you to see your way through tests and challenges, regardless of their level of difficulty. Trusting these forces is the key. When you wake up in the morning, visualize all the positive energy that is available within you and will be there for you in all situations. This expectation must be cultivated and consciously affirmed every day.

Look at things with a detached view. Instead of fearing any event in your life (especially failure), try viewing your experience with detachment, as if you had no stake in the outcome. Then the solution will come out of hiding. Whatever happens is meant to happen. In this state of mind we are free of fears that restrict us in our ability to deal effectively and creatively with life; we experience a natural connectedness with things. We can see clearly so that we recognize solutions which formerly were hidden from us. Fear keeps us from taking action, and if we don't act, we never get beyond where we are now. But our fears disappear when we confront them. And once we take charge of ourselves, we can have, do and be anything we've ever dreamed of. We all have fears and weaknesses, or some vulnerabilities that we carry from childhood and spend our lifetime concealing. That's why we respect people who seem completely at ease and impervious to mistakes and failures. By learning to shrug off emotional assaults, they come across as fearless. Part of the art of making life look easy is the ability to control nervousness and self-doubt. When you exhibit self-doubt, you no longer seem in control. People will instinctively pull away from you.

It is no longer possible to achieve alone in this world. Treat everyone you meet as a potential customer, someone with whom you may develop a strategic alliance in the future. Men and women with high level of self-esteem can get along with almost anyone and in almost in any situation.

Build on your past achievements for future success. Achievement is something which you enjoyed doing well and which gave you a feeling of pride. It stirred your emotions, gave you a lift. What others think is of no importance, all that counts is your own opinion of your achievement. For a man who knows his own abilities and uses them, there is no ceiling to success. Each step forward leads on to greater ones. And thus, in making a habit of success, he will find that success has made a habit of him.[5] When you see your future, it will start to happen. Determine what you intend to give (sacrifice) in return for achieving your goals. There is no such reality as 'something for nothing'. Self-esteem, when all said and done, comes from within. In an interview with the Los-Angeles Times, Grammy-winning artist, Alanis Morissette admitted that she was depressed for a year because she was not satisfied with her award winning album *Jagged Little Pill*. Selling millions of records and winning international acclaim had a downside for her. "I thought fame and success should solve your problem, that there would be a sense of peace or self-esteem raised by having all this external success," she said.

Fear dulls the mind. It destroys dignity. Be aware of every form of fear and wash it away. Don't let it remain with you for a single minute. "There is no innocence where there is fear, jealousy, attachment," says Indian sage J. Krishnamurti. Learning to live without attachment means that you don't have to put up with everything that happens and to let go if that is best for you. "Fear is like fire, If you don't know how to handle it, it can kill you. But, if you use it correctly, it can warm your house," said Mike Tyson's trainer, Gus D'Amato. That happens to be true in the business world as it is in boxing. Don't feel out of your element when things are not going well. With a positive attitude, you can take a losing proposition and turn it around. Crisis can be turned into an opportunity. The most important thing is not to blame yourself. Try to take it less personally. Be teflon-coated. Flexibility in the face of change is the most valuable source.

Be assertive. Assertiveness means respecting yourself, expressing your needs and defending your rights. It also means respecting the needs, feelings and rights of other people. When we are assertive, we usually feel better about ourselves and more self-confident. Speak positively, express appreciation, be optimistic, accept responsibility, be cooperative, say exactly what you mean and tell the truth. According to theorist Albert Bandura, who we are and what we do depends not only on our "competencies," or abilities, but also on "expectancies" based on our own experience. Not surprisingly, people who feel competent and expect to succeed are likelier to do so than those who don't. What we wish and expect for ourselves governs the response we get.

> *"Everything can be taken from a man but one thing:*
> *to choose one's attitude in any given circumstances, to*
> *choose one's way."*— *Victor Frankl*

> *"Your talent determines what you can do. Your*
> *motivation determines how much you are willing to do.*
> *Your attitude determines how well you do it."*—*Lou*
> *Holtz*

"The world is as you see it." — Yoga Vashista

"Meet with triumph and disaster and treat those two impostors just the same."— Rudyard Kipling

"Whatever the mind can conceive and believe, it can achieve." — unknown

"Nothing gives one person so much advantage over another as to remain cool and unruffled under all circumstances." — Thomas Jefferson

"The greatest discovery in our generation is that human beings, by changing the inner attitudes of their minds, can change the outer aspects of their lives." — William Blake

"Since I came to the White House, I got two hearing-aids, a colon operation, skin cancer, a prostate operation and I was shot." He paused. "I have never felt better in my life." — Ronald Reagan, about his first term in office

"Give every challenge the best shot you can, and then accept the outcome with equanimity."— Dr.Rosenfeld, M.D., author of 'Live now Age Later'

"No matter what, keep swinging."— Louis Armstrong, Jazz legend

"Face life, not as a victim, but as a master, in control of your life situations, circumstances, and environment."— unknown

"Strength, style, and attitude is what differentiates a winner from a loser."— Cliff Drysdale, tennis commentator

CHAPTER FOUR - DECISIVENESS

"You cannot end up a winner in a world where you
haven't decided what to conquer." — John P. Imley

Indecisiveness is a common obstacle to success . People who have trouble making decisions often are afraid of failure. Even people who know they have done careful research and given a project their best let themselves bogged down in indecisiveness. They fret and stew, and while they do this, they fail to make timely decisions. Failure is not the end of the world. In fact, you can make mistakes and still be a valuable member of the society. People who refuse to decide and act, even if they might be wrong, don't move up. Take a stand and make independent decision. Excessive concentration upon one's activity is detrimental. Once you have decided what to do, let it happen.

Men who succeed reach decisions promptly, and change them, if at all, very slowly. Men who fail to reach decisions change them frequently and quickly. Indecision makes an unsettled mind. An unsettled mind is helpless. Most people spend months deciding whether or not to get into a business, later finding out their hunch was right, and now it is too late to capitalize on the idea because so many others are doing it. The reason ineffective people take so long to make decisions is that they are afraid they will make the wrong ones. Generally, people get stuck in indecision when they have not successfully faced and dealt with setbacks in the past. If they got burned in the past, then they will tend to back off and doubt their decision even though they feel strongly committed to it. To remedy this situation, it is better to experience a lot of failures than not to have tried. Even if a decision is not perfect, it may still leave you in a better position than if you had done nothing. Believing in your ability to make decisions that are in your best interest is a crucial element to personal growth. Be prepared to experience successes and failures. Don't expect miracles or overnight transformations. Expect instead to learn some things about yourself, some things about the ways in which you make decisions. Such awareness of self should translate into wisdom and smart judgments.

To overcome discouragement, believe even more in yourself and your ideas, and trust your instincts. Persistence and belief in your inner guidance are fundamental to success. Effective people don't worry about making a mistake after they have made the decision. If things don't work out the way they planned they will make another decision to get them out of their present challenge and take with them the knowledge that they learned from the previous decision. Worry is a state of mind based upon fear. Worry is a form of sustained fear caused by indecision. Therefore, it is a state of mind which can be controlled. We don't worry over conditions once we have reached a decision to follow a definite line of action. Kill the habit of worry, in all its forms, by reaching a general blanket decision that nothing which life has to offer is worth the price of worry. With this decision will come poise, peace of mind, and calmness of thought which will bring happiness.[1] If you are unsure of a course of action, do not attempt it. Your doubts and hesitations will infect your execution. Timidity is dangerous: Better to enter with boldness. Everyone admires the bold; no one honors the timid. Boldness and hesitation elicit very different psychological responses in their targets. Hesitation puts obstacles in your path, boldness eliminates them. Entering action with boldness has the magical effect of hiding our deficiencies. When entering any kind of negotiation, go further than you planned. Ask for the moon and you will be surprised how often you get it. When you see several steps ahead, and plan your moves all the way to the end, you will no longer be tempted by emotion or by the desire to improvise. Your clarity will rid you of the anxiety and vagueness that are the primary reasons why so many fail to conclude their actions successfully. You see the ending and you tolerate no deviation.

Don't dilly-dally around. Make decisions in a hurry about what you want to do. This is the solution to intuitive avoidance. Make spur of the moment deals that you know are going to work. Get accustomed to proceeding with an incomplete picture (analysis). Tendency to overanalyze business problems stem from a lack of confidence.[2] Love and compassion for others give people constant direction. Implementation of our mission then becomes increasingly clear. In an article published in Fortune magazine of June 21, 1999 by Ram Charan and Geoffrey

Colvin on why CEOs fail, they argue that it is rarely for lack of smart or vision. Most unsuccessful CEOs stumble because of one simple, fatal shortcoming: bad execution – not getting things done, being indecisive, not delivering on commitments. They based their conclusions on careful study of several dozen CEO failures they have observed over the decades in their roles as advisor to fortune 500 CEOs and journalists respectively. The list of fallen CEOs include John Akers of IBM, Eckhard Pfeiffer of Compaq Computers, John Scully of Apple Computer, and Robert Stampel of General Motors Company. All of them were master strategists, but failed to deliver due to lack of execution. A recent example is that of Philip Murray Condit, erstwhile CEO of the Boeing Company. He was considered a brilliant engineer, obsessive problem solver with an ability to envision elegant design solutions. But these qualities proved to be of lesser use in an executive position. Although always a bold visionary, Condit was frequently indecisive as a CEO. When confronted with a challenge from the archrival Airbus Company's 555-seat, double-decked commercial airliner, Condit not only underestimated the threat but also waffled when he needed to respond decisively. Innovative new jets were proposed but no action was taken. A loss of market share, along with Pentagon scandals and allegations of improper conduct on the part of his executives led to his resignation in December 2003 at the age of 62.

The decisive person is one who is high in self-direction. Decisive people have confidence in their own ideas and can make decisions quickly. They can look at a situation and confidently form opinions, drawing their own conclusions. They set goals for themselves, determine their own priorities, and initiate action. They are resourceful. Decisive people shape the environment around them. Once aware of problems, they boldly plan ways of solving them.

All glory comes from daring to begin. The worst way to fail is by never getting started. You may lose, you may fall flat on your face, but, before you can accomplish anything great, you have got to have the courage to at least try. "Don't sit and worry about the risk to you. Go, do it. It will work out. Make it work out," says Jack Welch, former chairman of the General Electric Company. Cause something to happen. To be successful in life, you have to take serious risks. Move boldly. You can't be timid or half-hearted if you hope to seize the high ground on the other side of the trench. Military history is illuminating in this respect. Many opportunities have been thrown away by generals who spent too much time planning and probing and not enough time fighting.[3]

Real decisions demand clear and timely action and leave no alternative. To make anything happen, you simply have to be willing to change, grow and learn. And that can often be painful. Know what you want. Consider the best strategy for achieving it. Follow that strategy. Change that strategy when it does not work. W.C.Fields said, "If at first you don't succeed, try, try again. Then quit. There is no use being a damn fool about it." Learn to make and commit to the decisions that will effect your career.[4] If you simply say that I want in this life to be happy, it is completely meaningless. By being specific and defining your goal in as many different ways as you can, you'll develop a more intimate understanding of what you want. As a result, the choices you make along the way will be more goal-oriented. You'll be more likely to recognize your goal when you get there, since you'll have so many criteria by which to measure it.

Larry Tisch, erstwhile chairman of CBS, is a genius, not of planning and design, but of swift decisiveness driven by instinctively good common sense. Like bridge, (which he is expert in), he plays the hand he is dealt, not what he wanted. If he makes a wrong play, he forgets about it, and goes on to the next round. He plays bridge like he does business.

Self-doubt is the major stumbling block to becoming successful. That is why so many people have goals they never seem to realize. Write down your goals, make them specific; don't be afraid to change them as you grow and learn; write down the reason why you haven't acted yet; listen and get ideas from others and go one step at a time. Sam Walton, founder of Walmart, started his first store in 1962, now there are 1,259 with $21 billion in sales.

For most situations, success is easily measured by your ability to solve problems, problems from trivial to profound. The pioneer must have courage as well as intuition. Intuition is the ability to make good decisions with incomplete data. When you begin to act, the action changes you as you find resources inside of you that you did not know you had. Setting goals does help, but most emerge by chance. Just do it.

Every crisis we face is multiplied when we act out of fear. Franklin Delano Roosevelt said it better, "The only thing we have to fear is the fear itself." The essence of moral leadership lies in the ability to force us to face fears, and, by so doing overcome them. That was FDR's great talent, and he used it to lead the nation out of the depression and into victory in World War II. Fear is the disease that rots our will to succeed.[5]

Set aside all your distractions and go for your dream. Don't wait for ideal circumstances, they will never come; nor for the best opportunities. Keep your head erect; look up people in the eye, keep your composure under control all the time. Don't be afraid when you have no other choice. Be willing to make decisions. If you wait to make an important decision until all the information that you might want is in, you will never make it in time.[6] "All my life my answer to complicated circumstances has been to make a dramatic and decisive move," said J. Watson Jr., former chairman of IBM.

"Act as men of thought, think as men of action," said Richard Nixon. A lot of successful people are risk-takers. Unless you are willing to do that, to have a go, to fail miserably, and have another go, success wouldn't happen. There must be something risky between you and your dream, otherwise why wouldn't you be living it? Attaining dreams requires new behavior, and new behavior is taking a risk. Be daring, be different, be impractical. When you commit to a goal, the methods to achieve that goal will appear. When the methods do appear, they may not be (and seldom are) dressed in a familiar garb. To reach your dream, you will be called upon to do a lot of things you don't want to do. One great way of pursuing your dream is to maintain your inner stillness and follow your dream.[7] In order to meet your objectives, you should be both – thinker and doer –.

Donald Trump, in his book, *Surviving At The Top*, says, "one thing I have learnt about the construction business – and life in general – is that while what you do is obviously important, the most important thing is just do something. You can waste tremendous amount of time agonizing over which course of action to take when, in fact, any of the choices you are considering is probably preferable to continued pondering, which only heightens your fear of making a mistake." Being decisive also motivates the troops. George Stephanopoulis mentions in his best-seller, *All Too Human,* that the former President Bill Clinton seemed to have chronic bouts of indecision. He needed a person like Dick Morris, as political advisor, who spoke to the part of Clinton that wanted to be told what to do.

Fear has a real message for you. It is trying to tell you that there is something you need and have got to get before you can afford to take risks and have adventure. It may be practical preparation for emotional support. But, whatever it is you need, if you don't get it, and you try to go ahead without it, you really will get hurt.[8] May be there is a different way of doing what you want. Make a shift in your approach. There is always a way for you to get what you want, but it requires that you take a new and sometimes scary action.

> *"If you don't know where you're going, you might wind up somewhere else." —Yogi Berra*

> *"Whatever you can do or imagine, begin it; boldness has beauty, magic, and power in it." — Goethe*

"The easiest thing in the world is achieving your goals, the hardest thing is defining them." — James Woods, movie star

"Whatever the problem, don't get stuck with it. Take action. Do the very thing you don't want to do."— unknown

"I always wanted to be somebody, but I should have been more specific."

— Lily Tomlin & Jane Wagner

"Eventually, the time of action must come. When this happens, be a winner! Don't settle for mediocre results. Don't try to stay even. Go for it all!" — Deng Ming-Dao, in Everyday Tao

"The greatest risk is not taking one." — unknown

"Actions may not always bring happiness; but there is no happiness without action." — Benjamin Disraeli

"Whatever you can do or dream you can, begin it. Boldness has genius, power and magic in it. Begin it now." — Goethe, German Poet

"In flying, I have learned that carelessness and over-confidence are usually far more dangerous than deliberately accepted risks." — Wilber Wright

PART II:

YOU ARE WHO YOU ARE

INTRODUCTION

"You are who you are. For better or worse,
you can't be anyone other than you."— Joel Wells
"To know thyself will set you free."— Socrates

The reality of human personalities is that we cannot change who we are. We are stuck with ourselves, whether we like ourselves or not. We can grow and mature, and thereby expand and nurture our potential, but we will still be ourselves. We cannot change our past. You have the ability to transform your way of thinking and being, but to do so, you would have to merge what you used to be with what you could be. Old and new personalities had to become one. Even when we change, our history does not. We need to learn to work within the basic personality structure we have inherited and developed, and to make the best of it——fundamentally to accept who we are. What type of a person you are temperamentally depends on your biochemical base that dictates predictable emotional patterns and responses in any situation. You have a natural self that can't be changed. For example, if you feel that you need constant challenge and quickly lose interest when novelty wears off, whether in job, a hobby, or a romantic situation, then your emotional category is that of a seeker. You are prone to be drawn into excitement, thrills and even danger. A typical example is Jim Clark, the founder of Silicon Graphics, NetScape, Healtheon, and creator of Hyperion (computerized sail-boat). He is a person in constant need of motion and change. He is always fully occupied only by what had not yet happened. The part of his brain that keeps him interested in being alive gropes for what comes next. Studies indicate that a gene D4DR, that affects how the brain responds to dopamine(a chemical which produces sensation of satisfaction) occurs more frequently in people given to novelty-seeking. The other types are sensor, focuser and discharger.[1]

According to astrology, all human beings are definitely not created equal. They are divided into a complex array of different types that can at least be sorted out, if not partially understood, by looking at the position of the planets in the sky at the site and time of their birth. Furthermore, these various types of people are affected by the continued movement and rearrangement of those same planets for the rest of their lives. They come in and out of cyclical bursts of creativity, periods of deep depression, warm fulfilling experiences, horrible losses, and on and on. Therefore, you have to accept yourself just the way you are. Arrive at emotional well-being and genuine self-esteem. Be yourself always. Don't pretend to be somebody else because then you will make yourself miserable. You will cross the boundaries of your emotional comfort zone. When we are pushed outside our comfort zone, we are vulnerable to unpleasant emotions and bad moods. Believing strongly in yourself will help you feel better. Now researchers are beginning to link personality traits to brain scans and specific genes. Neuroscience shows us that our brains are all wired differently. Like two sets of fingerprints, no two people are exactly alike.

Are you essentially the same individual in this particular moment that you were in your early childhood, and that you will be for many years to come? This fundamental question about the nature of human personality is remarkably complex, one to be resolved partly in the realm of science, and partly in the realm of philosophy. Personality is defined as the sum total of the mental, emotional, social, and physical characteristics of an individual. It's personality that determines the way you react to others, the way you communicate, the way you think and express emotions. These are the outward manifestations of the basic traits that characterize a personality throughout life. Your thoughts, fears, hopes, reactions, behaviors, and dreams all come from this core personality. The evidence certainly demonstrates that individual personality attributes are, at least, partially inherited, observable from birth, and capable of exerting such powerful influences on your behavior, lifestyle, relationships and major life experiences. In spite of this, life experiences, such as the process of growing older with the passage of time or joining a powerful social movement, can affect your personality. Does this mean that your personality actually changes, or that you merely experience different aspects of the same personality you have had all along? Although this question has preoccupied philosophers for centuries, researchers are only beginning to understand the complex processes involved. Dr Mel Levine, professor of pediatrics and cofounder of All Kinds of Minds at the University of North Carolina, writes in his best-seller book *A Mind At A Time* that the brain of each human is unique. Each of us is endowed with a highly complex inborn circuitry, creating innumerable branching pathways of options and obstacles. Approximately 30 trillion synapses or nerve linkages exist within the human brain. That crowded network allows for plenty of strong connections, and misconnections – in short, a nearly endless combination of neurodevelopmental possibilities. Designated teams of neurodevelopmental functions join together to enable individuals to acquire specific abilities. Many individuals ultimately develop strong skills and functions within their niche.

The latest research in genetics, molecular biology, and neuroscience shows that many core personality traits are inherited at birth, and that many of the differences between individual personality styles are the result of differences in genes. Genes are the single most important factor that distinguishes one person from another. A person's genes are entirely in place at conception, but they are not all switched on. When a baby is born, its body is a collection of assorted chemicals: around ten percent protein, ten percent fat, one percent sugar and seventy-five percent water. Their assembly has been orchestrated by the 100,000 genes the body has inherited from its parents. These have determined what it has become, and they will continue to organize its body throughout life. Humans are designed to develop slowly and cannot do so without the help of other people. Different genes are constantly switching on and off, and responding to a changing environment. Shortly after birth, the brain begins to receive input from its new world. The dense forest of interconnecting nerve cells, or neurons, respond to sensory messages – sight, sound, smells. The bombardment of new information reaching the baby's senses stimulates its brain into a constant process of rewiring, so that all the time it is becoming better able to make sense of the world and to control its own body. The key is the interplay between the hardware we are born with and the software we add. You are who your brain thinks you are. This is the result of an intricate interaction of genes and life experiences.[2]

Are there not limits imposed upon us by heredity and environment on how radically we can depart from our customary identities? The answer to this question is far from being settled in any scientific sense. Genes give us shape of our bodies, as well as brain, which come with certain built-in predispositions – things we are driven to do and things we just can't do. We spend much of our adult life reprocessing our childhood. On the other hand, some believe that people can be forced to make astonishing changes in themselves. Environment – meaning everything that's not inherited – also plays a role. This can range from purely biological factors to unique experiences such as childhood injury or a special third-grade teacher, according to Dean Hamer's way of putting it. There are undoubtedly limits to how much a person can change over the course of a life, and to how many different selves can inhibit a single mind and body at one time, but we don't know what those limits are. Peter Guralnick, Boston writer who spent 11 years researching and writing about Elvis Presley, the king of rock-n-roll, writes in his second volume of king's biography, *Careless Love:The unmaking of Elvis Presley,* "No matter how many million records he sold, the king remained branded by his beginning as a poor boy from a shot-gun shack in Tupelo, Mississippi. Elvis always had the sense that people were laughing at him. He had a yawning emotional chasm in his life that ultimately could not be filled by drugs or women or food." On August 16, 1977, at Graceland, his heart stopped after too many pills and too much loneliness. Joseph Patrick Kennedy 11, a former congressman and son of Robert F. Kennedy, has a vulnerable, insecure side to him. He nixed a race for governership of Massachusettes for fear of failure fueled in him a lot by his mother, Ethel. She told Joe he would never be what his father was, that he was not smart, not as talented. Abraham Lincoln, the 16th president of the United States of America, was a lonely person. He avoided intimacy as much as he could, and didn't want to reveal himself to anybody. He just gave the appearance of intimacy. Herbert Donald, a retired Harvard University professor, writing about him in *We Are Lincoln Men: Abraham Lincoln and His Friends*, thinks that Lincoln's beard was an indication of his fear of emotional vulnerability. He was putting on a facade. He did not want his private face on display. He was hiding behind that beard. All this is attributed to his brains, his isolation, his difficult father and the death of his mother.

The architecture of a personality can't be totally transformed. It can, however, be renovated. The kind of formative experience makes it unlikely that a cheapskate will become lavish, a shy person the life of a party, or a compulsive one casual about details. Such 180-degree changes don't happen, because personality is embedded in the warp and woof of the brain, not just in one transmitter system or another, according to Michael Stone, a professor of psychiatry at Columbia University's school of physicians and surgeons. Our genetic inheritance includes a private reserve of about one hundred and fifty different brain chemicals to formulate our neurotransmitters. These neurotransmitters have certain pathways. They direct where the blood circulates and regulate how much of it flows to various brain centers. For example, introverts' and extroverts' blood travel on separate pathways, each pathway requires a different transmitter. Extroverts are activated by dopamine, a powerful transmitter most closely identified with movement, attention, alert states and learning. Introverts, on the other hand, use an entirely different neurotransmitter, acetylcholine, connected to many vital functions in the brain and body. It utilizes long term memory. That's why word retrieval is a problem with introverts because the information moves slowly.

DNA represents the secret of human life. A single human cell contains instructions within its DNA that would fill 1,000 books of 600 pages each. A molecule of DNA is 10,000th of a millimeter wide and a 10th of a millimeter long. It is a complex molecule made up of just four chemicals, or bases – adenine, thymine, guanine and cytosine – arranged in sequence in spiral strands that wrap around each other to form double helix. In the nucleus of every human cell are 23 pairs of chromosomes – tiny strands that bear the genes, the chemical units that determine heredity. Inside each chromosomes are myriad combinations of the four DNA bases in sequences that go on and on about 3.2 billion times. About 310,000 of them actually appear to group together to form genes. Arranged in sequences of three in endless variations, they comprise the genetic "codes" that produce our individual characteristics. These variations tell us who we are and what may await us. Some make us short or tall or give us straighter or curly hair. By now, researchers have nearly identified all the genes in the human body, and even more important, the chemical structure of each gene. The resulting "star map" will help scientists unscramble how our bodies work at the most fundamental levels. They already are intrigued, for example, by early data on D4DR, the so-called risk-taking gene discovered in 1996. D4DR has several variations. People with a particularly long series of seven repeated sequences of the amino acids making up the gene score high on tests measuring risk-taking behavior. These people also test as more exploratory, impulsive, fickle, excitable and quick-tempered. In contrast, people with only a four-sequence strand of D4DR test as rigid, slow-tempered and loyal, according to Mary Cauley, reporting in the Milwaukee Journal Sentinel. With every gene that makes up the human organism having been identified, could we manipulate DNA to design a person with only "superior" qualities? This opens the door to a debate on who decides what makes a better person. Also, although nature has created more than one-hundred amino acids, almost every creature on this planet uses the same twenty to build proteins. Would an extra amino acid give us an evolutionary advantage? Scientists are currently experimenting on this. However, this does raise a question: Why didn't nature do it to begin with, or, can we play God?

Psychoanalyst Alice Miller researched the childhood conditions of Adolph Hitler. She concluded that Hitler's childhood abuse was a factor in causing the death of 40 million people in the world war 11. Hitler was not a born criminal. His true self was "murdered" by a respectable yet unskillful father, who continually beat and shamed him. Hitler's natural human feelings of compassion and empathy had been turned off so that he could survive his father's beatings. To Hitler's unconscious mind, the fear and rage he could not safely express in childhood turned into a holocaust. Psychology suggests that much of our ability to function as well-integrated, mature adults is determined by how well our specific developmental needs were met in our early childhood. Our personality has been formed to compensate for these gaps in our development. The experience of our identity has shifted from our true nature to the shell of defenses that we have had to develop.

The perennial question "Who am I?" has been asked throughout the ages. The answer is socially biased and is deeply influenced by the cultural context in which we live. The fact is that we human beings cannot live without some agreed upon idea of what nature and life are all about. East and West certainly don't share a similar way of life. Superficially that is obviously true, but at a deeper level it is not true at all. Men and women in all times and cultures are alike with respect to their basic needs of life. We all face the same questions with regard to the meaning of life, and the nature of death. We cannot assume that other people's minds work the same way that ours do. How people see themselves depends on the situation they are in, the person they are interacting with, their fears, ideals, and personal goals. Without a smooth and relatively seamless interface between your internal vision of yourself and the external images of your personality that are reflected in the way other people approach and respond to you, you may eventually come to feel trapped, alienated, frustrated, or resentful. Furthermore, if others do not accurately perceive your true motivation and intentions, they may fail to open the doors of opportunity that could lead you toward personal, occupational, and intellectual growth and development. Over time, such interpersonal differences in perspective could create internal psychological problems for you as well, leading you to feel unsatisfied with or uncertain about your core sense of self.

Many philosophical and religious systems have emphasized the significance of letting go of the individual "ego" or "self" as a primary tenet of achieving a higher level of personal fulfillment. Viewed from a psychological perspective, this might imply that learning to overcome a limited self-centered view of your own existence is a crucial element in personal growth. One way to accomplish this objective is by learning to see yourself from many different perspectives, so that you may incorporate this more expansive view into your evolving self-image.[3] Carolyn See, the author of *Making A Literary Life* offers the following advice in her inimitable style to the new writers who might face series of rejections before their dream comes true: "Your ego is a big, messy, undisciplined, anxiety-ridden dog. It barks and whines and pees on the floor and sheds all over the furniture and takes nips at passing strangers and goes crazy when it sees another dog that might be bigger or smarter or prettier. This dog – at least in my experience – is untrainable. The only thing you do is try to keep it on a fairly short leash."

People are broadly classified into three basic Psychological categories: the compliant, the aggressive and the detached personality. The compliant type (moving toward people) are focused on love and relationship as the main solution for life's problems. The aggressive type (moving against people) try to dominate and control others and emphasize becoming tough-minded, hard-driving, and strong-willed in order to cope with life. The detached type (moving away from people) choose privacy, independence, and intellectual detachment and seek to become detached observers, onlookers who are able to treat life as a drama acted out by others. The compliant type manifests all the traits that go with "moving toward" people. It shows a marked need for affection and approval, and an especial need for a partner. This type feels helpless when left to his own resources; and has a tendency to subordinate himself. This lack of assertiveness and firmness does impair his capacities. The aggressive type takes it for-granted that everyone is hostile. His needs stem fundamentally from his feeling that the world is an arena where only the fittest survive, and the strong annihilate the weak. He needs to excel, to achieve success, prestige, or recognition in any form. The detached category of people put emotional distance between themselves and others. Among their most striking quality is the need for self-sufficiency. The underlying principle here is never to become so attached to anybody or anything that he or it becomes indispensable. Self-sufficiency and privacy both serve his most outstanding needs. He is no conformist. As a rule, he prefers to work, sleep, eat alone. Isolation is what he wants. His sense of superiority expresses itself in his wanting to feel separate and distinct from others.[4]

It goes without saying that to be an individual means you don't have to fit someone else's mold of what is "normal." The litmus test of accepting your temperament is setting your own standards, not allowing yourself to be defined by external standards. Stop trying to become a better person if that means comparing your insides to other people's outsides and denying your own temperament. Deliberately turn away from the world. Wean yourself away from the opinion of others – however talented, creative and celebrated they may be – as you continue to journey within. Instead, reframe your intention and strive to become more genuinely who you are. Your awareness and respect of your temperament will give you true emotional confidence. You will move through your world open to people and to challenges, alive to life's possibilities. The whisper of your own self will tell you which way to go. You will be shown the next step of your uniquely personal journey. Everyone has some forte, something he can do better than he can do anything else. Many men never find the job they are best suited for. And often this is because they do not think enough. Too Many men drift lazily into any job, suited or unsuited for them; and when they don't get along well they blame everybody and anything else but themselves. Everything that is happening to you is the outward physical manifestation of your innermost thoughts, choices, ideas, and determinations regarding who you are and who you choose to be. What happens is whatever you want to have happen. You create your own reality. More people than ever before are aware of the power of the mind, and are consciously creating the direct expression of who they really are, and the rapid manifestation of what they choose to be.

Don't accept somebody else's way of doing things or anybody else's carved-in-cement wisdom. Challenge it all. Never be intimidated by an authority figure. Scrap the dogma from your boot and go make things happen *your* way.

Bill Gates, founder of Microsoft, and the most famous business man in the world, was in the sixth grade when his parents decided that he needed counseling. His intellectual drive, curiosity and interests were different from typical sixth graders. He was at war with his mother Mary, an outgoing woman who harbored the belief that her son should do what she told him. After a year of sessions and a battery of tests, the counselor reached the conclusion that his mother Mary better adjust to losing because there is no use trying to beat him. Finally, she came around to accepting that it was futile trying to compete with him. A lot of computer companies have concluded the same. In the years since he dropped out of Harvard,

William Henry Gates 111 has thrashed competitors in the world of desktop operating systems and applications. In building Microsoft, he has come to symbolize the software and computing industries. Now he intends to do the same thing in the world of digital media, where information, communication and entertainment will converge in ways that will change how we think, work and live. His success stems from his personality: an awesome blend of brilliance, drive, competitiveness and personal intensity. He is still like a kid with a start-up who is afraid he will go out of business if he lets anyone compete; the same traits that his psychologist noted when Gates was in sixth grade.[5] Incidentally, Bill Gates exemplifies the sort of mind that succeeds in the software industry. He reportedly can recall the telephone extension numbers and car license plate numbers of countless Microsoft employees. It is said that whereas most people can memorize a seven-digit telephone number, good software writers have the sort of memory that can readily memorize strings of fifteen or more digits.

On the other hand, Michael S. Dell, the founder and CEO of the Dell Computer Corporation, had a business savvy from early childhood. He was twelve years old when he netted $2,000 selling stamps by mail order. In high school, Michael hustled newspaper subscriptions by using an Apple 11e to develop mailing lists targeting newly weds or families who had just moved to town. He made enough money to buy himself a BMW. As a freshman at the University of Texas in 1983, Michael took excess inventory from local computer dealers at cost, upgraded the machines, and sold them over the phone for less than the dealers were charging. Within a year he had left school to build a computer company operating on the same direct-sales principle. Today, Dell is a major global computer supplier with more than $18 billion in revenue.

Define your own self-worth, as opposed to somebody's idea of who you should be. Re-confirm what is important to you. Appreciate, esteem and celebrate the you you are. Instead of focusing constantly on your shortcomings and failings, think about all your strong points and accomplishments. No one can condemn or demean you but yourself. The most important thing is to be whatever you are without shame. "If you smile, the world smiles with you, cry and you cry alone." It is a universal truth.[6] Jackie Kennedy said, " No matter what the future holds for you, weather it with intelligence, courage and incomparable style."

Some experts claim that the notion "You are who you are" is a defeatists tendency. You can be what you want to be through a tenacious commitment to self-improvement. John F. Kennedy is known as one of our finest political orators. Yet, early in his presidency, he was so nervous about speaking in public that his left hand would shake uncontrollably.

61

That fact didn't stop him from making memorable speeches and presiding at witty informative press conferences. As for his shaky left hand, he put it in his pocket. With his firm right hand, he gestured with vigor. Kennedy, like his hero Churchill, used words to forge his place in history. It is interesting to mention at this point that in a 2001 book about Jacqueline Kennedy by Barbara Leaming, Jackie has been described as a woman whose tormented childhood resulted in a feeling of crippling insecurity. The source of this self-doubt lay in shame over her parents' ugly divorce and in her mother's relentless criticism of her unusual looks (especially her kinky hair). That's why Jackie spoke frankly of her lack of interest in politics. Her emotional survival depended on her ability to keep the world at a distance and her polished reserve hid a core of insecurity. CEOs get into the executive suites only through tenacious commitment to self-improvement; doing it better the next time. All people have untapped potential. There are, of course, clear differences between individuals in nature and nurture, that is, genes and development, as to how much untapped potential there may be. But no matter what level of performance a person currently exhibits, he or she can make quantum improvement. Not everyone can be the CEO of a multibillion-dollar corporation, just as not everyone can be an Olympian or win at Wimbledon, but with coaching and practice we can all be better than we are.

Aristotle said, "All men desire by nature to know." Successful people have boundless curiosity. Whatever limitations the accident of birth imposes on them, they seek to overcome. Creative imagination is expressed in varying ways and in varying proportion. Some people contribute in brilliant flashes of form; others through their steadfastness, persistence or the grueling grind of hard routine work. Each individual should be given opportunity to exploit his talent to the fullest and in the way best suited to his personality. Try as we will, we can create no synthetic genius, no composite leader. Men are not interchangeable parts like so many pinion gears or carburetors. " Genius", as John Adams said, " is bestowed imperiously by nature upon an individual, and behind every advance of the human race is a germ of creation growing in the mind of some lone individual, an individual whose dreams awaken him in the night while others lie contentedly asleep. It is he who is the indispensable man. With all our technical advances, creative genius is not yet machine made, and can not be produced by crash programs. He cannot be stockpiled, prefabricated, or improvised."

Is there a purpose in life at all? No one can tell another what this purpose is. Each must find out for himself. If he succeeds, he will continue to grow in spite of all indignities. Under worst conditions, the last of human freedoms is the ability to choose one's attitude in a given set of circumstances. Never in your life are you without problems and challenges. Learn to take charge of your life and hold on. Commit to resolve rather than endure your personal problems. You are responsible to life for something, however grim your circumstances may be. Life ultimately means taking the responsibility to find the right answer to its problems and to fulfill tasks which it constantly sets for each individual. The sort of a person an individual becomes is the result of an inner decision, and not the result of external influences. Fundamentally, therefore, any man can decide what shall become of him - mentally and physically. It is the spiritual freedom which cannot be taken away - that makes life meaningful and purposeful. Human life, under any circumstances, never ceases to have a meaning. Meaning of life differs from man to man, and from moment to moment. Thus it is impossible to define the meaning of life in a general way. For some one it could be simply to meet a loved one, to finish an unfinished manuscript, to establish your own enterprise, position in society etc., etc.. [7] Life has a purpose. Everything is happening for a specific reason. Everything is continually unfolding, and we are connected into that unfolding in ways that we can't even imagine. By our willingness to grasp the possibility that life is unfolding as it must, we have a head-start. Therefore, according to the world-famous physicist and thinker, David Boehm, "Live your life by participating in the unfolding. This means seeing what is needed in the moment. Doing exactly what is required of us, right now, right here." We don't have to let our anxieties and our desire for certain results dominate the quality of the moment, even when things are painful. Our purpose is unfolding constantly, although we may not be aware of it. We were born with an inherent driving force that wants us to fulfill the mission.

"There is always some kind of a yearning deep inside us. It never gets quite quenched. It is a seeking of completeness. I think that is one quality of life that is common to all of us." says Nick Nolte, the veteran movie actor.

"To ponder interminably over the reason for one's own existence, or, the meaning of life in general, appears to be shear folly. And yet everyone holds certain ideals by which he guides his aspirations and judgments," said Einstein.

In the last two decades, many Americans have turned inwards in search of frontiers. The enormous influence of yoga, meditation, psychiatry and psychotherapy can be adduced as evidence for this, as can the enormous body of literature about self-improvement. There is a desire to concentrate on the first building blocks of life, to go back to basics and find an answer to this crisis of self-identity.

> *"Everybody is unique. Compare not yourself with anybody else lest you spoil God's curriculum."* — Baal Shem Tov

> *"Recognizing and honoring all your desires is the basis of finding your true self."* — John Gray

> *"Every decision you make stems from what you think you are, and represents the value that you put upon yourself."*— A Course in Miracles

> *"There is only one success——to be able to spend your life in your own way."* — Christopher Morley

> *"Unless mankind redesigns itself by changing our DNA through altering our genetic makeup, computer-generated robots will take over the world."*— Stephen Hawking

CHAPTER FIVE - ONE
LIFE TO LIVE

"There is plenty of evidence that human beings are not primarily driven by genetically determined instincts, but are rather free to make their own choices." — Hunter Lewis[1]

As youngsters we develop simple presumptions about life, people and ourselves. These presumptions determine how we perceive the world and deal with problems. We essentially remain childlike, letting others determine our destiny. Therefore, as we grow chronologically, we need to mature in the art of self-observation. Some of the methods to improve self-knowledge include seminars or getting feedback from family, friends or your behavior. Through successive self-improvement, you reach a point when you start loving and accepting yourself unconditionally. You become who you are in a natural and organic way. You exhibit a cheerful curiosity toward possibilities, and willingness to see what will happen today as you wake up. Key to successful self-improvement is knowing when to stop.[2]

One thing Americans have done better than any other culture in history is handle chaos and change, and invent the future. Americans are a part of a wildly individualistic, determined culture and believe that for every problem, there is a solution. Responding to a challenge by doing nothing is not their long suit. What will be will be is no more their language than the phrase, "It is God's will." Once Americans have chosen a future, it is open to being molded and shaped. Sooner or later, Americans usually clean up their new order and get it something close to right – no matter how terrifying it appears at the beginning. Americans have a dream of reinventing, redefining, restoring themselves. Search for the future inside them beats strong.[3] A case in point, a Wisconsin sailor, Tim Kent, age 50, will try to circle the globe in his 50 foot vessel as a part of the annual 'Around Alone' competition. It is the greatest mental and physical challenge in any sport. For Tim, it has been a huge dream and he says that if you have the opportunity to fulfill a dream, you have to go for it. "When I finish this race, my daughters will grow up thinking there's nothing that is not possible to do," says Kent.

There is only one success – to be able to spend your life in your own way. Things always happen that you really believe in. Each handicap is like a hurdle in a steeple chase, and when you ride up to it, if you throw your heart over, the horse will go along too. Don't give up the conviction that it's possible to be in control of our life. "If something did not work out, I had choice: drop it, or simply make a modification in my plan of attack," says financial world guru, Charles Given. Ted Turner, once owner of CNN TV network, does not believe in failure. He does believe in taking the initiative. His visions are unfailingly grand. He is very unstructured, but very determined. His approach can be captured by two words - "Do it." In an article published in the September 1998 issue of the Reader's Digest, Ted Turner is described as a man in perpetual motion. By repeatedly reinventing himself, he has achieved what would take others many lifetimes. He says, "I am trying to set the all-time record for achievement by one person in one lifetime." He further asserts that to get to the top in virtually anything today, you really have to make a superhuman effort. You wouldn't ever find a superachiever anywhere who wasn't or isn't motivated, at least partially, by a sense of insecurity. Call it luck, instinct or vision, but when Turner is told something can't be done, he's gone ahead. He needs crises and disapproval and skeptics to motivate him. Ted Turner believes that his father committed suicide partly because his goals were too limited. When he realized his three dreams – to be a millionaire, own a yacht and a plantation – he became a man without a future. Ted Turner confides that in order to feel engaged with life, he needs goals that are so high he can never accomplish them. Today, with a net worth of $4.8 billion, he is the 26th richest man in America. He founded CNN(Cable News Network), the most influential television news channel in the world, and is now vice chairman of the world's biggest media conglomerate, Time Warner Inc. If you want to live everyday with passion, design a project that's bigger than your life, one that you don't know how to accomplish. This project may not even be completed in your lifetime. Perhaps you will create a legacy, a gift that will outlive you, affecting future generations.

According to the Harvard Business School, "A successful entrepreneur is one who believes that he can control his own destiny." Not everyone can or should be an entrepreneur; most people work effectively for another person, or a corporation. Security is a reasonable and proper concern for most people. " Entrepreneurs are people who understand there is a little difference between obstacle and opportunity, and are able to turn both to their advantage," according to Victor Kiam, owner of Remington and New England Patriots.

Starbucks, the ubiquitous retail chain that sells coffee beverages, beans and accessories, today has more than 1500 outlets staffed by more than 25,00 employees. Its 1997 revenues exceeded $1 billion. Howard Schultz, the CEO and mastermind behind Starbucks astonishing growth shared his thinking about how to be successful entrepreneur in his book *Pour Your Heart Into It*, written with Dori Jones Yang: "You got to have a great tolerance for pain! you have to work so hard and have so much enthusiasm for one thing that most other things in life have to be sacrificed. So many times I've been told something can't be done. But if I believe in it, I can't let it go. Part of my determination comes from my enthusiasm, and part is fear of failure. I believe life is a series of near misses. A lot of what we ascribe to luck is not luck at all. It's seizing the day and accepting responsibility for your future. It's seeing what other people don't see and pursuing that vision."

Love yourself and your people. Believe that you can do anything that you set your mind to do. Let no circumstances remove you from the center of your dream. Find a vision of who you want to be, and put your energies and power behind it . Then for you, the best years will lie ahead.[4]

It is not good enough to merely play as well as you can, but you must also think that you can beat or be the best as well. Be a tough competitor. This is what professional business is all about. Break psychological barriers and, in doing so, expand hugely the possibilities of winning. Get rid of modesty and self-effacement. Grab the moment to realize that you are not merely trying to play well, but to win. A self-discovery like that is tremendously exciting. Try to give it to yourself. Suspend the judgment that you cannot win. Give yourself license to win. You might discover that you are better than, for whatever reason, you gave yourself credit of being.[5]

Prepare yourself for the moment when destiny will knock on your doors. Believing in yourself is first step in your ascending future. The reason that so many hesitate is that turning that belief into practice always challenges us to abandon our reliance on the past. If the jump is big enough, you have to abandon whole aspects of your personality and acquire new ones. Growth always involves parting with the past, the greater the growth, the more the path we must shed.[6] "I shall seize fate by the throat. It shall never wholly overcome me," said Indira Gandhi. She would not allow a shadow of self-pity to touch her mind.

Where most psychologists used to contend that one's personality is etched in stone during childhood, many now say that profound developmental changes often occur in young adulthood and throughout mid-life. Personality may be more fluid, adaptive and innovative than is usually thought. It is never too late to find your passion. In nature, nothing retires. What, where and how you do what you do is something well within your control, whether you are 20 or 70. At the age of 83, Gordon Parks, a writer, photographer and musician, who received twenty-eight honorary degrees and national medal of arts from President Reagan, says that he refused to be type-cast as a black artist. His mother used to say, "You can do anything if you want it badly enough. Nothing limits you, unless you allow it to." He says, "Creativity is in everybody's blood. But you have to develop it; and it does not depend on age."

Researchers are finding an unexpected potency from deliberate practice in world-class competitions of all kinds, including chess, musical rituals and sporting events. Relentless training routines of those at the top allow them to break through ordinary limits in memory and in physiology and so perform at levels that had been thought impossible. Extensive practice can break through barriers in mental capacities, particularly short-term memory. If you are determined to succeed, you can find a way around any obstacle, even memory.

Everyone has a right and the duty to grow and reach beyond his circumstances. If you trust fate, you have one chance in a million. If you trust your goals, you have every chance in the world. Make clear pictures of your most intensely sought goals, hold them clearly in mind to pursue and win. We are born with ability to determine our destiny and to alter the course of everything around us by the goals we picture into existence and leave behind us. A goal is not a goal if it is not measurable. Visualize the objects of your desire and make them real to your inner, goal-striving mind. This is how you can change your future. By burning into our minds the goals we picture, we can work toward success twenty-four hours a day, since that part of our brain does not sleep.[7] To get luck, you have to put yourself in a position to receive it. Positioning yourself for potential opportunity and advantageous situation is the whole basis of the entrepreneurial approach. Someone said, "I did not want to be an old man sitting around regretting that I didn't take a chance." Take charge of your personal destiny. Anything is possible if you believe you deserve it. Build on your strength.

Just because you are good at something doesn't mean that you have to do it for the rest of your life. People change. Times change. What you felt passionate about in one phase of your life may not be what turns you on fifteen or twenty years later. It is important to gravitate toward those things that infuse your life with gusto, whether you are twenty-eight, forty-eight or eighty-eight years old. Winning is loving what you are doing and doing what you love. Leaders are proactive thinkers and doers with the courage to take risks and challenge the status-quo. They know that the ability to invent a desired future is dependent upon the willingness to break with the past.[8] Somerset Maugham said, "It's a funny thing about life; if you refuse to accept anything but the best, you very often get it."

The success stories of the next few decades will not be about people who are educated from age five to twenty-five and who then apply that schooling until they retire forty years later. Winners will be those who are both willing and able to grow throughout their lifetimes. Don't assume that you cannot continue to develop, and develop greatly as you age. This perspective is nicely summed up in a poem by Samuel Ullman, the beginning of which reads:

"Youth is not a time of life, it is a state of mind;
it is not a matter of rosy cheeks, red lips and supple knees;
it is a matter of the will, a quality of the imagination,
a vigor of the emotion; it is the freshness of the deep springs of life.
Youth means the temperamental predominance of courage over timidity,
of the appetite for adventure over the love of ease.
This often exists in a man of sixty more than a boy of twenty.
No body grows old merely by a number of years.
We grow old by deserting our ideals."

"The people who get on in this world are the people who
get up and look for the circumstances they want, and if
they can't find them, make them."
— *George Bernard Shaw*

"Destiny is no matter of chance. It is a matter of choice:
it is not a thing to be waited for, it is a thing to be
achieved." — *William Jennings Bryan*

"Don't let your past control your future"—unknown

"Love yourself and your people. Believe that you can do anything that you set your mind to do. Let no circumstances remove you from the center of your dream."— John F. Kennedy

"You only live once – but if you work it right, once is enough." — Joe E. Lewis

"Don't get boxed in by life. We are in control of our lives." — unknown

Most Oriental faiths proclaim a worldview that personal extinction (Mukti) is the highest goal, because otherwise one keeps getting recycled for another go at this planet where external life is considered pointless. On the other hand, western approach preaches a one go-round in life, and, therefore, claims to foster life-enhancing goals and daring achievements. I shall discuss this opposing viewpoint in the next chapter.

CHAPTER SIX - KARMIC CYCLE

"A man can surely do what he wills to do, but he cannot determine what he wills." — Schopenhauer

The Sanskrit term, Karma, has been adopted in English dictionaries as the all-embracing term for that universal law, the harmonic law of adjustment, of compensation, action-reaction, to which all natural processes are subject. Karma is the unerring law which adjusts effect to cause on the physical, mental, and spiritual planes of being. It is law of harmony that continually restores the naturally harmonious state of the cosmos whenever it becomes disturbed. Karma is involved in the vast sweeps of cyclic life that wheel behind evolution, which are preordained by karmic law. The law of karma is one of the most important laws governing our lives. The system involving reincarnation and the karmic law is the only plausible explanation for our world. The doctrine of karma offers the basis for a sound philosophy of life.

Karma, the law of cause and effect, shows that we make our own life situations through our past actions. According to this doctrine, we ourselves are responsible for our lives, our opportunities and limitations, our character traits, talents and personality. Everything about us is the outcome of forces we ourselves have set in motion, either in this life or in some distant past. Our past is reflected as clearly as though in a mirror, manifesting itself in the present. Our body and circumstances are the memory of our past actions. Just as one can tell from the leaves of a tree the type of seed that was planted years earlier, an open and honest look into our present circumstances can lead to the insight into their causes. The accumulated energy of repeated negative patterns of behavior resurfaces and projects them into the situation and lifestyles that are most suited to such patterns. The way we experience things is dependent upon such accumulated energy. There can be no lasting peace until we have dealt with all past karma, good or bad. We are the inheritors of our past actions, and this life presents us with a wonderful opportunity to meet their effects with a bow of acceptance. We can't escape the ripening of past karma but we can choose how we want to deal with it. There is no running away from this. Sooner or later, the things that we don't want to deal with and try to escape from catch up with us. We, in fact, carry our "Karma" around with us. We are all work in progress, striving to refine our spirits and our lives. We are growing up in a spiritual sense.

Life is like an experiment, and everything we do is improvisational. Right action essentially requires of us only that we be perfectly sincere, appreciate things as they are, understand causality and its ethical implications, and try to do our best. For doing our best is the very best any of us can do. Karma has given us back the actual consequences of our own actions. All the thoughts, motives, emotions which we generated in the past have gone into the complex strains that make us what we are today. Karma is the succession of the forces which built up the personal man, reproducing themselves in one personality after another. Every cause that has not yet produced its effect is an event that has not yet come to completion. Cause of rebirth is the unfulfilled desires of past life. Whatever a man is, it is the result of his own past. It is an imbalance of energy that is in the process of being balanced. That balancing of energy does not always occur within a span of single lifetime. Therefore, it is not always possible to understand the significance or the meaning of the events in our life. Continual incarnation and reincarnation of the energy of the spirit into physical reality for the purpose of balancing its energy in accordance with the law of karma is the basis of our evolutionary process. We cannot erase influences we generated in the past, but we can influence the course of our lives at any time by pouring in new energies in new directions. We may not see the results immediately, but karma assures that they will come, as any energy we generate must have its effect. If we counteract negative elements within us, we set up new causes which alter the karmic outcome of past actions. The results of our actions are sometimes delayed because any event can be a mixture of many karmas ripening together.

Our minds are certainly pre-programmed considerably with genetic patterns for making sense of the world around us and our position in the world. An important element in transcending negative programming of the human mind is to introduce new programming, a new habit, a new behavioral and cognitive pattern that is more rewarding. When this happens, the old programming simply stops receiving energy to function, and falls dormant. Only through the input of a vast amount of perceptual information as we grow up does this genetic programming receive the stimulation for the mind to form functional concepts of how to succeed in life. If there were a way available to avoid the grip of karma, that would be the way to attain the state of eternal being.

We inherit genetic karma from our ancestors. It may be attitudes, situations, or illnesses. If an ancestor has created a strong imbalance, this can be handed down in the structure of the DNA, causing descendants who are open to this particular thing to come under its karmic influence. Attituditional karma relates to attitudes or ways of being that a person carries from life to life. This type permeates all that a person is and all that a person does. Some of the attitudes commonly carried over are egotism, fear of failure and a sense of not belonging. Many times people do certain things that seemingly have no relevance to their current life. These actions are probably from past life desires. Life is a constant self-creation. If the present state of man is the product of a long past, he can change what he has made. His past which he has built for himself and his present environment may offer obstacles to him, but they will all yield in the end to the will in him in proportion to its sincerity and insistence. Karma is complete only when we have balanced our previous actions through consciousness, commitment, and new actions. Our soul knows these situations and relationships, and will create opportunities for us to resolve them. Without karmic understanding, the events occurring in our lives appear arbitrary.

Many religions teach that we have only one life experience, but this teaching doesn't really fit with modern research and experience. Almost anyone can begin to remember past lives through guided meditation, says Dr. Brian Weiss, former chairman of the department of psychiatry at Mount Sinai medical center, and author of the book Many lives, Many Masters. According to Dr. Weiss, past life memory is accessed in the same manner as other transcendent information: by going within. EEG (Electroencephalograph) studies show that past lives are being tapped when brain levels measure 8.3 cycles/second. Flickering eyelids or REM (Rapid Eye Movement) accompany this state. Captain Robert L. Snow, commander of the homicide branch at the Indianapolis Police Department, tells the true story of his search for his past, hints of which he discovers while under hypnosis. In an enthralling journey as reported in Looking for Carroll Beckwith, he proves that most every recollection he had while hypnotized actually happened, nearly 100 years ago. As a result, he was convinced that belief in past lives and reincarnation is no longer limited to Far-Eastern philosophies and religions, but is a universal truth.

Karma is the force that impels to reincarnation, and that karma is the destiny man weaves for himself. At birth, the individual is placed in an environment which he has chosen, that which answers to his character. The karmic connection between lives is made by characteristics which are passed on from one personality to its successors. They correspond to the DNA, gene, chromosome arrangement of inherited qualities in the physical bodies. They are, as it were, the seeds of character, representing innate faculty and capability – or lack of it. At death they remain as karmic effects, as germs, in the atmosphere of the terrestrial plane to attach themselves to the new personality when it reincarnates. The new entity bears complete responsibility for all our actions. Thus, karma is the web of life, the total pattern of cause and effect. From intellectual point of view, the law of karma means that nothing happens in this world without a definite cause. It follows that we can control any specific kind of happening by suitably changing its cause. The characteristics of a personality, the qualities that make one personality different from another, cannot be appreciated without an understanding of the karma that created those characteristics. The dispositions, aptitudes and attitudes that you are born with serve the learning of your soul. As your soul learns the lessons it must learn to balance its energy, those characteristics become unnecessary, and are replaced by others. This is how you grow. What is not learnt in each lifetime is carried over into other lifetimes, along with new lessons that arise for the soul to learn. This is how the soul evolves into eternity. Reincarnation may mean our energy or consciousness lives on after death, not that we as specific individuals are born repeatedly. Just as when a leaf dies, its energy becomes something else. Arthur C. Clark, the leading science-fiction writer and futurlogist, who lived in Sri Lanka where almost everyone believes in reincarnation, has a problem in accepting this view. He does not see any mechanism that would make it work; the input-output devices; the storage medium. But, he agrees that we are long ways from explaining the celestial designs as yet. Modern-day scientists are of the opinion that our consciousness is based on the phenomena occurring in the neurons and other cells, and that the brain and mind are not two separate, independently existing entities. Mind is conceived by them as nature's most complex phenomenon rather than as a mystery with an unknown nature. Dependence of consciousness on the body, and more particularly on the brain, is the weightiest argument against reincarnation. But the best argument that the memories can survive the destruction of physical tissues comes from the reincarnation cases witnessed in many parts of the world. There might be a non-physical process of storage of memories. It might be in some dimension of which we are just beginning to form crude ideas through the study of paranormal phenomena.

The nature package includes your heredity, your environment, all of your personality characteristics, all of the opportunities that exist at this moment, all of your attitudes, all of your predispositions – the whole package – functions under the laws of Karma or the laws of the universe. In other words, the package is unfolding. It is just lawfully working itself out. Once you realize this, then you know how it came about. Everything in the universe enters the field of existence at the place and time to which it belongs. It appears there and then because at that place and time a particular need exists which it can meet. A newborn is conditioned by the past ancestral, social or personal reincarnational link to successfully meet a particular cosmic need, and thus to perform a specific role on this planet. This conditioning is the newborn's karma. When you surrender, you allow yourself to flow with the rhythm of life, rather than struggling against it. The peaks and valleys that mark your personal path become easier to traverse when you surrender to them. This is not to say that you should remain passive and just let life happen to you. Rather, you need to learn to surrender to those circumstances over which you never really had any control anyway. Surrender the illusion that you are the choice maker. Westerners find the use of word "surrender" so horrible because they think of an ego surrendering to another. Surrender is not the same as giving up. To surrender means to get your ego out of the way and let go of what is stubbornly holding you in the state you are in. When the tendency to conquer and control is not balanced with a letting-go, it leads to exhaustion, dissipation of energy and defeat. Learn to relinquish your need to predict outcomes and understand exactly what is happening from moment to moment. We must be willing to let go of control. According to Dr. Herbert Benson, author of The Breakout Principle, letting go of a problem triggers the internal release of nitric oxide, which has been linked to the production of neurotransmitters such as endorphins and dopamine, the body's natural tranquilizers. They enhance greater creativity, memory, and productivity. Also, nitric oxide (NO), is a highly active oxygen carrier to the brain cells. As a result, the blood vessels open up, the heart rate decreases and inner tranquility takes over. These observations have been recorded at the Harvard medical school's Mind-Body Institute using functional Magnetic Resonance Imaging (fMRI), brain-mapping, and innovative techniques of blood analysis. Everything is running off Karma. You give up dualism. Surrender is complete only when your will should become non-existent; Lord's will taking its place. Things may turn out differently from what they look apparently. Surrender unreservedly and the higher power will reveal itself. That is what surrendering truly is. It is not my, but Thy will. Then you leave it in the hands of God whether or not you are going to live or die, serve or not serve; and you don't decide for yourself what's best.[1] When we develop the integrity to be in a state of surrender, we alter our relationship to the future and become a part of the unfolding universe.

Our religious and moral teachers have broadly classified actions into three categories: fatalism, determinism, and free will. According to fatalism, our actions are predetermined by external circumstances which are beyond one's control. Some call it God's will. Thus we are made to play our part in the universe. Fatalism takes the view that all our actions are in vain. Determinism means that all actions are determined by the environmental conditions in which a person is born and works in the course of his life. This law says that every effect must have a cause adequate to produce it. It removes our ability to act freely. Advocates of free will believe that every person is a free agent of his actions and has the power to choose between several options to direct his will. In choosing between these alternatives, one may follow tendencies created by his past karmas, but also may struggle against them to exercise his free will. Thus a man's actions are not entirely determined, for he is endowed with free will. Only past is determined, future is not. Past deeds resulting in the present were also free actions, and they can be wiped off by free volition of the present. According to the theory of karma, fate is not a blind chance but is the result of our own work of the past and the present. "Whatever the man is, wherever he is, whatever he suffers or enjoys, is the result of his own actions," says Manu, the Indian sage. Thus, no God's will is involved in our life. Fatalism has no role in the philosophy of karma. As you sow, so shall you reap.[2] Quantum mechanics rejects Determinism. It says that, up to a point, what happens in the universe is random, a matter of pure chance. There are uncaused events. In fact, physicists now tell us that some subatomic events have no cause. They just happen. There is a certain amount of uncertainty in the the universe. Even when acting on free-will, what happens on each occasion is made to happen by laws lying entirely beyond our control. The choice is fixed by what is going on inside the brain(consciousness). Not everything can be explained or understood by science, at least at this juncture of time.

Be willing to listen to your inner voice that helps guide us as our journey unfolds. The underlying component of this kind of commitment is our trust in the playing out of our destiny. In this state of being, our life is naturally infused with meaning. Then "free will" gives way to "grand will". In fact, all physical events in our lives are caused according to the laws of nature. We believe that our actions are free because we are ignorant of their causes. They are not revealed to us in their precise and detailed character, but only confusedly. Rather than being in a state of confusion over whether you do or don't have a voice over what is called your destiny, it's far better to surrender and be willing to hold two opposing ideas in your mind simultaneously. You live in a body with boundaries, and in a boundary-less inner world at the same time. Thus you are in charge and you aren't in charge at the same time.

A man is nothing but a puppet of past actions (karma) and of nature (or environment). Each man's intellectual reactions, feelings, moods and habits are merely effects of past causes, whether of this or prior life. Karma is the feedback of one's action. It stipulates the conditions under which a person would return in the next life. The soul is believed to transmigrate upon death into another living incarnation on its' journey toward 'Moksha" or 'Nirvana' (liberation of atma or soul) from cycles of life and death. A ceaseless series of reincarnations ultimately leads to release from the painful world.[3] To achieve final salvation in the Lord is indeed to find that the human body has completely fulfilled its purpose. One method of achieving salvation is to first get finished with the desires. However, this approach is very risky. Most people who attempt to use it are not successful and succeed only in creating more karma. Using powers in the service of the ego creates new karma and new attachment which ultimately lead to the loss of the power. there is no end to the search. There is no position from which we can say, "Now I have arrived. I can stop working." There is no end-point. Therefore, the best route is to avoid fulfilling of the still-active desires, using the energy instead for specific acts of purification.[4] Some experts claim that desires are genetically coded and cannot be changed. They motivate our actions and define our personalities. The ultimate perfection of a person is seen to lie in self-realization, in identifying oneself with the ultimate source and power of reality. Consequently, the goal is to realize that one is not merely body, not merely biological life.

According to the *Upanishads,* the great power that energizes the cosmos *(Brahman)* and the spiritual energy of the self *(Atman)* are ultimately the same. This vision of the unity of self with ultimate reality provides the foundation for methods of liberation which constitute the practical core of the Hindu philosophy and is considered to be the greatest contribution made in the *Upanishads.* Wholeness is the central theme of mystical revelations the world over. The Hindus seek unity of the individual soul or

"Atman" with "Brahman" or "World Spirit" or all. The ancient Chinese "I Ching" is based on a holistic cosmology in which the relationship between Heaven and Earth, mountains, fire, wind, and wood are reflected in the state, family, and lives of individuals. The natural processes on Earth are indivisible, constituting a holism that must be nurtured and maintained. Scientist James Lovelock has explored the idea of a holistic Earth in which organic and inorganic systems are interlocked together in a way that can be envisioned as a single living cell he calls "Gaia", after the ancient Greek Goddess of Earth. The Earth, as Gaia, is a complex coevolving entity comprising micro-organisms, grasses, trees, animals, climate, and even the movement of continents.

We and we alone are responsible for what we are and our condition on earth. we have made our present, and we are continuously making our future. Today is the result of yesterday, and tomorrow is the result of today. It is a continuing process as life is continuous. There are many circumstances or conditions for which we can see no cause or reason unless, we are willing to recognize a link with the past. We are the combination of all that we have ever been, done, felt in this and all our other past lives. Therefore, not only do we make daily choices, but we have made choices in former lives for which we are responsible. Everyone with whom we interact in a meaningful way, whether positively or negatively, has ties with us from a previous life or lives. We are free to choose but we must realize that within each choice lies our future choices. We must face the consequences. This is karma, the law of cause and effect. Acceptance of karma necessarily includes a belief in reincarnation. Unless there is rebirth— reincarnation—the effects of former lives cannot exist.[5] The range of the fruit of karma is far beyond the reach of human understanding. Our immediate assessment of affairs cannot be trusted, because we don't know what lies ahead. Whether or not a grand plan is at play, unseen twists farther downstream make current events merely a segment of a process that is, at minimum, rather mysterious. The events in our lives are too intricate to be perceived by our limited vision.

Rudolph Steiner, the famed Austrian scholar introduced new dimensions to the mystery of karma and reincarnation, recognizing the world of spirit as a reality. Based upon his intensive research on spiritual and psychological phenomena in life, spanning from the turn of this century until his death in 1925, he affirmed that what people prepare themselves in one incarnation organizes their bodily existence in the next. People with specific abilities and strengths come into this world as the result of causes for which they themselves laid the groundwork in earlier incarnations. We are not inserted into the world order through chance.

We should not feel it a coincidence to find ourselves in our particular place, but rather that a subconsciously willed decision underlies this, as it were.[6] Through its actions, each human spirit has truly prepared its own destiny. It finds itself linked in each new lifetime to what it did in the previous one. The physical body is subject to the laws of heredity. The human spirit, on the other hand, must reincarnate over and over again, and its law consists in having to carry the fruits of previous lifetimes over into following ones. Karma presents us with situations that are predetermined, and to which we are inevitably guided through necessity, as a result of our past lives on earth. However, by using our free-will in the present life, we can create conditions for future to the extent that our capacities allow. Life has a dynamic evolving quality. Gradual development of virtues and capacities that otherwise lie dormant is the true hallmark of freedom. Our free-will breaks the bond of necessity within karma. Karma continues to operate, constantly bringing balance to our actions. The more our knowledge expands, the more we learn to make a judicious adjustment between the karmic dynamism of the past and the creative urge of our inner potential oriented to the future. The motivations flowing from such interaction ultimately determine our course of evolution. It is now widely believed that our mental consciousness and faculties are not because of something physical, the computer-like operating system of our brain. They are, in stead, the result of a soul force that we inherit at birth and which determines who and what we are, including how we think and the level of our intelligence.

Is one totally predestined or totally free? Neither of these absolute views seems to be correct. One can accept one's destiny or break from it, day by day, decision by decision. There are pitfalls along the way, of course. The examples of Stephen Hawking, who has had a brilliant career as a physicist despite extraordinary physical odds, or that of the Irish artist and writer Christy Brown, whose story is told in the film, *My Left Foot*, demonstrate something of the presence of freedom to overcome enormous odds given by destiny. Hawking must use mechanical means to communicate his insights to students as he suffers progressive paralysis due to Lou Gehrig's disease. Brown, because of the limitations imposed by cerebral palsy, paints and writes with his left foot. One could, of course offer examples in the other direction of persons with seeming "golden paths" set by their destiny who somehow go awry and fail to achieve what is expected.[7]

Karma is simply cause and effect. It is not the purpose of karma to reward or punish. Its purpose is to educate the subconscious, and to purify it. Once the subconscious is purified, it no longer needs karma, or the

"Karmic Cycle", as we refer to it. The karmic cycle is the chain of lives we live in order to workout all of the negativity we have earned in previous lifetimes. When the balance-sheet is zero, the subconscious is purified. We then no longer need to come back again to learn. The most important way to look at death is as part of the cycle of descending into matter – earth, and then ascending into pure spirit – heaven worlds, and doing this over and over again until we have attained our full development and become at home or at one with the divine forces. (The subconscious mind survives death, so that a new life means merely exchanging one body for another.)

Spiritual development of humanity leads progressively to the ego's control of the astral, etheric and physical bodies. Spiritualization of matter is the goal of humanity, according to the Hindu Upanishads. We are spiritual beings, our bodies themselves are only atoms in a particular vibration. We, human beings, look like we are material stuff, flesh and blood, but we are atoms, pure energy. When we look deeper into atoms, we first see particles, and then, at deeper levels, the particles themselves disappear into patterns of pure energy, vibrating at a certain level. Every thing in nature has some sort of counterpart in the nonphysical world. Outer space is not vacuum as we understand it. It is teeming with energy. The entire cosmos, at every plane and in every form, is energy. Our body is a form of energy and so are our thoughts and feelings. These forms of energy differ from one another in terms of the rate and amplitude of their vibrations. Every quantum of energy is interchangeable with every other one, and there is a continuous transformation of energy from one form to another. Thus, everything in the universe is interrelated. When you have succeeded in breaking the identification with your body, senses, and thought, you merge into pure consciousness – Universal Energy. Virtual particles appear and disappear continuously in what we think of as empty space. We don't understand this energy or where it's coming from.

Life has a purpose. Events happen for a reason. Begin the process of finding meaning behind each life event. Live by letting yourself be guided. Know that you are fulfilling your life's destiny. Only when complemented by a surrender to a higher order can the efforts of the personal – will bear wholesome fruit. Be alert to some kind of a message or intuition. Coincidences lead us toward the attainment of our mission. There are no chance encounters; everyone comes to our life for a reason and has a message for us.[8] The karmic law requires that every human wish find ultimate fulfillment. Non-spiritual desires are thus the chain that binds man to the reincarnational wheel. The physical karma or desires of man must be completely worked out before his continued stay in astral world becomes possible. Our soul has certain intentions for this lifetime.

In order to fulfill those intentions, we select the parents and the early circumstances that would help us develop along certain lines. Those who still have earthly karma to dispose of and who must, therefore, reinhabit a gross physical body in order to pay their cosmic debt. One of the strongest forces affecting our lives is that of karmic drive which consists of strong desires or expectations carried over from past lives. The unfulfilled desires or expectations become karmic in nature in that they are looking for fulfillment. Evolution moves, and moves through us. Therefore, action is necessary part of life. We need to be aware of right action and do it. Living right helps us transcend into the higher spiritual level. Our future in this life and others is temporarily planned, based on forces we have either set in motion or previously blocked. We are coming into a period of greater intuitional, mental, and spiritual development which will help us be more aware of what is or is not manifesting in our lives and what we can do about it. The more aware we are of the future, the more we can, with our understanding, intent, and actions, reprogram this life and future lives. Dreams, intuitions, and insights all let us know some of what is transpiring. The main thing is for a person to open to overall development that can bring greater awareness, so better choices can be made.[9]

Sri Aurobindo, considered to be the greatest spiritual- evolutionary theorist, writes in his classical work, *The Life Divine,* that each being reaps what he sows; from what he does he profits, from what he does he suffers. This is the law and chain of karma, of action, and it gives a meaning to the total force of our existence. It is evident on this principle that a man's past and present karma must determine his future birth and its happenings and circumstances. Man is the creator of himself, he is the creator also of his own fate. All this is perfectly rational and may be accepted as a fact, as part of the cosmic machinery; for it is so evident, rebirth once admitted, as to be practically indisputable.

To expect anything is always a mistake. If you act without feeling that you are the doer, then there will be no impediment. Problems come from the internal conflict between what you expect to happen and the way life actually unfolds. "History is so full of unexpected things that some of the simplest facts in our lives we cannot foretell," said the famous Russian novelist, Alexander Soltznitsyn. Everything happens only when its time comes. No matter what plan you may have, with all the world's expertise put into it, it can go awry for some excuse or the other. There is someone else's hand into it. That's what we need to recognize. All affairs of heaven and earth are ruled by a single divine being. Events occur in accord with the dictates of a single natural law or principle. "I have spent years tussling with loss. But you finally get to realize it's not necessary for things to work out the way you want them to, in your own little mind," says the famous film star Nick Nolte. There is such enormous complexity in life, so little understanding of why things happen as they do, that it is folly to believe we are able to know what is about to happen.

To achieve greatness, you must be willing to surrender ambition. You set goals, but don't be driven by them. Trust that you are being guided to the fulfillment of your destiny. Larger forces than yourself are at work in your life. Give up the demand for the outcome you think you want and learn to appreciate whatever it is you get.[10] Hear the voice that God has given you and let your mind obey that. Joe Pesci, the character actor says, "I have come to believe you can't chase success. You can chase it your whole life and never get it. Turn your back on it, all of a sudden you have got it." One day while he was working as a restaurant manager in New York, he got a call from Robert De Niro to play a role in *Raging Bull*. That changed his life.

"What matters is not what happens to you, but how you react to what happens to you. More important than what you do is what God does through you, and you will never find that out except in those moments when you have no choice but to surrender yourself completely," says Chuck Colson, aid to Richard Nixon and now a reborn-Christian. "When I was in prison for Watergate scandal, I realized that I must have been put there for a purpose – to help prisoners," he says.

It is possible for the individual to realize his potential beyond his own dreams. But, when dreams come true, they do so at a price. No one escapes the weight of natural justice which may give with one hand, but invariably takes with the other. Do the best you can, and rest content with that. Be prudently adventuresome! Don't be so risk averse as to lose out opportunities. Calculate the odds and try to keep them on your side. Be cautiously optimistic. Do not let the prospect of failure in chancy situations prevent you from exerting plausible effort in trying to bring a matter to a successful conclusion. Before self publishing his book on economic cycles in 1984, Dr. Ravi Batra (hitherto an obscure professor at Southern Methodist University, Dallas, Texas) had sent it to Lester Thurow at M.I.T. Thurow agreed to help out the young Batra by writing a brief introduction to the book. In 1987, Simon and Schuster, Smelling a market for a sensational book to coincide with the stock market crash of October 19, 1987, purchased the rights to Batra's book under the condition that it be rewritten and retitled *The Great Depression of 1990*. [The original title, *Regular Cycles of Money, Inflation, Regulation and Depression*]. It became the best-seller of its time.[11]

All great men and women have been people of faith, believing that everything was unfolding as it should, in its own time. They have had an attitude of calmness and confidence and a belief that there was a power greater than themselves. That was helping them. "Over the centuries, the great beings of all traditions have told us to turn within if we want to experience the highest truth. When we are able to touch the divinity within our own hearts, we understand that everything is happening through the will of God. Then, wherever we are, whatever we are doing, we have the experience of perfection," says Gurumayi Chidvilasananda. Act without motive of fear or consequences. Right action is necessary. It does not matter what the results will be. You must trust your Master, you must trust yourself. Unless there is a perfect trust, there can't be the perfect flow of love and power. There is nothing you can't do if you will, because you are a spark of God's own fire. The process of karma is not such a tough thing to figure out. When you are putting out supportive, loving energy into your universe, you will surround yourself with supportive, loving individuals. People who are honest and trustworthy usually believe that others are the same way. Karma is the belief that everyone is like us, so if we are doing good things, we begin to view the occurrences of our life as good. When we do bad things, we begin to view the occurrences of our life as bad.

Each of us must look at the significant turns in our lives, try to perceive the sequence of interests, important friends, coincidences that have occurred in our life. Weren't they leading you somewhere? All the twists and turns of our lives are preparing us for a purpose, a mission we have been pursuing without being fully aware of it, and once we bring it completely into consciousness, our lives can take off.[12] Gary Cooper, the veteran actor, had very clear thoughts about fame, glamour and other pitfalls of civilized life and society. He once said, "I don't like to see exaggerated airs and exploding egos in people who are already established. No player ever rises to prominence solely on talent. They are molded by forces other than themselves. They should remember this – and, at least twice a week drop to their knees and thank providence for elevating them from cow ranches, dime-store ribbon counters and book keeping desks." "To assure something worthwhile happening, first pray about it, and test it according to God's will; then put a picture of it on your mind as happening. Put the matter in God's hands – and follow God's guidance," said Norman Vincent Peale in his masterpiece book, *The Power of Positive Thinking*. Unconditional surrender to God's will is the only way to achieve happiness. Be at peace with what you are, while endeavoring to achieve your defined life's goals; keeping in mind the hand of power beyond you.

The basic elements such as internal drive, intelligence and integrity, which determine our course of action in life are in place before puberty. Some combination of genes, parental care, nutrition and schooling create building blocks. We are not merely the physical creation of our parents, we are also their spiritual creation. That is why we are born there: to take a higher perspective on what they valued. Your path is a higher synthesis of what these two people believe. The problems your parents were unable to reconcile, they left for you. This is your evolutionary question. Your quest this lifetime. "It was not quite late in life that I began to understand my father and mother as human beings, and to realize how their personalities and mine had been shaped by their circumstances," wrote Dennis Healey, Ex-Chancellor of Exchequer, England in his memoir *The Time of My Life*. In his book *The Clinton Enigma*, Pulitzer prize winning journalist David Maraniss has covered a four-and-a-half minute speech delivered by president Bill Clinton on August 17, 1998 confessing that he had misled the nation about his relationship with Monica Lewinsky. He analyzes the familiar patterns of Clinton's personality starting with his troubled childhood. He took attributes from two women who raised him in his infancy – the freewheeling spirit of his mother, the stubborn will of his grand mother – with him into his adult life.

Psychologists suggest that, throughout their lives, people arrange themselves in hierarchical orders based on deeply ingrained perceptions of their personal abilities and importance. Often, an individual's view of whether he should be a general, a lieutenant, or a foot-soldier is formed early in life. It evolves from birth order, or perhaps from favored status with a parent. In his important 1996 work, *Born to Rebel*, the American social historian Frank J. Sulloway has demonstrated that people respond during personality development to the order in which they were born and thus the roles they assume in family dynamics. Later-borns, who identify least with the roles and beliefs of parents, tend to become more innovative and accepting of political and scientific revolutions than do first-borns. They do it by gravitating toward independent, often rebellious roles, first with the family and then within society at large. In his new edition of the book *"Birth Order,"* the eminent psychologist, Dr. Kevin Leman, claims that in any family, a person's order of birth has a lifelong effect on who and what that person turns out to be. Birth order makes sense most of the time for a vast majority of people. Citing an example, Leman explains why Lee Iacocca had style and all the tools to be a master CEO of the Chrysler Corporation. He is aggressive, decisive, straightforward, compassionate, volatile, funny and always someone who could tell it like it is. All these traits can be traced right back to how a first-born son grew up in a loving Italian home in Allentown, Pennsylvania. The values inculcated by his parents, particularly his father, gave him incredible resilience and steely resolve. According to Leman, if you are a perfectionist, reliable, conscientious, list-maker, hard-driving, natural leader, chances are that you are a first born in the family. If you are a mediator, compromising, diplomatic, avoid conflict, you are a middle child. If you are a manipulator, charming, blame others, attention seeker, you are likely to be the baby in the family. On the other hand, if you display the traits of being very thorough, high achiever, self-motivated, fearful, cautious, voracious reader, have very high expectations for self, it describes the only child.

The desire to make a difference in one's world manifests itself in early childhood. Indira Gandhi reached the heights which, from childhood, she had felt was her destiny. Both our physical characteristics and temperament are fixed before birth. We cannot escape our inner person, the core that makes us what we are. If you try to make yourself into some ideal person, you will fail. You can't escape that inner core. We are what we are. There is a law of nature that governs the extent of any change we initiate ourselves. "The man who wishes to succeed must never pretend to be other than you are; for all pretense is a hindrance to the pure light of truth - which should shine through you as sunlight shines through clear glass. You must work for the sake of the work, not in the hope of seeing the result. You may face without fear the trials and difficulties of the path. They are the result of past actions. You cannot alter them. So, it's useless to trouble about them. You must bear your Karma cheerfully."[13]

People need a sense of purpose to maintain a will to live under the starkest possible way. Dr. Viktor Frankl, the psychoanalyst and a Nazi death camp survivor, in his masterpiece treatise on *Man's Search for Meaning* raises a pertinent question, "Are you sure that human world is a terminal point in the evolution of cosmos? Is it not conceivable that there is still another dimension possible, a world beyond man's world; a world in which the question of an ultimate meaning of human suffering would find an answer?" Even Leo Tolstoy at one stage in his life pondered with the questions: "Why should I live? Is there in life any purpose which the inevitable death that awaits me does not undo and destroy?" A karma yogi answers those questions by saying, "To achieve final salvation in the Lord is indeed to find that the human body has completely fulfilled its purpose; a master then uses it in any way he deems fit." A master, one who has achieved salvation, is able to materialize and dematerialize his body and move with the velocity of light, and to utilize the creative energy of light rays in bringing into instant visibility any physical manifestation. His mass is infinite. This is in agreement with the famous equation outlining equivalence of mass and energy ($E = m \times c^2$). The release of the atomic energy is brought about through annihilation of the material particles.

Gary Zukav writes in *The Dancing Wu Li Masters* that every subatomic interaction in the physical world consists of the annihilation of the original particles and the creation of new subatomic particles. The subatomic world is a continual dance of creation and annihilation, of mass changing to energy and energy changing to mass. Transient forms sparkle in and out of existence creating a never-ending, forever-newly-created reality. In other words, science advances the hypothesis that a microscopic form of rebirth underlies everything in the physical world. In the *Tao of Physics*, Fritjof Capra refers to these subatomic particles as being 'destructible and indestructible' at the same time. This is precisely what is implied by reincarnation: even as we die we are capable of activating another body. Destructible yet indestructible. Dead yet very much alive.

Many modern-day scientists on the cutting edge of the computer technology revolution are convinced that information is the key to immortality. Yoneji Masada, a leading figure in the Japanese plan to become the first fully developed information society, writes enthusiastically of the newest vehicle to earthly immortality: "Unlike material goods, information does not disappear by being consumed, and even more important, the value of information can be amplified indefinitely by constant addition of new information to the existing information. People will thus continue to utilize information which they and others have created, even after it has been used." Information is impervious to the ravages of time. It is of this world but does not die with the flesh. Just as some religions might contend that the body is merely a temporary vessel for the everlasting spirit that resides in it, the new cosmologists would contend that the body is merely a temporary vessel for the information that is embedded in it. Similarly, many molecular biologists see the information contained in DNA as immortal. In their limitless possibilities to reconstruct and reinvent the body, move DNA across species boundaries, erase the genetic past, and pre-program the genetic future, the biotechnologists think of life as an unfinished work of art with untold possibilities. Some scientists claim that DNA governs everything human, and that in two or three decades, using genetic technologies, human kind would have the power to direct its own evolution. This volitional evolution is bringing into question the definition of being human, the relationship of human beings to their genetic heritage, and the very existence of God. Freeman Dyson, physicist, and author of the book *The Origin of Life,* writes: "It is impossible to set any limit to the variety of physical forms that life may assume. It is conceivable that in another 10^{10} years, life could evolve away from flesh and blood and become embodied in an interstellar cloud – or in a sentient computer." Human cells are building blocks of life, just as matter is made of atoms. Cells are chemical computers full of computational tricks and can transform inputs into outputs, the way computers do. Compared to even the best of human computers, the living cell is an information processor extraordinaire. Cells make their protein versions by manipulating the bits and bytes stored in the cell's nucleus, in the form of DNA. The DNA in a cell contains enough information not only to make a human body, but to operate one for a lifetime. DNA is the master information storage molecule. A gram of dried-out DNA stores as much information as maybe a trillion CD-ROM disks, according to Leonard Adleman, the eminent molecular biologist, and author of *Computing With DNA*. DNA computing has become a vast research enterprise. It is too soon to say whether DNA logic gates will ever steal the computing show from Silicon. Understanding DNA's computational capabilities might reveal unanticipated insights into the nature of life itself, says Tom Siegfried in his book *The Bits And The Pendulum*. Quantum transportation is the latest in information technology where the original is moved from one place to another, unlike sending a copy. It has not yet reached the sophistication of transporting humans, like in the popular science fiction television series, *Star Trek,* evoking images of captain Kirk dematerializing and then reappearing on some alien world. Here, a sophisticated computer converts matter temporarily into energy. The human body is transformed into billions of bits of information, which are then sent through space by way of electronic pulses. The information is then downloaded and reassembled at its destination, restoring the body to its original form. People could even be suspended in transit until a decision is reached to rematerialize them. To transport humans in reality, a good teleporting machine must put every atom back in precisely its proper place. That information would require a billion trillion desktop computer hard drives, or a bundle of CD-ROM disks that would take up more space than the moon. And it would take about 100 million centuries to transmit the data for one human body from one spot to another., according to Samuel Braunstein, a quantum physicist at the Wezmann Institute in Israel.

Nancy Cooke de Herrera narrates a true story in *'Promises to Keep'* about teleportation, the ability to be in two places at the same time. It was the spring of 1963 when Millie Hoops, a longtime follower of Maharishi Mahesh Yogi, famed for transcendental meditation, was ill with cancer and praying to see him before she died. Maharishi had promised to be with her and guide her across to the other side. He had just returned from a trip to Canada and was describing the success of his mission to a select group of followers in a meeting when he suddenly grew silent. Then, in a hush, he said, "I will leave you for a few minutes." He walked upstairs in the same building and, after a few moments only, he came down the steps to continue his conversation. At about the same time, nurses at the hospital confirmed that just before patient Millie died, they saw a person in a long white gown come down the corridor out of the darkness. As the figure came closer, they realized it was a bearded man in white robes. He was carrying a bunch of red roses. He smiled as he passed the nurses station and walked right into Millie's room. One of the nurses saw him make a gesture over Millie's head. A few moments later, he turned and left the room. Shortly after, she died. St. John hospital was at least a half-hour drive from where Maharishi was conducting the meeting. It was physically impossible for him to be there, but he kept his promise.

Another story is about a miracle man from India named Sai Baba. It is acknowledged that Sai Baba often manifests a gray, sweet-smelling ash (*vibutti*) out of thin air and pours it into the hands of visiting devotees. Visitors are astounded to see a bluish-white glow surrounding his head and shoulders. Perhaps, these halos are more than just a symbolic image.

A part of the study conducted by U.S.Intelligence and the military on outer-space/extra-terrestrial/UFO since early seventies uses remote viewing (RV), (a psychic ability to mentally perceive a person, place or thing from any distance by other than normal five senses). The researchers were convinced that something very real was transpiring on a subconscious level. The remote viewers sighted not only the vehicles flying around with living beings inside, but towers located on airless worlds throughout the galaxy. They seemed to be sort of relay towers. They claimed that these towers appeared to fling vehicles beyond light-speed from one part of the galaxy to another, bypassing time and space, technologies far ahead of us out there. They describe other planets filled with beings both strange and wonderful. One group of aliens that remote viewers came into mental contact with were shapeless, phantom like entities able to manifest themselves in any way, shape or form. They exist in other dimensions and therefore outside of our time. They can apparently "pop" into time at any point they choose, often carrying out operations in different times concurrently. In our hemisphere, nothing can travel faster than the speed of light (about 300,000 Km or 186,000 miles/sec). This is because, as a body approaches the speed of light, its mass increases until, at the point of light speed, a spacecraft would need access to an infinite amount of thrust, which means using an infinite amount of fuel. Thus the speed of light is the absolute universal limit to how fast a spacecraft can travel. When spiritual adepts reach certain states of ecstasy, their bodies allegedly free themselves of gravity, allowing them to levitate, and sometimes move at a considerable speed. Teleportation of objects by human beings is said to be accomplished through the manipulation of universal energy. The capability of objects to appear and disappear at will have their origin to a different electromagnetic frequency to ours as they enter our dimension in the visible spectrum. Reporting in their publication, *Here Be Dragons*, (The Scientific Quest for Extraterrestrial Life), David Krorner and Simon LeVay state that humans have succeeded in engineering lifes that owe nothing to carbon chemistry, nothing to chemistry of any kind, nothing to evolution, and nothing even to nature. The quest to understand how the spark of life ignites from non-life has intrigued the minds of many eminent scientists, however. The main problem, of course, is that life as we know it depends on very long and specifically ordered polymers to catalyze reactions and to hold and transmit genetic information. The probability of even one such polymer assembling itself by chance is extremely small, according to some experts. Others believe that through autocatalysis, life could take on by itself.

Such wondrous visions of space strengthen our religious beliefs. "Once you know that death is not the end of your existence, then you are truly liberated," said David Morehouse, former army major, who entered the remote viewing unit in 1988. He went on to have a wide variety of experience beyond earth. "The only thing I can imagine it being like is going into the presence of God and standing there in a four-dimensional world where you can go forward in time- any thing at any given distance. Omniscient, omnipotent, that's how you become. That is the realm of God."[14] Psychic phenomena should convince even the most ardent skeptics that there is definitely something beyond the five human senses at work.

"The virtues we acquire, which develop slowly within us, are the invisible links that bind each one of our existences to the other – existences which the spirit alone remembers, for matter has no memory for spiritual things." *Seraphita,* Honore De Balzac, the French novelist).

"The mystery of life, coupled though it be with fear, has given rise to religion. To know that someone impenetrable to us really exists, which our dull faculties can comprehend only in their most primitive forms - this knowledge, this feeling, is the center of true religiousness. In this sense, I belong in the ranks of devoutly religious men". Einstein.

Shirley MacLaine, famous actress and spiritualist, found a link between grounded earth realities and the cosmic spiritual reality.[15] She became aware of the "coincidences" in her life and started feeling some "preordained plans" unfolding according to her willingness to accept for what she was ready. She believes that every one is a soul, of divine origin, and one that has lived many times before and will live again. She is a staunch believer in the reincarnation of life and transmigration of soul. She further states that our life is a colossal cosmic joke because it would continue its own course regardless of what we did or didn't do.

> *"I have felt it necessary to seek divine guidance for whatever decisions I have made. If you want to be fulfilled, you must find your purpose in life. To do that you must need to realize it's not your decision. It is what God wants from you. I have always felt that if God wants me to do something, he will see me through, and he has."— Coretta King*

> *"Life is a chaos anyway. Things happen by happenstance. You are under an illusion if you think you are in control."— William Shattner*

> *"What happens to a person is characteristic of him. He represents a pattern and all the pieces fit. One by one, as his life proceeds, they fall into place according to some pre-destined design." — C.G. Jung*

> *"Fate, karma, destiny———-call it what you will——— —there is a law of justice which somehow, but not by chance, determines our race, our physical structure and some of our mental and emotional traits." — Parmahansa Yogananda*

> *"Wherever we go, wherever we remain, the results of our actions follow us."—unknown*

> *"Be not one whose motive for action is the hope of reward, since happiness lies in the doing."— Lord Krishna advises Arjuna in the Bhagavad Gita*

> *"All actions take place in time by the interweaving of the forces of nature, but the man lost in selfish delusion thinks that he himself is the actor." — The Bhagavad Gita*

"When there is no search for a result, but only continual movement of thought, then that's creative thinking. That's the purpose of life To think creatively is to bring about harmony between mind, emotion and action. The desire to arrive at an end or achieving your goal is but an escape from the present turmoil." — J. Krishnamurti

"We go through life with a series of God-ordained opportunities, brilliantly disguised as challenges."— Charles Udall

"A spiritually mature person is one who acts without worrying about the fruits of his action, a person who is unmoved by acclaim and by criticism." — Bhagavad Gita

"I feel myself driven toward an end that I do not know. As soon as I shall have reached it, as soon as I shall become unnecessary, an atom will suffice to shatter me. Till then, not all the forces of mankind can do anything against me."— Napoleon Bonaparte

"I know with absolute certainty that we live many lifetimes on this earth. The more we understand about our past lives, the more sense our current lives make. Death is not an end but simply another transition in the ongoing, eternal journey of our spirits. Our spirits are nothing more or less than pure energy, and energy can't be destroyed. Spiritually, I was already convinced that reincarnation existed. Regression hypnosis confirmed it."— Sylvia Browne, a renowned psychic, and author of 1999 book, "The Other Side And Back"

"And may I, recognizing all things as illusion, Devoid of clinging, be released from bondage." — lojong, Tibetan spiritual writings by Langi Thangpa

"Lead me from bondage to freedom; lead me from death to immortality." — Upanishads

"It is the neophyte who thinks renunciation and disciplined action are separate."— *The Bhagavad Gita*

"Everything returns that has not been resolved to the end. When all cravings and compulsions have been stilled, then the ultimate must happen."— *Siddhartha*

"Our future is not a predetermined, static destination. In reality, it is a movable object, a set of probabilities, and most important, a karmic consequence of the lives we lived yesterday and the lives we live today." — *Marianne Williamson*

"If there were no karma, mind wouldn't be."— *Maharishi Mahesh Yogi*

"If we find the answer to why the universe exists, it would be the ultimate triumph of human reason. For then we would know the mind of God." — *Stephen Hawking, Theoretical Physicist*

"We must infer our destiny from the preparation. We are driven by instinct to have innumerable experiences which are of no visible value, and we may revolve through many lives before we shall assimilate or exhaust them."— *Ralph Waldo Emerson*

"Tendencies deeply rooted within our nature require a future life for their realization." — *unknown*

KARMA

What is this life, O' God, I wonder?
I think and weep, sleep and ponder.
I wake and find the same old thunder.
I walk, but slip like a wavering younger.
But, the voice of duty beholds and cries,
"Beware you man, the slave of karma.
You do your lot and seek my sharna.
I judge and fix your deeds and dharma."
Thus I kill my grief and sorrow.
And take this verdict as a hope for tomorrow.
And keep on my efforts to an endless chain.
Like a common passenger in a long journey train.

Pritam Ahuja

Notations :
YOUNGER – Youngster
KARMA – Actions born of cause & effect
SHARNA – Refuge
DHARMA – Our true purpose in life

CHAPTER SEVEN - SELF
AND SPIRITUALITY

*"As it becomes harder to achieve material success as a result
of one's efforts, people are looking elsewhere for meaning and
purpose - often to the spiritual realm."*— *Gail Sheehy*[1]

A man is made up of three personalities, three elements, each partly dependent and independent of the other. First there is body; second, there is mind, constantly making decisions that body may refuse to comply with; and third, there is something else, which seems to become stronger instead of weaker as time goes by; an element of spirit, a directive force which takes control over both mind and body. As far as our physical heritage is concerned, no matter how much change and progress mankind has experienced in the external aspects of life, man's real core, his true being has not changed.

Spirituality is not meant to be separate from the body. Nature balanced mind, body and spirit as co-creators of our personal reality. When the material, psychological and spiritual dimensions are brought into balance, life becomes whole, and this union brings feelings of comfort and serenity.[2] Within you is a divine capacity to manifest and attract all that you need or desire. You are both a physical body in a material world, and a non-physical being who can gain access to a higher level. That higher level is within you and is reached through the stages of development. To reach the ability to know and use your divine inner energy, you must move beyond your identification as being exclusively a physical body. You are an infinite, limitless, immortal, universal and eternal energy temporarily residing in a body. You know that nothing dies, that everything is an energy that is constantly changing. Individual consciousness and universal consciousness are one and the same. Your mental picture provides a direction for the flow of energy and gives substance to its eventual appearance in material form. Some people stand out over others. They seem to have an inner glow, that little spark of enthusiasm that shines through. Our inner glow expresses our level of energy and exuberance for life.

A growing number of us are coming to understand that there need be no discrepancy between spirituality and success in the work place. Material abundance is simply not enough to make people fulfilled. The key factor seems to be a moving beyond purely materialistic and competitive concerns to the discovery of a deeper meaning. In fact more and more of us have come to know that it is from our most deeply held beliefs that our greatest success can come. "No other nation has invested such profound thought in understanding the process of human development as India", says Frederick Harmon, author of *The Executive Odyssey.* "It is here that I received the strongest reinforcement of the idea that all growth in life is fundamentally an internal process (spiritual growth), and that external conditions are shadows of the inner self." Bill McCartney, after more than 30 years in sports and 13 years as head-coach of the top-ranked college football team at Colorado University, before announcing his resignation in 1994 said: "I believe part of the reason God called me out of coaching is to pray for and speak to the spiritual blindness sweeping our country." Now, as a co-founder of Promise Keepers, he has dedicated his life asking men to vows of commitment into spiritual and moral purity.

In 1943, the psychologist Abraham Maslow published a now-famous paper in the Psychological Review, entitled "*A Theory of Human Motivation,*" in which he identified what he termed a hierarchy of needs. At the bottom of the list are the basic needs for food, water, and oxygen which ensure our day-to-day survival. When these are satisfied, we turn to warmth, safety, shelter and long-term survival. At the third level is the need for love and procreation, ensuring the survival of the species. Once this has been looked after, people crave for esteem and social status. At the top of the hierarchy comes the need for self-actualization, the need to become our true spiritual selves. At present most people see growth in predominantly material terms. With general shift toward higher states of consciousness, we would begin to see growth in a much wider context; personal and spiritual growth would become as important as material growth. Peter Russell, author of *The Global Brain Awakens*, states that rapid as the growth of the information industry is, it may not be the fastest growing area of human activity. There are indications that the movement toward the transformation of consciousness is growing even faster. We, the human beings, are by no means a finished product; we are evolutionary work in progress. As we evolve, we become less separate, moving our boundaries so as to become a part of the universal wisdom.

We have the power and the knowledge to become anything we want to become. The acknowledgment of our seemingly invisible spiritual power would hasten our improvement. As a society, our ultimate purpose in creating technology may be to mirror our collective striving for a connection with a deeper spiritual sense of ourselves and our fellow human beings. Einstein said, "Science and spiritual understanding are the same thing. So, if you have gone as fast as you have with higher technology, why not try to make connection with the spiritual stuff?" Spiritually, this goal manifests itself in a burgeoning interest in meditation and the exploration of Eastern religions. Technologically, the world of radio, TV and cyberspace make us aware of limitless realities outside ourselves. This new awareness contributes to a stronger sense of self – an awareness of individual capabilities.[3] It is the phenomenon of spiritual force that is operating behind the changes we notice daily.

The Western day is nearing when the inner science of self-control will be found as necessary as the outer conquest of nature. The human mind can and must liberate within itself energies greater than possible with external matter. Perhaps, the most unexpected development of our time is that religion and science are ceasing to point in opposite direction. What, precisely, is the mind, the elusive entity where intelligence, decision-making, perception, awareness and sense of self reside? Where is it located? How does it work? Does it arise from purely physical processes – pulses of electricity zapping from brain cell to brain cell, helped along their way by myriad complex chemicals? Or is it something beyond the merely physical – something ethereal that might be close to the spiritual concept of the soul? According to the renowned neuroscientist, Dr. Candace Pert, intelligence is located not only in the brain but in cells that are distributed throughout the body. Brain is not the source of intelligence. It is simply a data processor. It takes in data through receptors called senses. It interprets this energy information according to its previous data on the subject. It tells you what it perceives, not what really is. Based on these perceptions, you think you know the truth about something, when actually, you do not know the half of it. In reality, you are creating the truth that you know. These are questions probed in an interesting article published in the *Times* magazine of July 17, 1995, entitled *Glimpses of The Mind*. Until recently, unraveling the relationship of mind and brain was beyond the realm of observation and experimentation. But, science has finally begun to catch up with philosophy. According to expert view, all the research does not mean that science is on the verge of understanding consciousness. It may be that scientists will eventually have to acknowledge the existence of something beyond their ken – something that might be described as the soul.

Non-dualistic reality is a state in which physical and spiritual merge and become one. This is called flow-state. Such states are accompanied by mental efficiency as a feeling of effortlessness. When you feel alive and attentive to what you are doing. In this state, you are at your best performance level. The common features of flow experience are high challenge, clear goals, a focus on psychic energy and attention, and continuous feedback. Effortless activity happens at the highest level of performance in every area of human endeavor. There is nothing like thinking in the usual methodical way. What takes its place is more akin to an informed instinct. Consciousness vanishes and you feel free of all mind-body constraints. When acting and thinking become one, there is no room left for other thoughts. Problems are not shelved – they don't exist during the flow state. Years of practice and experience combine on some occasion, giving rise to a new capacity to let execution unfold beyond technique, beyond exertion, beyond thinking. Action then becomes a pure expression of art, of being, of letting go of all doing – a merging of mind and body in motion. When all that we have realized has become the very basis of our being, we have gained the final path of no more learning. That brings in a natural spontaneity and joyful freedom. An unknown mechanism hidden in the extremely intricate yet unexplored nervous structure of the body is the spiritual energy called "kundalini." Coiled like a snake at the base of the spine, Kundalini is the spiritual force that lies dormant in every human being. Once awakened, often through meditation and yoga practices, it rises up the spine and finds expression in the form of spiritual knowledge, mystical vision, psychic power, and ultimately, enlightenment. It leads to the emergence of a conscious personality possessing such astounding attributes as to make the phenomenon appear to be the performance of a supernatural agency. Efforts to translate this form of spiritual energy into the electromagnetic energies with which physicists are familiar has been largely unsuccessful. The precise nature or source of this energy and how it finds its way into our material world remains unknown. The idea that enlightenment has a biological basis for evolution and development of personality is growing in acceptance as scientists discover more about the brain and consciousness. It is here, perhaps, that the physical and the nonphysical meet, where spirit and matter intertwine, and where the unknown and the knowable touch each other. Some of the terminology and techniques used to attain this level of maximum performance when body and mind become one are described below: [4] [5]

Conscious State

Conscious state is an awareness of body and breath. It means totality of one's thoughts and feelings. As one up-levels his own consciousness, he sees more creative solutions to the problems that he is confronting.

Sub-Conscious State

This state is active in dreamless sleep, and is associated with temporary mental separation from body and breath. In deep sleep or dreamless sleep, one takes journey into the unmanifested. One merges with the source. You draw from it the vital energy that sustains you. This energy is much more vital than food.

Super Conscious State

Is a freedom from the delusion that existence depends on body and breath. [Our exploration of the outer space may someday reveal the mysteries of astral residents (liberated from earth through salvation) living in super consciousness.]

During sleep, the muscles relax, but the heart, lungs and circulatory systems are constantly at work; they get no rest. In super consciousness, all internal organs remain in a state of suspended animation [life, motion], electrified by cosmic energy [i.e. through yoga]. Using this power (cosmic universal energy), the yogi finds it simple to unite his mind at will with divine realms or with the world of matter. He sees more creative solutions to the problems that he is confronting. [Yogi is the person who practices yoga.]

Cosmic Energy

Streams of highly penetrating charged particles bombarding the earth from outer space.

Yoga

(The science of mind control). Yoga literally means to join or yoke. It helps integrate the mental and the physical plane or alignment. It is a method of restraining the natural turbulence of thought which prevents communion with the spirit. Through the practice of yoga over an extended period of time, one learns that the mind itself has a higher state of existence, beyond reason—- a superconscious state. There are various progressive stages of yoga practice. The first step is an intellectual exercise of concentrating the mind on one point (dhyan). Subsequently, the intellectual function drops off when the inner sound kills the outer sound and the union of the self with Higher Self is attained. Yoga is the science of mind-wave quieting. In order to psychically see the world or the moon reflected in a pool of water, we must wait until every ripple is stilled. Then the clear image will appear.

Right postures (Asanas); control of breath (Pranayam); withdrawal of senses from external objects; concentration (holding the mind to one thought) Dharna; meditation (Dhyana) and super-consciousness (Samadhi) are some of the essential steps to attaining unison between body and mind. Yoga is a perfect, scientific, and appropriate method of fusing body and mind together so that they form unity. This unity creates a psychological disposition which makes possible intuitions that transcend consciousness. Total detachment (oneness of soul and body) is the ultimate form of yoga.

Yoga is perfect evenness of mind. It can be achieved through various paths: karma yoga, raja yoga, bhakti yoga and jnana yoga. Karma yoga is the path of right action—a selfless service for personal good as well for the good of all, not for the reward or for the satisfaction of personal desires. The holy book, Bhagavad Gita, is an expression of karma yoga, which Lord Krishna teaches to Arjuna in the battle field at a dramatic moment. The metaphor is that there is a battlefield inside every man; the battle is against the ego and its attachments. Raja yoga is the interface between ordinary consciousness and knowledge of the absolute through meditation.. It controls the mind, strips down the layers of the ego, and helps in attaining samadhi, the universal state of consciousness. The aspirant then attains nirvana, which is the state of abiding joy and peace. Bhakti yoga fills the yogi's mind with God, with love for God and worship of God. Jnana yoga is a deeper inner search for self-realization. The goal of all the yogas is the attainment of consciousness of the unity of individual soul (Jivatman) with the over-soul (Parmatman).

Meditation

Control of sensory mind and intellect. You cease being a prisoner of the body, and are in communion with your spirit. Under this state, nature automatically obeys the will of the man. The body becomes merely a piece of clay. Sensory organs come to a halt, permitting the yogi to achieve identity with cosmos. In this state, nourishment is derived from the finer energies of air and sun light, and from the cosmic power that recharges your body.

During meditation, you slowly learn to relax before you can connect with and channel universal energy. By gaining access to nature's inner, effortless computing system, you liberate huge amount of energy and creativity. New circuits, new areas of brain become available to you for your thoughts, perceptions and actions. Brain wave integration takes place during the practice of meditation. Through meditation, one can enter silent spaces between thoughts, the gap in which the thinker, the process of thinking, and the object of thought are revealed as one.[6]

Meditation awakens and frees the mind helping us develop clarity. It is an unconditional way of living moment by moment. Meditation is used to transcend human limitations, gain self-realization and experience the divine. Meditation explores, investigates, unveils, and illumines what is hidden within us and all around us. In simple language, meditation is the practice of thinking about or perceiving one thing at a time. It's a way of personal development through fusion of the disciplined mind and the creative spirit. It brings in a unity of being that is not divisible into thoughts and feelings. One is thus able to transcend the normal chattering of mind and achieve a much higher ability to function in the affairs of everyday life. Modern researchers have noted that during meditation, a practitioner's heart rate slows down, his brain rhythms go into a different mode, he becomes detached neurologically from his surroundings and actually sensitive to the object of his contemplation. This leap into the unknown is the most powerful shift of energy that can occur within human consciousness.

According to the *Yoga Sutras* by Patanjali, meditation is an unbroken flow of thought toward the object of concentration. In other words, meditation is prolonged concentration. Ordinarily, a thought-wave arises, remains in the mind for a moment, and then subsides, to be succeeded by another wave. In the practice of meditation, a succession if identical waves are raised in the mind; and this is done so quickly that no one wave is allowed to subside before another rises to take its place. The effect is, therefore, of perfect continuity.

It has been said that if the mind can be made to flow uninterruptedly toward the same object for twelve seconds, this may be called concentration. If the mind can continue for twelve times twelve seconds (2min & 24 sec), this may be called meditation. If the mind can continue in the meditation for twelve times two minutes and twenty-four seconds (28min & 48sec), all mental distractions disappear and mind becomes one-pointed. Then similar thought-waves arise in succession without any gaps between them and it enters the state called *Samadhi*. As the aspirant grows in concentration, he may find himself suddenly possessed of psychic powers—-he may be able to foresee the future or control certain other natural forces.

Enlightenment[7] Enlightenment is the absolute knowledge founded on the identity of the mind with the object. During enlightenment, the enlightened mind succeeds in breaking through the multipartite functions of the brain, thus creating a unified whole mental module maintaining the conviction that he is one person, of one mind, in charge of his affairs in an ordered universe (cosmic unity). Each of us harbors not one but many minds, which, if true, suggests that one's individual brain is a galaxy of various intelligences. Once we better understand the human nervous system, we may be able to explain the phenomenon of enlightenment more logically.

There are many different perspectives on enlightenment.

Some think it happens suddenly, in a flash of light; others believe it only comes about through a gradual process of deepening awareness. Enlightenment is not about becoming divine; instead, it is about becoming more fully human.

Renunciation Renunciation doesn't mean walking away from responsibilities and loved ones; it does mean doing our best and abandoning our emotional attachments and compulsive preoccupations. Renunciation means to let-go, to accept things as they are, trusting the process and to live in the moment.

Liberation Liberation means freedom from want; letting things be as they are; freedom from both fear and hope. A man must cease to identify himself with the mind in order to win liberation. When he knows beyond doubt that he is the real Self (*Atman*), and not the mind, he is made free from his karma. The universe exists in order that the experiencer may experience it, and thus become liberated.

Consciousness is not a destination at which we finally arrive. It is an ongoing, ever-deepening, infinitely expanding process, a journey that perhaps has no end. According to Sri Aurobindo, considered to be the greatest spiritual evolutionary theorist, "The spiritual evolution obeys the logic of a successive unfolding; it can take a new decisive main step only when the previous step has been sufficiently conquered: even if certain minor stages can be swallowed up or leaped over by a rapid and brusque ascension, the consciousness has to turn back to assure itself that the ground passed over is securely annexed to the new condition. A greater or concentrated speed does not eliminate the steps themselves or the necessity of their successive surmounting."

The natural evolution of consciousness is toward a spiritual breakthrough that liberates mind from the chain of logic and reason and achieves a superior, more reliable vision of reality. We must have patience and compassion for ourselves, knowing that real change takes time. Once we have established a relationship with our own inner teacher and guide, we have an access to an unerring source of clarity, wisdom and direction, right inside us at all times.[8] Ideas are stored in our mind-body system. Beneath the surface crust of ordinary consciousness, we are filled with ideas and associations linking with other ideas – the very stuff of evolution moving in us to emerge as innovation.

Some scientists believe that consciousness (when self becomes whole) may result from certain properties of subatomic particles in the brain. Others claim that consciousness emerges from the binding effects of electrical oscillations in our neurons. Yet another viewpoint is that consciousness exists in the form of a field spread throughout space. Individual minds can tune in to this field and so "resonate" with one another. But in the end, all fail to bridge the gap between brain states and feelings, or explain consciousness as a derivative of brain function.[9]

According to Hindu scriptures, each person is an embodiment of an individual soul, which is perceived as consciousness. The soul is atomic in size and is situated within the heart. It is believed that there are innumerable particles of spiritual atoms which are one ten-thousandth of the size of human hair, smaller than the material atoms, and thus beyond the appreciation of the material scientists. This very small spiritual spark is the basic principle of the material body. It is a form of energy which can be raised by accessing ourselves to super consciousness (for example through yoga, meditation etc.) This current of the spirit soul is felt all over the body as consciousness. Material body minus consciousness is a dead body. When the soul is purified from the contamination of material atmosphere, its spiritual influence is exhibited.[10]

The unconscious part of our mind is the possessor of extraordinary knowledge. It knows more than we know. "We" being defined as our conscious self. Awareness is a process of the conscious mind coming into synchrony with the unconscious. It is difficult to define unconscious except to hypothesize it with God. Ultimate goal of the individual is to become as one with God, since the unconscious is God. Healthy choosers intuitively cultivate their spiritual intelligence. They trust an internal compass and conduct their lives from a self-directed reason that, at times, can seem illogical. Understanding our life's unique design, its beauty and inherent wisdoms, comes slowly and only with discernment. Disciplines such as yoga, prayer, meditation are potent growth tools. When we flourish outwardly as sturdy, distinctive persons, we're spiritually intelligent. Spiritual intelligence injects faith and wisdom into everyday matters. It is our integrated mind. Seeming delays, rejections, criticism, our own fears, apathy, sloth, and dullness, the ups and downs of normal creative cycles add fodder for discouragement. Deprived of reward, it is the spiritual guidance, where it comes from, which regenerates faith, ability to persevere, and belief in a goal as if it already exists. By faith, the heart rests in simple trust. Authentic communion with the spirit sparks that faith. Awakening of our spiritual side, no matter what the circumstances, is always a precursor to future greatness. This is seen in great leaders such as Albert Einstein, Abraham Lincoln, Mahatma Gandhi, mother Teresa, Martin Luther King Jr., and thousands of others. Each felt spiritually awakened and believed that his or her accomplishments were directed by a greater force operating spiritually in the universe. They felt that they could personally tap into that force and use it. The same force exists in you and me. It is just waiting for us to awaken to it.

The Vedic system of Hindu philosophy envisages creation of universe out of atoms which are eternal. The shape of things is directly related to the individual souls left over unredeemed from the previous cycle of creation. Combination of these atoms causes creation, and their disintegration results in dissolution of the universe. Thus soul is the fundamental and only reality from which everything else has evolved. Modern science has been able to create various objects out of the fundamental particles of matter (atoms), but has not yet been able even to define in unambiguous terms what mind, consciousness and life are.

At the end of last century, theosophists Annie Beasant and Charles Leadbeater described in a book called *Occult Chemistry* the physical make-up of then every known chemical element, including some isotopes not yet discovered. This extraordinary feat they claimed to have accomplished by means of intensive yoga which provided them with faculties known as "siddhi." This psychic power allows yogis to develop an inner organ of perception that enables them to attune their vision to microscopic levels. With uncanny details, they had described every element known in their time, including several isotopes as yet unknown, now named quarks and sub-quarks, the subject of today's intensive inquiry. Also, using the extraordinary power of "siddhi," an adept can focus on particular organs, tissues, and cells of the body for healing or transformation. This ability may involve the release of bodily forces that science does not yet understand. It is conceivable that such experience involves exchange of energies that entail atomic and molecular reformation that transforms the look, feel, and capacities of tissues and cells.

"In order to psychically see the world, or the moon reflected in a pool of water, we must wait until every ripple is stilled. Then the clear image will appear," said the 4th century B.C. Indian sage Patanjali in his famous work *Yoga Sutras*. After twenty years of research supported by the Army, the Navy, NASA, the CIA and others, it is clear that the Indian philosopher had it right when he said that one obtains psi data by accessing the akashic records (the aspect of non-local mind) which in the Hindu tradition contain all information past, present and future. Akasha is a Sanskrit term that refers to a primordial substance upon which is imprinted the events of our lives. The information imprinted on the akasha includes our actions, desires, hopes, dreams, all of our life and our reactions to it. This includes past lives, what they were and what they are destined to be; the present as it is and as it is destined to be. It also includes the probable futures that we have and the destiny proposes for them. The records also contain information regarding the overall evolution of the person. Almost anyone can experience regressing to a past life. There are two ways of checking the akashic records. One is viewing and the other is experiencing. Patanjali taught that we can see into the distance and know the future by becoming what we wish to see, and creating a single-pointed focus of attention on our desired objective. He tells us that in order to see the world in our mind, we must quiet our mental waves(vriti, in Sanskrit). We have learnt to call these waves mental noise. When you reach the level of wholeness with the cosmos, then past, present, and the future become arbitrary illusions. All things, events, entities, objects flow into one another. The spectator and the spectacle are one. It is this way that the 'mediums' or paranormals say they regard the world at the moment when they are acquiring the information paranormally. It's the same way a mystic regards the world – a part of the whole. All actions and events are a part of the harmony. "As a psychic medium, I have the ability to perceive the vibrations and frequencies of those who have crossed over. Through meditation and prayer, I'm able to synchronize my energy level with those I wish to communicate with on the other side, and thereby receive their thoughts, feelings, and images," says John Edward in *After Life*.

Metaphysicists proclaim that consciousness is a non-physical, but real entity. It is not produced by the physiology of the brain, instead the reverse is true: it is consciousness that directly influences the brain. Quantum physics demonstrates the existence of consciousness. Quantum waves moving faster than light serve as the connecting agent between our minds and the physical world. Conscious thoughts occur on such a minute scale, involving such infinitesimal exchanges of energy, that only a quantum mechanical explanation could properly account for the actual phenomenon of consciousness.[11]

Thus something very strange goes on in the conscious brain which appears to be beyond what we can understand in terms of our present day physical world picture. The future of consciousness are being supplied by fields as diverse as neurology, psychology, cosmology and quantum physics. And added to this is the growing sense that a merger between the highest teachings of science, religion and mysticism is long overdue – a grand synthesis that will finally help us solve the greatest mystery in the universe. New discoveries in the science of mind are likely to challenge many deeply held religious beliefs about mind and body relationship. In order to understand the functioning of the mind, logically the most obvious way to explain consciousness would be to show how conscious experience can be built of material that is itself unconscious. We have no private insight into the unconscious state because, by definition, such a state cannot be experienced. We close our eyes to fall asleep (unconscious state) and then (barring dreams) morning comes immediately. The search for the secret of consciousness is certainly one of the most important projects in human history.[12]

Many scientists believe that consciousness is an emergent behavior, that an individual neuron in the human brain is not conscious but that the billions of neurons in the brain working in a multitude of varied and interlocked assemblies, some cooperating, some competing, give rise to consciousness. Various levels of consciousness ally at least to some degree with corresponding levels of neuronic complexity and functionality. Stimulation or suppression of various neuronal patterns affects consciousness, as anyone who has ever fallen asleep can attest. Spiritual awareness is a matter of passing through a series of steps to broaden our perspective. We must intend to integrate each increased degree of awareness into our daily routine. Humans are, in essence, a field of energy. However, our normal energy levels are weak and flat until we open up to the absolute energies available in the universe. We have finally reached a point where the idea of a personal transcendent experience (also called enlightenment, nirvana or cosmic consciousness) has reached a significant level of acceptance. How consciousness and the physical world interact is now much less of a mystery; consciousness is but energy in its finest and most dynamic form. This helps explain why events are affected by what we imagine, visualize, desire, want or fear, and why and how an image held in the mind can be made real.

In his book, *The Conscious Universe*, Dean Radin, Director of the consciousness research lab at the university of Nevada, Los Vegas, states that while the idea that the mind can affect the physical body is becoming more acceptable, it is also true that the mechanisms underlying this link are still a complete mystery. Besides not understanding the biochemical and neural correlates of "mental intention", we have almost no idea about the limits of mental influence. Many geneticists and molecular biologists believe that after we get a grip on the remaining mysteries of DNA, we will finally be on the road to the golden age. And after the human genome has been fully unmapped, we will really understand human behavior at its most fundamental level. Sooner or later, biologists claim to succeed in understanding almost everything about the human organism and the role of each gene in shaping the mind and body. Incidentally, the biological differences between various human populations are minimal. There are, for instance, only six of some thirty-thousand human genes that are thought to influence human color. Genetically, we are all part of the one family. Stephen Hawking, a distinguished physicist, views genetic engineering as the power to accelerate the choices that evolution takes thousands of years to make. Likewise, many neuroscientists fully expect that once they have unraveled the electrochemical complexities of the brain, they will then finally understand the nature of consciousness itself. (The complete system of human genome was published in 2001. It was announced that the human genome contains not 100,000 genes, as originally postulated, but only 30,000. That is, scattered throughout the genome are 30,000 distinct stretches of digital information that are directly translated into protein machinery to run and build the human body. In the coming decade, geneticists will identify genes that differentiate us from chimpanzees, infer which of them were subject to natural selection during the millions of years our ancesters evolved into humans, identify which combinations are associated with normal, abnormal, and exceptional mental abilities, and begin to trace the chain of causation in fetal development by which genes shape the brain system that lets us learn, feel, and act. The source of difference between a chimpanzee and a human being lies not in the different genes but in the same set of genes used in a different order and pattern. The difference between two individual human beings amounts, on average, to 0.1 %. The human genome contains three billion "letters" of code. That amounts to three million different letters between any two individuals.)

All life stems from two very different classes of molecules: nucleic acids and proteins. These groups form the very heart of what is meant by life. Nucleic acids store life's software; the proteins are the real workers and constitute the hardware. The two chemical realms support each other only because there is a highly specific and refined communication channel between them mediated by a code, the so-called genetic code. This code, and the communication channel – both advanced products of evolution – have the effect of entangling the hardware and software aspects of life in a baffling and almost paradoxical manner.[13]

Many people nowadays are having experiences of profound change in their personal consciousness and sense of self because of chemicals designed to cause such experiences. Although there is immense amount unknown about drugs – why and how they do what they do – it is certain that many of them have the ability to alter the quality of human life. Drugs can enable people to discover quite different personalities within themselves and to change dramatically over rather short periods of time. Drugs, in short, can be changers both of the self and of fundamental ideas about self. Drugs, for example, might help us find out which part of the brain controlled certain things. We might learn something about mental illnesses which might be caused by an imbalance in the chemistry of the brain. Psychopharmacology is a recognized field of medical practice and research, an enormous worldwide industry, and an intimate part of the personal lives of millions of people. What we have at the present time is the enormous range of chemical substances – all the way from milk chocolate to crack cocaine, from ginseng tea to LSD – that have effect on how we feel or think. The late astronomer and author Carl Sagan was a secret but avid marijuana smoker, crediting it with inspiring essays and scientific insights, according to Sagan's biographer. In one of his essays, Sagan said, "I can remember one occasion, taking a shower with my wife while high, in which I had an idea on the origins and invalidities of racism in terms of Gaussian distribution curves. I wrote the curves in soap on the shower wall, and went to write the idea down." Society may not be comfortable with the idea of drugs as tools for spiritual exploration, but it is obviously willing to accept drugs as tools for psychotherapeutic and even cosmetic purposes. Current research in genetics and neuroscience guarantees that there will soon be much more information about what role the genes (and the chemicals the genes make) play in our emotional lives. This may imply that human consciousness, including the sense of self, is mediated not only by genes and childhood experiences, but also by the chemicals that we take into our bodies. The future of the self will be determined, in part, by the drugs that are available and how we use them.[14] Spiritual values are becoming an integral part of optimal health for individuals and institutions alike. While organized religion has eroded over time, modern Western medicine has begun to encroach on the infinite complexities of the spiritual domain.

Some scientists believe that robots will facilitate the transference of human consciousness into computers. They will scan the functions of each cell in the brain, then simulate them through a computer program until slowly the simulation duplicates the brain's entire contents and functioning. The range of human experience – thought, emotions, physical sensations – arise not only from the electrical activity in the brain, chemicals play a part too through the endocrine system and neurotransmitters in the brain. But if all information can be digitized, then presumably chemical and hormonal influences can as well. All this promise teeters perilously on two assumptions, of course: that consciousness is emergent, and that it is computable. And what if consciousness is not local but universal, if the boundaries between minds are not rigid but fluid, and if, as attested by mystics, we contain within our apparent individual minds the continuum of all minds? Rodney Brooks, director of artificial intelligence at MIT, says in his 2002 book *Flesh And Machines* that the complexity of our body makes it unlikely that we will simply be able to download our brains into a computer anytime soon.Humans will remain ahead of pure robots because of the bioheritage to augment whatever machine technology may have to offer.

Frank Tipler, a professor of mathematical physics at Tulane university, has proposed a similarly universal simulation. According to Tipler, "The human being is a biochemical machine completely and exhaustively described by the known laws of physics. A person is a particular type of computer program (very complicated), and the soul is nothing but a specific program being run on a computing machine called the brain." And so, religion, he concludes "is now a part of science." He bases his arguments on quantum and relativity physics.[15] According to the modern-day scientists, the study of consciousness is a scientific problem. There is no justification for the view that only philosophers can deal with it. We also can not be driven to embrace religious beliefs; only an act of blind faith can make them acceptable. According to the Nobel Prize winner, Francis Crick, if the scientific facts support the hypothesis that neurons are the link between mind and body, then the idea that man has a disassembled soul is unnecessary.[16] Each one of us is the behavior of a vast interacting set of neurons. Brain is attached to the rest of the body and communicates with it. The nervous system receives information from the various transducers in the body. A transducer turns a chemical or physical influence, such as, light, sound or pressure into an electrochemical signal. We need to understand just how all these chemical and electrochemical processes interact. Thus, brain has an operating system, just as a modern computer does, and its actions correspond to consciousness. The ebb and flow of neural traffic is mediated by the neurotransmitters dopamine, serotonin and adrenaline, and any disturbance to these chemicals, or damage to the tissue that is sensitive to them, can have catastrophic effects on the way we think, feel and behave. Thus, when we do some nice thing to others or ourselves, the brain is flooded with serotonin, the "feel-good" neurotransmitter that helps to energize us. By the way, experts claim that serotonin normally hits the system full force at about ten o'clock in the morning. Neuroscientists now believe that mind and body are not different. The thoughts and emotions that we think emanate out of our mind are, in fact, the result of complex interactions within and between nerve cells in the brain. What allowed Mozart to compose an entire symphony in his head or the Indian mathematical prodigy Ramanujan to discover complex theorems without the benefit of formal education? Neuroscientists now claim that such special traits arise from the activity of neurons in specific parts of our brain and that our sense of having a nonmaterial soul is really an illusion. Although, in the long run, an all embracing theory taking in emotions, imagination, dreams, mystical experiences and so on will be necessary, Francis Crick assumes that all the different aspects of consciousness employ a basic common mechanism (or perhaps a few such mechanisms). Understanding the mechanism for one aspect will go most of the way to helping us understand them. V.S.Ramachandran, a famed neuroscientist at the University of California, San Diego, author of *A Brief Tour of Human Consciousness* and *Phantoms In The Brain* claims that a specific part of the brain associated with temporal-lobe epilepsy is also associated with intense religious experience, thus pointing to the physical existence of the soul. Yet, there are unsolved puzzles to the point that one feels impelled to invoke divine intervention.

Majority of evolutionary biologists and psychologists are in agreement that,so far, every one of our mental traits (except for those obviously learned) is a product of natural selection and we have no control over it. There is a specific component of brain tissue that gives rise to our understanding. Such a state could not be replicated in a computer. In a recent compilation of articles by eminent scientists in her book, *Mapping the Mind,* Rita Carter has summed up the views with the statement that we are machines, but we will continue to feel and to act as though the essential part of us is free of mechanistic imperatives. But, future generations will take for granted that we are programmable machines just as we take for granted the fact that earth is round.

The sheer genius of modern technology and its achievements encourages the belief that, however complex life's design, it must eventually be equaled in a machine. Possessing a technology (such as nanotechnology) so sophisticated that we can contemplate the design and construction of objects, which are every bit as complex in terms of number of components per unit volume as living cells, encourages the belief that machines will one day be built which are capable of self-replication, and that artificial life based on a completely different design to that on earth will finally be achieved. Nano is a prefix and measured in nanometers it means billionth's of a meter, not quite a quarter-millionth of an inch. Compared to bulk processing, nanomachines can build one atom at a time by placing them just where they ought to be. Nanomachines could link atoms together precisely into the exact molecular structure that you desire. Picture nanomachines inside your body, breaking down plaque on your artery walls, tearing apart invading microbes (such as HIV), delivering molecules of medicinal drugs to the cells where they are needed, destroying tumors, rebuilding torn or diseased tissues wherever they are found. Yet, the undeniable fact remains that many characteristics of living organisms are still without any significant analogues in any machine which has yet been constructed.[17] Nanomachines exist today only in dreams of farsighted engineers and scientists.

Bill Gates, founder of the Microsoft computer company, thinks that there is nothing unique about human intelligence. All the neurons in the brain that make up perceptions and emotions operate in a binary fashion. "We can someday replicate that on a machine," he says. Earthly life is carbon based, and computers are silicon based, but that is not a major distinction. Eventually we will be able to sequence the human genome and replicate how the nature did intelligence in the carbon based system. He doesn't seem to be convinced that there's something special or divine about the human soul. "Evolution is many orders of magnitude ahead of mankind today in creating a complex system. We will understand the human mind someday and explain it in software-like terms," he conjectures. Together, the computer and the gene create a powerful new mind/body dualism. In the coming years, humanity will come to use the computer more and more as a "substitute mind" – or language – to manipulate, redirect, and organize the vast genetic information that makes up the physical substance of living nature. The final integration of the information and life sciences comes in the form of the "molecular computer," a thinking machine made of DNA strands rather than silicon. Scientists have already constructed the first DNA computer, and it is predicted that in the near future, much computing will take place along DNA pathways rather than on the integrated circuitry of a microchip. DNA's ability to compute information greatly exceeds the most advanced supercomputers that exist. Unlike most conventional computers, which are sequential and can handle one thing at a time, DNA is a massive parallel computing machine and can theoretically compute a hundred million billion things at once. DNA stores the information in much the same way as computers. DNA is essentially digital. This means it can count. With the mapping of the approximately 100,000 genes that comprise the human genome having been completed, new breakthroughs in genetic screening including DNA chips, somatic gene therapy, and the imminent prospect of genetic engineering of human eggs, sperm, and embryonic cells is paving the way for the wholesale alteration of the human species and the birth of a commercially driven eugenic civilization.[18] As a corollary to the above, IBM scientists have now constructed a basic computer component using a single carbon molecule which would theoretically result in computers far more powerful and cheaper to build and run than today's silicon-based computers. Within the next decade or so, chip designers will be unable to pack more transistors and capacitors into small spaces on computer chips using traditional technology. At that time, the electronic industry will embrace this new technology that can continue to miniaturize computer components. The results of their findings were deliberated in the 2001 August meeting of the American Chemical Society. It is likely that, in the distant future, a biological machine might perhaps be grown and put together artificially that understands.

Jeff Hawkins, inventor of the Palm hand-held computer, says he has discovered a new framework to understand how the brain works. His hypothesis is that the brain works by anticipating and completing patterns more than it does through inputs and outputs of information, a commonly accepted theory. His concept of pattern-completion memory is based on the belief that memory triggers itself—-just like someone mentioning the name of a familiar person to you brings to mind his whole imagery. Mr Hawkins hopes to build a silicon machine modeled on pattern-completion memory. He is a new convert from digital technology to neuroscience, and believes that a new understanding of our brain will lead to the creation of truly intelligent machine with processors as powerful and as integrated as human neurons.

The human genome, the so-called "Book of Life," will be used for diagnostic tests that can spot the telltale changes in a cell before a cancer begins to grow, to DNA microchips that someday may provide a complete readout of a person's genetic virtues and flaws, to a new generation of drugs that compensate for shortcomings of a patient's genetic material. With this information, we will be in a position to unimaginable insights into what it means to be alive, to be conscious, and to be human. According to computer scientist Carl Feynman, "We have discovered that the gray mush in our heads is probably not the best material for thinking." In the Life magazine's projection of what the world will be like in years 2001-3000, Paul Horn, senior vice president of research at IBM, says that sometime down the road, people will be phased out of the process. Computers will soon be using their superior thinking material to make themselves even smarter. Humans and computers are already collaborating on the design of new generation of such computers. That might change our perception of the world profoundly, if all this happens to come true.

According to John R. Searle, professor of philosophy at U.C. Berkley, machines might have conscious thoughts in the same sense as any human being. Humans are machines of a special biological kind, and it might be possible to produce a machine out of different materials that can also think. Thinking is merely the formal manipulation of symbols, and that is what a computer does; the mind is to the brain as the program is to the hardware. Nature's way of doing things might not be the only way – or necessarily the best way. It could be that trying to give silicon circuitry the same kind of intelligence as that displayed by protein-based system simply isn't the way to go. Even more so, if the particular traits we try to imitate turn out to be "fixes" adopted by nature to overcome some shortcoming that an engineering approach starting from scratch doesn't have to be stuck with in the first place. But, despite nearly forty years of astounding technological advances that have exceeded all predictions, the early artificial intelligence (AI) vision of reproducing all-around humanlike reasoning and perception remains as elusive as ever. Daniel Dennett supports this observation of elusivity in his classic book *Kinds Of Minds* by arguing that the molecular keys needed to unlock the locks that control every transaction between nerve cells are glutomate, dopamine, and norepinephine, among others. The function of each of these chemicals depends on its fit with the lock. This distribution of responsibility throughout the body makes this changing of the locks practically impossible. Too much of the information processing and storage is enbedded in these particular materials(all carbon-based). Therefore, it really does matter what you make a mind out of. You could not, for example, make a sentient mind out of silicon chip, he thinks.

According to Howard Gardner, professor of neuropsychology at Boston school of medicine, human mind is better thought of as a series of relatively separate faculties, with only loose and unpredictable relations with one another, rather than a single, all-purpose machine that performs at a certain horse power, independent of content and context. Thus, a person's strength in one area of performance simply does not predict any comparable strength in other areas. Each category of intelligence rests on its own neurological substrate, and can be nurtured and channeled in specific ways, depending on a particular society's values. Which genes control which aspect of intellectual functioning and how genes work together to produce intelligent behavior remains a mystery as yet. In his 1999 book, *The Age of Spiritual Machines,* Ray Kurzweil projects that before the next century is over, human beings will no longer be the most intelligent or capable type of entity on the planet. Computers will achieve the memory capacity and computing speed of the human brain by around the year 2020. The number of transistors in the Intel's computer chip has increased from 29,000 in the model 8086 in 1978 to 7.5 million in the pentium in 1998, and the microprocessor's capability has grown ten thousand-fold over the same twenty years. By 2011, Intel expects to deliver chips that have one billion transistors. This exponential improvement stems from Moore's Law, which says that the power of microchips doubles every eighteen to twenty-four months. Now Robots move large number of wafers between the processing steps instead of the technicians using tweezers early on. The tools of the digital age extend the capabilities of our minds. They magnify our ability to think and articulate our thoughts. The question will arise in the long run whether computers can match the human subtlety and complexity of thought, and can we call them conscious? Will they also claim to have spiritual experience? Kurzweil prefers to leave this issue for future generation to resolve. However, he does make a claim in a later article published in *Psychology Today,* of February 2000, that if freeing of the human mind from its physical limitations is a necessary step in evolution, then technological evolution, such as scanning of the brain onto a computer, moves us inexorably closer to becoming like God. This freeing of our thinking from our biological form may be regarded as an essential spiritual quest. The freeing of our thinking from our biological form may be regarded as an essential spiritual quest. Ray Kurzweil is now predicting that the coming technology explosion will make infinite life span possible. Millions of blood cell-sized robots, which he calls 'nanobots,' will keep us forever young by swarming through the body, repairing bones, muscles, arteries, and brain cells. Improvements to our genetic coding will be downloaded via the internet. We wouldn't even need a heart. He believes that humanity can achieve immortality in no more then twenty years from now. This is the subject of his 2005 book *Fantastic Voyage*. In an interview with the News Magazine of September 1, 2001, the famed British physicist, Stephen Hawking states that if humans hope to compete with the rising tide of artificial intelligence, they will have to improve through genetic engineering. Science could increase the complexity of DNA and 'improve' human beings. He thinks that we should follow this road if we want biological systems to remain superior to electronic ones. Astronomer Carl Sagan in his book, *Billions and billions*, said, "The prediction I can make with the highest confidence is that the most amazing discoveries will be the ones we are not wise enough to foresee." Our computer scientists and cyberneticists are even now discussing the possibility of one day downloading the entire personality of a human being into a mechanical container, an artificial body that would, for all practical purposes, be virtually immortal. Indeed, these cyborgs would be the ideal future explorers of far flung worlds, unhindered by the dietary requirements of fragile human flesh.

In a recent publication, *The Science Times Book Of The Brain*, developments on the status of consciousness over the past five years have been summarized elegantly. Some neuroscientists believe that brain is an image-making machine. In its default mode it generates the random images that we call dreams. In waking mode, the images are modulated by incoming sensory data into precise representation of the external world. The relationship of these images to consciousness is a matter of interest to philosophers as well as neurophysiologists. Some believe that once we understand how the images are generated – a formidable problem but one that seems to be within reach – we will also understand everything we need to know about consciousness. Others argue that consciousness is more complicated than mere perceptions; we not only see the world, we feel it, and these qualitative sensations cannot be explained by the mechanics of the brain's operation. The theologists argue that we need to examine the experience of mystics, who experience their own consciousness in its simplest form, a feeling of oneness with the universe, the highest experience that the conscious brain has to offer. So, there are still far more questions than answers. The award-winning science writer, John Horgan concludes in his book, *The Undiscovered Mind,* that the more intelligent or aware or enlightened we become – whether through drugs or meditation or genetic engineering or artificial intelligence – the more we will be astonished, awestruck, dumbfounded by consciousness, and life, and the whole universe, regardless of the power of our scientific explanations. We can not make a science of God for God is not an object like other objects of thought. According to the Vedas, God is possessed of a celestial non-material form which has the attributes of being, conscious, bliss, and all-pervasiveness.

Dr. Candace Pert, a research professor in the department of physiology and biophysics at Georgetown University, states in her book *'Molecules of Emotion'* that chemicals in our bodies form a dynamic information network, linking mind and body. The neuropeptides and receptors, called information molecules, use the code language to communicate our emotions. The decision about what sensory information travels to our brain and what gets filtered out depends on what signals the receptors are receiving from the peptides. So, there is a biomolecular basis for our emotions. According to her, this concept of information-network as a mind-body link is replacing energy and matter as the common denominator for understanding all biological life and environmental processes. Since information transcends time and space, placing it beyond the confining limits of matter and energy, then our emotions must also come from some realm beyond physical. In her view, information theory seems to be converging with Eastern philosophy to suggest that the mind, the consciousness, consisting of information, exists first, prior to the physical realm, which is secondary.

Increased blood flow to a given part of the brain correlates with heightened activity in that particular area and vice versa. Using image technology called SPECT scanning to map the brain, neuroscientist Andrew Newberg, at the University of Pennsylvania National School of Medicine, has taken snap shots to demonstrate that during the peak moments of meditation, the blood flow in brain's left parietal lobe is dramatically reduced. This region, called Orientation Association Area, is responsible for drawing the line between the physical self and the rest of existence, a task that requires a constant stream of neural information flowing in from the senses. As the orientation was deprived of information needed to draw the line between the self and the world, the scientists believe that the subject would experience a limitless awareness melting into infinite space. The boundaries of the self fall away, creating the feeling of being at one with the universe. This altered state connects with a deeper, more spiritual part of ourselves perceived of as an absolute universal reality. The subject of this study is cogently reviewed in the Times magazine of October 25, 2004, and published by Dean Hamer in his book The God Gene. In essence, it tends to project the view that God is an artifact of the brain; there is no soul; and that the mind is just chemistry.

Dr. Melvin Morse, a pediatrician, has recently published a book along with Paul Perry entitled *Where God Lives.* From a study of hundreds of critically ill children with near-death experience (NDE), he observed that those who have survived NDE were spiritually more settled than others. They trust their intuition and feel they can connect again with the divine presence they saw when they nearly died. Drawing on scientific evidence, Morse details how the right temporal lobe of the brain (he calls it God-spot) enables people to develop their sense of self and find greater fulfillment. As one child who nearly died of bacterial meningitis described it, "It's the light that told me who I was and where I was to go." He concludes that prayer would be the most likely means by which a well person could stimulate the right temporal lobe. This region is responsible for vision as well as psychic powers and vivid spiritual experiences. It is not a system that stores memory within the brain. Rather, it is a transmitter and receiver, communicating directly with a source of memory that exists outside the human brain. In the best-seller book, *Tuesday with Morrie*, professor Morris Schwartz afflicted with the Lou-Gehrig disease and approaching the end of his life, responds to Ted Koppel for the *Nightline* ABC television interview as follows: "The closer you get to the end, the more you see your body as a mere shell, a container of soul. This disease is knocking at my spirit. It'll get my body. It'll not get my spirit. I am bargaining with Him up there now. I am asking him' Do I get to be one of the angels'?" It was the first time Morrie admitted talking to God.

Jodi Foster, winner of two Oscars and graduate of Yale university, while playing the role of an astronomer in her movie, *Contact*, based on a novel by Carl Sagan, has the following to say: "Believe in the beauty and the awe-inspiring mysteries of the universe, but I believe there are scientific explanations for phenomena that we find mystical. We just don't know them yet." She hopes that the movie *Contact* would enliven the debate about life on other planets and what that could mean to religion here on earth. "Some people use God to fill in the gaps between what we know and what we don't know. As science increasingly fills the gaps of mysteries we have, where does God go?" she ponders. However, religion has come around to the view that even things that can be explained scientifically can have an underlying purpose that goes beyond the science. The more we learn, the more we realize how little we know. Humans may continue to dream of the power of prediction and control, but most self-organized systems are laced with countless uncertainties and many subtle varieties. Scientific theories may be modified or even destroyed at any moment because they are mostly based on hypotheses which can be confirmed or rejected by others. In the end, only religion claims to deliver certainty. Faith alone is immune from doubt. We dream of eliminating uncertainty by conquering and controlling nature, but chaos is central to the creation of the universe. Chaos is nature's creativity. We are so limited when facing the infinite creative power of nature.

About ninety-five percent of the universe is made of stuff that we have yet to identify. Another four percent is made up of clouds of extremely hot hydrogen and helium gas. Nearly one-half of a percent is made up of neutrinos left over from the big bang. That leaves half-a-percent for the material locked up in stars – all the stars and galaxies. The chemical elements that we are made of accounts for so little of the universe that's mostly rocks, gas, dust, and emptiness. Dramatic progress is being made in understanding how the universe is put together. When the real world of space, time, and matter is well enough known, will that knowledge reveal the creator's presence? That is the question raised by the best known scientist E. O. Wilson in his 1998 book called *Consilience, the unity of Knowledge*. He says that these hopes are vested in the theoretical physicists who pursue the goal of the final theory, the theory of everything, T.O.E., a system of interlocking equations that describe all that can be learned of the forces of the physical universe. The prospect of a final theory might seem to signal the approach of a new religious awakening. There is a debate going on presently whether this biophysical universe was created by an intelligent designer, or, is it a part of the natural evolution in which everything proceeded by chance and necessity, including the emergence of life? The evolutionary scientists think of God being used as a stop-gap for ignorance. Stephen Hawking, yielding to the temptation, in *A Brief History of Time (1988)* declared that the scientific achievement would be the ultimate triumph of human reason, "for then we would know the mind of God." Is spirituality embedded in our DNA? Dean Hamer, Chief of Gene Structure at the National Cancer Institute, writing in his 2004 book *God Genes* claims that human spirituality is an adaptive trait. He has located one of the genes responsible for production of neurotransmitters that regulate our moods. He thinks that our most profound feeling of spirituality may be due to brain chemicals governed by our DNA. According to Hamer, every thought we think and every feeling we feel is the result of activity in the brain.

Winifred Gallagher, while researching a story about the neurophysiology of orgasm, learned that because it is a reflex, the nerve impulses that generate orgasm don't reach the cognitive areas of the brain; thus the event can be neither exactly remembered nor simply produced by will. This universal yet evanescent, novel, giftlike quality is also characteristic of profound spiritual experiences. Perhaps they too are rooted in the instinctual, emotional midbrain – which in turn may help explain why intellectuals are so often uneasy about spiritual matters.[19] In our quest to understand why is it that we and the universe exist, science and mysticism often connect and sometimes overlap. In an article published in *Psychology Today* of October 1999, Dr. David N. Elkin claims that spirituality is the fastest growing – one of the only growing – sector of the publishing industry. He further stresses that spirituality is essential to human happiness and mental health. Spiritual interventions heal – sometimes when traditional psychotherapy fails – because they untie the mental and emotional knots that prevent the life force from doing its work. Gerald Celente, the founder and director of the Trends Research Institute, predicts that a new world religion will arise in this millennium. It will be based more on something loosely defined as "Spirituality" than on specific creeds, and it will appeal to the new generation.

Some of the spiritual experiences of outstanding personalities of the present era are narrated below:

"When I began to integrate spiritual recognition with my intellectual education, I felt like a complete person for the first time in my life. That 'something' that had been missing was the awareness of my spiritual self", says Shirley MacLaine in her book, *Dancing in the Light*. Wally Amos, chocolate-chip cookies fame, credits his religious faith and daily meditation with giving him strength and serenity to work through the crisis, after loosing it all.

Chuck Colson, former Nixon aid and now a reborn Christian, while being interviewed by Larry King on CNN TV network, stated that in spite of all wealth and affluence, there is a sense of despair, unrest and skepticism in the life style of Americans today. People have now begun to discover flaw in their basic values, and are, therefore, leaning toward spiritualism as a means of self-improvement and self-awareness.

Medical experts in USA are leaning toward faith-healing as complimentary to professional treatment of chronic patients. It is believed that raising their spirits using techniques, such as, meditation, chanting, psychotherapy leads to accelerated recovery.

Hitler felt himself to be a prophet whose feelings and thoughts derived from a higher source; a 'possessed servant' who goes the way providence dictates. "I am now and then aware that it is not I who is speaking, but that something speaks through me." People were moved by the emotional communion established between Hitler and his audience. By hearing Hitler speak, the crowd felt transcendent presence and passion of the man about whom they had read and heard so much. In responding to his magnetic performance, the audience discovered themselves revitalized and powerful: and filled with devotion and awe for the man who had brought them together. Through him, they saw not only the vision of the future, they could partake of the ecstasy in the present.[20] Although some facets of charisma can be attributed to having an inspired gift, many aspects of it can be developed. If you believe that, then you move charisma away from mystical realm.

In order to win, you have to raise yourself to a higher level of consciousness where you become immune to fear, greed or failure. To win, you have to make sacrifices. Inertia, fear, and the pull of old habits warn us to remain where we are. To make our deepest desires come true, we must commit ourselves to reach a higher state of consciousness. Fear then becomes meaningless, replaced with immense relief at the true simplicity of life. In this way, life proceeds more naturally and effortlessly.[21]

Can you really reach the unlimited? The response is provided by the seventeenth century mystic, Angelius Silesius, "To reach the highest, it is first necessary to find yourself. Then it is necessary to lose yourself." Knowing and understanding ourselves can be acquired through books, but the second step needs transcending our limited beliefs and let spirit take control of the infinity.

> *"Right livelihood is a work consciously chosen, done with full awareness and care, and leading to enlightenment."— Buddha*

> *"The true value of a human being is determined primarily by the measure and sense in which he has attained liberation from self."— Albert Einstein*

> *"The meaning of earthly existence lies in the development of the soul." — Alexander Solzhenitsyn*

"Pay no attention to your thoughts. Don't fight them. Just do nothing about them, let them be whatever they are. Your very fighting them gives them life. Just disregard. Look through. You need not stop thinking. Just cease being interested. Stop your routine of acquisitiveness, your habit of looking for results and the freedom of the universe is yours." — Nisargadatta

"People travel to wonder at the height of mountains, at the huge waves of the sea, at the long courses of rivers, at the vast compass of the oceans, at the circular motions of the stars; and they pass by themselves without wondering." — St. Augustine, A.D. 399

"If you can make a machine that contains the contents of your mind, then the machine is you. To hell with the rest of your physical body."— Gerald Jay Sussman, MIT Professor of Electrical engg. & Computer Science

"All things and events we perceive are creations of the mind, arising from a particular state of consciousness and dissolving again if this state is transcended."— Upanishads

"Life is a journey of discovery into the most secret corners of our mind." — J. Krishnamurti

"The only journey worth taking is the journey within."— Yeats

"Be a light unto yourself."— Buddha

"The idea flow from the human spirit is absolutely unlimited. All you have to do is tap into that well."— Jack Welch, former CEO,GE

"There are no unnatural or supernatural phenomena, only very large gaps in our knowledge of what is natural."— Edgar Mitchell, Apollo 14 Astronaut

"The spirit can not be 'seen' or revealed unless the conscious mind is subjugated." — Edgar Cayce, Psychic, An American prophet

"The most pleasurable journey you take is through yourself. And that is what I have been trying to do all my life."— Shirley MacLaine

"I don't believe in God anymore, for I have experienced God."— Carl Jung, in later years of his life

"Two birds,
inseparable companions,
perch on the same tree.
One eats the fruit,
the other looks on."— Mundaka Upanishads, 5th century B.C.

The following famous verse refers to an essential unity between our individual self (feeding on the pleasures and pains of this world), and the Universal Self that transcends our body, emotions, and patterns of thought.

"What I want to achieve is self-realization. All that I do by way of speaking and writing is directed to the same end."— Gandhi

"Spirit and mind are not celestial sprinklings. Thought, like life, is matter and energy in flux. Our memory, instincts, and adaptations are all neural processes. Thinking and being are the same thing. Thinking results from lively interactions of a being's chemistry."— Lynn Margolis, in "What is Life?*

"It could be that as genetic knowledge grows in centuries to come, with ever increasing individuals coming to understand themselves as products of random throws of the genetic dice – a chance mixture of their parents' genes and a few equally accidental mutations – a new gnosis will be sanctified. Our DNA, the instruction book of human creation, may well come to rival religious scriptures as the keeper of the truth."— James D. Watson, in "DNA", The Secret of Life, 2003, Alfred Knopf

PART III:

SO, CAN YOU BE
WHAT YOU WANT TO BE?

INTRODUCTION

*"For better or worse, most people's lives seem to turn
out rather differently from what they had expected."*—
Oliver North [1]

The very purpose of our life is to seek happiness. But, basing our
happiness on our ability to control everything is futile. While we do control
our choice of action, we can't control the consequences of our choices.
Thus, we are not in control of our lives; universal laws or principles do.
We don't invent our mission in life, we detect it. It is within us waiting to
be realized. As we tap into our conscience can we discover our unique
purpose and capacity or contribution. No one can define it for you. And,
each person has his own specific mission in life. [2]

Most of us have learnt to pursue life with our egos alone, waking up in
the morning and thinking we must take complete control of our day. Yet
the mystery is always there. Each person has his or her own purpose and
distinct path, unique and separate from anyone else's. Thus, there is no one

answer to a meaning or purpose of life. The meaning of life is different for every individual. Universe always creates circumstances that lead every person to his or her own true path, and everything happens for a reason as part of a divine plan. Our subconscious mind knows what we are here for; it reaches out to us, sending messages through our dreams, intuitions, and innermost longings. The call of our destiny manifests as the hidden force behind our personality. The ultimate meaning of existence lies beyond the rational grasp of human beings, and therefore, outside the province of science.

According to western philosophy, you can rise above any circumstances and decide to be what you want to be, at any stage of your life. There are no boundaries to what you can become or do. You learn it when you know that your evolution (spiritual, mental, emotional) is never-ending and your potential for growth reaches to infinity. It is an erroneous assumption for a man to disregard his capacity to take a stand toward any condition whatsoever. Man does not simply exist, but always decides what his existence will be, what he will become in the next moment. By the same token, every human being has the freedom to change at any instant. Therefore, he can predict his future only statistically. The basis of any prediction is represented by biological, psychological or sociological conditions. Yet, one of the main features of human existence is the capacity to rise above such conditions and transcend them. The concept of predetermined life (karma), as in Hinduism, according to some critics, is a myth. Man's freedom of decision must be recognized. One's lifestyle does not necessarily depend on one's early childhood experiences or past life. Man is ultimately self-determining. What he becomes - within the limits of endowment and environment - is up to him. Man has potentialities to be a saint or a swine. Which one is actualized depends on decisions, but not on conditions.[3]

Do we make things happen or are our future states all plotted out for us by physical laws? Is there something that we can do called "exercising our will"? These are the issues that our culture is presently dealing with. Life often has its own agenda and we are destined to suffer unless we give up our attachment to things working out exactly as we would like. Being unattached does not mean being disinterested or removed; rather, it means remaining neutral in your judgment of circumstances and in your desires for a specific outcome. Unattachment means you are not bound by your expectations of how things should turn out, and that you are willing to let go. Ultimately what we choose to do for a living is best left to our intuition and values as well as to our needs and circumstances. Our best responsibility is to allow our deepest drives and talents to find expression through whatever form of service or career we choose, in the most positive, altruist way we can.

You can do whatever you set your mind to do. The idea of natural ability, genetics, education and environment, according to some pundits, is irrelevant, if not necessarily invalid. However, the most common consensus is that truly outstanding people have the critical qualities hardwired into them and if those qualities are not part of the mental architecture to begin with, any amount of developmental opportunities in their careers may not suffice to take them to pinnacle of success. To be successful, you need to have or develop great vision, ambition, thick skin, immunity to discouragement, and ability to live in isolation. Presenting a consistent personality, being yourself, saying what you mean, meaning what you say, and having everybody know it is more likely to lead to lasting, satisfying success.

Work hard to overcome your old self-defeating behaviors. What you can learn to do is leave that stage of your life behind you and walk through the gate into a new way of being. This process of leaving behind old habits begins in your invisible dimensions – that is, your thoughts. You picture yourself no longer needing to rely on those self-defeating patterns. New thoughts will ultimately lead you to new and miraculous behavior. Open yourself to the use of universal energy within you before it could happen in the physical world. Constantly remind yourself that all you have become is the result of that you have thought. Your intellect, levels of confidence, talents, fears, habits – all are physical-world manifestations of a mental equivalent. The way to change those mental equivalents is by thinking quietly, constantly and persistently of the kind of person you truly want to become. Look deep within yourself to uncover your unfulfilled needs. Pursue vocations and areas of interest that fit your inborn make-up.

Most of us start off with talents and abilities that are more or less average. Your individual potential is inside you, but it has to be developed if you want to get more of what is really possible out of yourself. You have to go looking for your calling, guided only by your muse. In order to be what you want to be, cherish your choices and maintain a control of your own life. Be geared to change, diversification, flexibility and openness. Commit yourself to your passion in work and embrace the conflicts and juggling involved. Risk being yourself, who you really are. The hallmark of people who continue growing and developing is that they become more and more authentically themselves. You don't care so much what other people think.

Be there now. Being there, in the moment, is what matters. If we are unaware of what we are doing a great deal of the time, and we don't particularly like the way things turn out in our lives, perhaps we could experiment with trusting the present moment, accepting whatever we feel or think or see in this moment because this is what is present now. This very moment is worthy of our trust. Somewhere deep within us resides a profoundly healthy and trustworthy core, and that our intuitions are worthy of our trust. Worry comes from trying to be in control of the past and the future, when the present is the only true time we have to be productive. Let go of the outcome (the future) and just enjoy the act of creating without worrying about the result. Surrender to the here and now. Many people believe that they will be happy once they arrive at some specific goal they set for themselves. However, more often than not, once you arrive 'there' you will still feel dissatisfied, and move your 'there' vision to yet another point in the future. By always chasing after another 'there' you are never really appreciating what you already have right 'here.' You end up living your life at some point just off in the future. The mind is always comparing and contrasting the present level of attainment with an ideal level of attainment. And as soon as a goal has been reached, the mind creates new levels of ideal attainments to strive for. Thus there is no chance of a relaxed sense of happiness in the present moment. Your challenge is to focus on the present, and on what you have right now, while simultaneously holding the intention of your future goals. Concentration is the ability to focus all your attention on what you are doing. When you are fully concentrating, you are wholly absorbed in the present. You are not even aware that you are performing. You pay attention to only those things that are important, and distractions don't affect you. Researchers have found that when people are successfully concentrating, their minds are relaxed but alert. This attitude is essential for taking in all the information you need in order to make good decisions.

Risk new things, risk new ways, risk failings, risk mistakes, risk pain. Be a part of the changing community, live it all. Be open to whatever life is handing us: all of it – pain, disaster, surprises, unexpected openings and losses.[4] Mahatma Gandhi said, "My imperfections and failures are as much a blessing from God as my success and my talents."

People who experience prosperity in their lives achieve a state of concentration so that everything else becomes non-existent. Their activities, instead of being a tedious set of chores to finish, become more like a meditation, only they are active and involved rather than sitting quietly. They are in the "flow." Flow has a great deal to do with purpose in our activities. When you are able to suspend your physical body as well as your ego, and allow your invisible self to emerge totally into what you are doing, your higher self is directing and producing and your body is merely going through the motions without any judgment from you. You are fulfilling your grand mission. You are experiencing magnificent joy or bliss, and nothing can get in your way. You are on purpose, and you are having the kind of peak experience that others can dream about.

Understanding how people perform at their very best is a critical undertaking. Only in the area of sport has the mind/body connection and its relationship to performance been researched seriously. Famed sports psychologist, Dr. Jim Loehr, in his article published in the *Tennis* magazine of February 1998 says that whenever we see a great player achieve sustained success, there is a psychological strength on and off the court that he or she exhibits in his or her character besides the rare talent, skill and toughness. For example, Boris Becker is a decisive, independent thinker, tremendously driven to be the best. He was not the most talented of the young Germans when he was coming up, but on psychological tests that measured passion and drive, he scored off the charts. He believed that it was his destiny to be the best tennis player in the world, and he had that belief from the time when he was very young. That's why the German coaches chose him for the national team. He then built a game that suited his own personality. "The lessons to learn from this example," says Jim Loehr, "are that you set your goals, and put your heart and soul going after them." Believe that you are on the road to success, that you have a destiny. Take the risks necessary to succeed. Choose a game that suits your personality and stick with it. It is not enough just to be good at what you do. It takes other talents to win – intangibles such as determination, experience, competitive focus, tough-mindedness, and staying power.

The state of your life is a reflection of your state of mind. Your thoughts create your physical reality. We, the humans, have the ultimate awareness of choice. We can choose to function at a lower level of awareness and simply exist, caring for our possessions, eating, drinking, sleeping, and managing in the world as pawns of the elements, or we can soar to new and higher levels of awareness allowing ourselves to transcend our environment and literally create a world of our own. Your inner transformation cannot be completed from an intellectual or scientific perspective. This is the job for your mind and your soul, the invisible segment of you that is always there but often ignored in favor of that which you can grasp with your senses. By raising yourself to a higher state of awareness, you get your life on purpose. But you must be willing to go within and discover it for yourself. This other realm defies our laws of science and logic. It is a place within each of us that is free of ordinary boundaries, rules and limitations. It is real and available to each person when he or she is ready. When you examine the lives of the most influential people who have ever walked among us, you discover one thread that winds through them all. They have been aligned first with their spiritual nature and only then with their physical selves. Albert Einstein summed it up all nicely: "Imagination is more important than knowledge." To be spiritual being means that you allow yourself the option of going beyond five senses. Hence, a whole new world opens up. As Gary Zukav writes in *The Seat Of The Soul,* "The experience of the multisensory humans are less limited than the experience of the five-sensory humans. They provide more opportunities for growth and development."[5]

Taking control involves risk. Daring to change requires courage in the face of possible failure. Making such decisions seldom seems courageous at first, but think about civil rights pioneer Rosa Parks, who made a personal decision to take control by refusing to sit in the back of a bus. She set off consequences that shook the nation and continue to fuel the ongoing civil rights struggle. This fascinating notion of innately knowing what is right has been exemplified from the time of the prophets to the modern age of Gandhi, Mother Teresa and Martin Luther King, Jr. Such individuals expressed profound certainty about the decisions they made based upon their instincts. Even during times of great personal risk or threat to their lives, they experienced little fear or doubt in making these decisions. Once they made a decision, their subsequent actions were characterized by certainty and direction. Their well-considered resolutions to exercise control came out of a deep, intuitive sense of conviction and purpose, after all the rational alternatives had been explored and exhausted. Control is a dynamic, ongoing, lifelong process that involves an interplay among rational thought, intuition, conviction, and external circumstances, as well as among individuals and the people in their lives.

The human way of growing is unique. It has no rules, and can occur in many ways. Sometimes people realize their goals instantaneously. They get a flash of insight that changes their lives forever. Sometimes growth is slow and cautious. For example, people have known for ten or more years that they would take a certain life step, but that they were waiting until they were emotionally able to do that. Identify the things that light us from within. Help your unconscious mind feel supported, valued and dignified. Say 'yes' to things that are important to you, and 'no' to things that discount your values. You will, thus, grow in self-esteem, and find what you want. There is something strong within you that directs your actions. Have faith in the power of your mind and talent to take you through life. See all problems as opportunities for creativity, growth and new answers.[6]

Creative people have frequently claimed that in their greatest works they radically transcended themselves, receiving inspiration from the gods, a higher self or divinity itself. It appeared as if one is merely incarnation, merely mouthpiece, merely a medium of overpowering forces. Like lightening, a thought flashes up. Everything happens involuntarily, with a completeness and power beyond ordinary thought. Such knowing is vision. It needs disciplined commitment to creative work as well as developing self knowledge to develop such cognitive abilities. Deep concentration, clarity of goals, loss of a sense of time, lack of self-consciousness, and transcendence of a sense of self are the main dimensions of this type of creativity. Profound intentions and highly focused activity seem to trigger startling events or meaningful coincidences that reveal a new path to be taken, a long-sought discovery or something else of significance to those who experience them. It is conceivable that such empowerments involve processes that neither science nor religion has adequately described. Does this activity result from transmission of electrical, magnetic or other forms of energy? Even if we don't comprehend all of its complexities, consciousness and living matter have a profound resonance with, and formative influence upon, each other. While such attributes require long-term cultivation for their fullest development, they frequently appear to be freely given, sometimes when we do not seek or expect them. Something beyond the ordinary self exerts an influence, raises our center of personal energy, and produces effects unattainable in other ways.[7] Daniel Amen, the neuroscientist and psychiatrist, suggests in his book *Healing The Hardware Of The* Soul that prolonged meditation may solidify new neural circuits. Distinct changes in brain activity, specifically involved in generating a sense of three-dimensional orientation in space, result in losing one's sense of physical place thus accounting for the spiritual feeling of transcendence, beyond space and time.

While making predictions for the future, Kevin Warwick, professor of cybernetics at Reading University, England, surmises that the implant technology will open up all sorts of possibilities in terms of enhancing people's capabilities. Electrochemical signals on the human nervous system can be transmitted to, and received from a computer via a fairly straightforward chip implant in a person's body, perhaps directly connected to the brain. Implants could deliver precisely controlled squirts of neurochemicals, or small, controlled electrical signals to relevant brain centers. Emotional feelings could thus be enhanced or suppressed. Living cells in our body have a whole set of sensors, switches, and timing devices, which must all be based on interactions between the molecules inside them. Advances in chemistry, biophysics, and microscopic imaging will make it possible to analyze these reactions within a single cell. A complete understanding of the working of a cell will provide a real insight into the nature of life.[8]

The pursuit of improvement in performance leads to victory, but the pursuit of victory leads to deterioration in performance. Whatever the mechanism by which it is achieved, relaxation is essential to successful performance. To be aggressive is appropriate, it serves the purpose of the game: to perform better than the opponent - to win. The determined person responds positively to challenges. Difficulties, obstacles, setbacks, seem only to incite him to further effort. The more unlikely success appears, the more the determined person strives to succeed. He has extremely high endurance. The handicaps which the determined must overcome (fear, depression, feelings of inadequacy) are best handled by disregarding them. The mentally tough person is objective under pressure. He is not concerned about what others think, or embarrassed by past mistakes. Not preoccupied with what has happened, he is free to concentrate on what should happen.

Self-assurance derives from an inner strength, a state of mental toughness that is impervious to the recognition of an inferior performance, the presence of a superior competitor, or the threat of failure. Trusting frees the individual from distracting concerns about the motivation of others. Learn to trust and be trustworthy. When we get insecure with ourselves we start doubting the integrity of others. It is essential to team work within a crew. Distrust is characteristic of losers. Continually reassess your performance to determine what should be continued and what modified. Courage is a degree of emotional stability that permits one to face reality calmly, to apply rational methods to problem solving, and to act in one's long-term best interests in the presence of fear, threats, guilt, despite anxiety or depression. All psychological studies demonstrate the major contribution of this trait to success. Courage permits us to set aside the fear and carry on.[9] In all realms of life it takes courage to stretch your limits and fulfill your potential. You must believe that you can do it, and you must take actions necessary to achieve your goals. That's the difference between people who triumph over adversity and others who succumb to it. Rosabeth Moss Kanter of the Harvard Business School coined the term 'Kaleidoscopic thinking'. It is a winning strategy to keep looking at a problem and turning the kaleidoscope until you see a different pattern. Sometimes you can develop an idea that's very different and a solution that hasn't been thought of before. The key is to recognize that there is almost always a different way to approach the issue and many times it is not the conventional way you have been doing it in the past.

You came here for a particular reason, and your divine purpose would be thwarted if you understood how everything is put together. Some things will always remain a mystery. It will unfold itself in due course. Some people discover their purpose in childhood, and others spend their lives searching for it. We must look into our hearts to discover our calling. If we look back over our life experience, we can determine when we have been most fulfilled. It is helpful to look at the talents and abilities that seem to come easily to us. Virtually every individual is driven by a deep and abiding sense of purpose. This strong sense of purpose is like a guiding light that comes from within, from their innermost intuition. They feel they have a role to fulfill in the universe. This role is their life's true work, and there is no turning back. It's not their egos that motivate them but rather this personal mission to serve a greater cause. Mary Kay Ash, founder of Mary Kay Cosmetic company, attributes her success to her mother's simple mantra, "You can do it." That was constantly reinforced over her formative years. She advises her colleagues to "fake it until you make it." She knows a great secret: If people can see themselves as the person they hope to become and act as if they are that person, soon they will not be acting. They will actually become that person.

Be governed by your inner compass, not by some clock, calendar or a schedule. The power to create quality of life is within us – in our ability to develop and use our own inner compass so that we can act with integrity, in the moment of choice. On the other hand, if things don't develop at their appropriate time, they are not going to develop at a later date. Eric Erickson, the noted psychologist, uses this notion to spell out the various phases of a person's life cycle. Each stage of life is characterized by a central task. If the task is successfully negotiated, a person moves on to subsequent stages of life more complete and fulfilled. If not, the person moves on to subsequent stages of life, but always remains troubled by the issue that he or she failed to come to terms with at the appropriate time.[10] You do certain things at certain times or never. You must begin while you have vigor to pursue a goal. Hitler, at the age of forty (1939), felt that he was running out of time. He decreed the launching of World War II, overruling the concern of military staff that they were not fully prepared. He incorporated a new concept of timing into warfare through the 'blitzkrieg' (the lightening war) – which used rapid modern technology to shorten conquest time.[11]

Within reason, you can get whatever you want if you are aware of your options, if you take shrewdly calculated risks based on solid information, and if you believe you have power. (Power of investment, authority, risk-taking). Try to regard all encounters and situations, including your job as a game, as the world of illusion. Pull back a little and enjoy it all. Do your best, but don't fall apart if anything does not pan out the way you would like it to. There is nothing that wastes the body like worry, and one who has faith in God should be ashamed to worry about anything whatsoever. It is a difficult rule, no doubt, for the simple reason that faith in God with the majority of mankind is either an intellectual belief or a blind faith.

Patience pays. When you don't know what to do, do nothing. Remain calm, but keep alert for the favorable moment to act. Sometimes the greatest acts of commitment involve doing nothing but sitting and waiting until you just know what to do next. When we believe in this approach, there is a flow around us. Things just seem to happen. We begin to see that with very small movements, at just the right time and place, all sorts of consequent actions are brought into being. Rather than getting things done through effort and brute force, we start to operate subtly. A flow of meaning begins to operate around us. There is a specific time for everything, a moment when you are in synch. That's when you give out your best. When creative people seem to be doing nothing, they are actually connecting to the time of the work, to its subtle rhythms and fractal structures. Actress Glenda Jackson referred to the time needed for a character to grow during rehearsal as "putting bread in the oven."

Scientists claim that with the advances of genetics and molecular biology underway, hereditary changes will depend less on natural selection than on social choice. Medical researchers, motivated by the need to understand the genetic basis of disease, have begun in earnest to map human genes. Gene therapies raise the prospect of elective genetic enhancement, through which individuals could introduce, boost, minimize, or delete in their sperm or eggs certain genes associated with a wide range of human traits. Reproductive biologists have cloned sheep, and presumably could do the same for human beings. In fact, on February 12th, 2004, for the first time scientists at Seoul National University, South Korea, announced that they have successfully cloned several human embryos and extracted valuable stem cells from them. Scientists are also experimenting with a limited form of molecular engineering, in which genes are altered in a desired direction. Still another fast-moving enterprise in the biological sciences is the tracking of individual development from genes to protein synthesis and hence to the final products of anatomy, physiology and behavior. It is entirely possible that within fifty years we will understand in considerable detail not only our own heredity, but also a great deal about the way our genes interact with the environment to produce a human being. Couples contemplating having a child could decide which of their own inherited predispositions they would like to accentuate or play down in their offspring. If these advances in knowledge are even partly attained, humanity will be positioned godlike to take control of its own ultimate fate. It can, if it chooses, alter not just the anatomy and intelligence of the species but also the emotions and creative drive that compose the very core of human nature.[12] Jeremy Rifkin, author of *Biotech Century*, claims that customizing genetic changes into a child, either before conception in the sex cell, just after conception in the embryonic cells, or during fetal development, is likely to become a reality within the next ten years. New breakthroughs in reproduction technologies, including the freezing and long-term storage of sperm, eggs, and embryos; in vitro fertilization techniques; embryo transplantation; and surrogacy arrangements, are revolutionizing human reproduction and conception and making possible, to an ever increasing degree, the artificial manipulation of the unborn. These developments are likely to change our notion of life in the coming century.

> *"It's a funny thing about life. If you refuse to settle*
> *for anything less than the best, that's what it will give*
> *you."— W. Somerset Maugham*

> *"You see things: and say 'why'? But I dream things that*
> *never were: and say 'why not'?"— George Bernard*
> *Shaw*

> *"You realize you aren't a superman. You're just a human*
> *being. Things happen in life for reasons you only figure*
> *out afterward."— Former New York mayor Rudolph*
> *Giuliani citing prostate cancer quit senate race against*
> *Hillary Rodham Clinton on May 19, 2000*

> *"Man's potentiality exceeds his actuality. He's never all*
> *that he can be."— unknown*

> *"The goal ever recedes from us. The greater*
> *the progress the greater the recognition of our*
> *unworthiness. Satisfaction lies in the effort, not in the*
> *attainment. Full effort is full victory."— Gandhi*

> *"Just when you think you're a big shot, something*
> *happens."— Jack Welch, former CEO, GE, in his*
> *autobiography*

CHAPTER EIGHT - JUST BE YOURSELF

"Do whatever will make you the greatest in your own eyes. You are the purpose in life."— Ramtha [1]

Our physical characteristics and temperament are fixed before birth. We can't escape our inner person, the core that makes us what we are. You are who you are. For better or worse, you can't be anyone other than you. There has never been anyone quite like you. Your creative gifts, your finger prints, your expressions, your DNA, your dreams, are unprecedented and unique. The arrangement of the atoms along the helical strands of your DNA determines how you look and, even to a certain extent, how you feel and behave. DNA is nothing less than a blueprint for building a living, breathing, thinking human being. Each individual's DNA differs from others in the same species (with the exception of identical twins), and differs even more from that of the other species. When we know who we are, we understand the values of our life, we find our worthwhile purpose. Let your answers arise from within: in their own way and time. Our inward conflicts can inform us about directions. Look into your mind, connect with it, and trust the richness of your own thinking. Have faith in the power of your mind to take you through life. Outstanding people recognize the power of their mind; they seize that power and direct it toward whatever they choose.[2]

You are the way you are for a reason. Trust your instincts. It is believing in yourself and allowing the circumstances to change that matter. It is falsehood to assume that you can be somebody else. People who refuse to obey anything but their conscience can change their destiny. Each of us has an inner compass that helps us know where to go and what to do. Trust it. People who really get things done in the outer world are continuously inspired and energized by a passion for the possible coming from the inner world. Their projects grow from inside out rather than the other way around. Important part of becoming successful is what goes on inside your own mind. Learn to adapt to each new circumstance, seeing events through your own eyes. Ignore the advice that people constantly peddle your way. Throw out the laws that others preach, and the books they write to tell you what to do. Don't seek to follow in the footsteps of others. Each of us must find our own way, at our own speed, and in our own place.

You can't will yourself to instantly forge exciting new directions. You have to give change chance to happen. Doubt and crisis would never be completely vanquished, but you must choose to have faith in your work, and accept the idea that it was what you loved to do and were meant to do. Faith and hope are hard to come by, but one has to develop necessary hope along with the faith for dreams to come true. One of the reasons many of us have trouble getting our work out into the world is that unconsciously we're competing instead of creating, which short-circuits the flow of inspiration. We squander our precious natural resources comparing the size of our talents to those of others. Turning within, observe your own true nature and maintain awareness of your natural mind. One has seen nothing until one has come face to face with oneself. For when we are illumined, the whole universe is illumined. Spirituality is a matter of self discovery. It is up to you to gauge each new situation. Rely too much on other peoples' ideas and you end up taking a form not of your own making. Feel good about yourself and how you are working with your life. Let those feelings permeate your entire body. This can help give courage and inspiration to do more or be more.

It is often said that when the student is ready, the teacher arrives. It is not always as we think, however. Sometimes the teacher may be a life situation to work through, or it may be a book, or the teaching may come through your own meditation and insights. It is best to become involved in learning that leads you to develop answers from inside yourself. Finding meaning and purpose through work is a major part of finding out who you are and what you are here to do. It's very important not to miss out on this element of truth in your life. Other times in our life the only thing we can do is try to find more satisfaction in the work that we already have. Your true vocation or calling is knowing yourself and being yourself.

The purpose of life is happiness. Some researchers have recently argued that an individual's characteristic level of happiness or well-being is genetically determined, at least to some degree. Even then, our feeling of happiness at any given moment is a function of how we perceive our situation, how satisfied we are with what we have. One of the most widely accepted definitions of happiness is that it is a state in which one does not desire anything else. Happy people tend not to value material possessions highly, are not driven by desire for power and achievement. To achieve tranquillity, you have to live your life according to your own lights. An inner peacefulness rests in the knowledge of what is of import and what is not; and a refusal to fully subject oneself to the arbitrary will of another. It involves having attained a substantial level of freedom from anxiety and a genuine commitment to something beyond oneself, such as indulging in a creative endeavor. Happiness comes from within. When we fix our problems, all we end up with is newer problems. We feel better only until the next problem crops up, which it inevitably does. In fact, we keep fixing forever without ever creating real happiness. Many economists believe that money does buy happiness – but the contentment fades as expectations rise or the signs of others induce envy. True happiness comes from finding your own inner voice and executing it, not necessarily from achieving fame and fortune. For example, Mel Gibson, the award-winning actor/director, talking about the 12 year spiritual journey that led to his controversial film 'The Passion of the Christ' said, "It might look like I'm living the high life, making movies and jetting around the world. But true happiness resides within." He had achieved everything he hoped for – except a sense of purpose. It led him to the faith of his boyhood, to a spiritual realization – the message of faith, love and forgiveness, as depicted in his movie. It is the story of a man who submits himself to his fate, who tells God, "Let your will be done."

Part of success is taking risks and building confidence in yourself. Leadership is the quality that transforms good intentions into positive actions. Throughout their lives, productive individuals grow increasingly authentic. They relax into who they are and realize their creative powers without the phoniness so common to some others. Our authentic being frees us to be fully ourselves, thinking, feeling individuals with a distinctive life. We must further our sense of self.

Self is instincts, intuitive senses, awareness, our destiny; your inner voice that tells you what is right and wrong for you. Pay attention to your inner voice to the best of your ability, no matter how ridiculous they might sound. They are the link to all the knowledge already stored within you. Remain conscious to that inner spark which shows up as bold impulses, and honor it. Respect the wisdom of your natural instincts, because they are probably superb when it comes to weaving everything you need into your life. All those who have ever made a difference in any profession have

139

listened to their inner voice and proceeded independent of the opinion of others. By honoring this voice, you fulfilled your own divine purpose. Acting according to your will is your spiritual journey. Don't do a thing to change yourself. Instead of designing yourself to fit the world, you can design a life to fit your abundant gifts. A commitment to challenging work gives life meaning. You need to learn to plan and enjoy going after what you want instead of waiting for it to come to you. Even if you don't get what you want, if you give it your best try, you will find yourself mysteriously fulfilled and able to move on with the rest of your life. You may feel some hurt, but when you have played out your hand, your heart will set you free. So don't concern yourself with the outcome.[3]

The urge to pursue your own goals, to determine your own destiny, has been termed by psychologists as "Self-Actualization." It is generally considered to be the highest stage of human development outside more esoteric spiritual stages of development. This stage evolves as we move from survival and security to finding our own unique role in society on our own terms, based upon what we have learned or experienced in life.

All around, during the acquisition binges of the 1970, Estee Lauder cosmetic company saw business firms becoming conglomerates. There was pressure for them to do the same. The Lauder's inner voice said no, stick to what you know best and don't change it lightly. Today, the same firms are spinning off the subsidiaries because they weakened instead of strengthening the original product. Estee Lauder, who concealed her real name Esther Mentzer and Hungarian parentage so as to completely disconnect herself from her past before entering the world of cosmetics, says, " The voice grows stronger with each success, each observed failure. All one has to do is listen—and watch. I have discovered that pondering facts and other people's judgments usually leads me down the wrong path. My first reaction is almost invariably the right one. My body, my mind, my heart, tells me yes or no, and I've learned to act on my visceral reaction." Incidentally, names have power. Catchy ones stay with us, dull ones earn obscurity. Which is why Reginald Dwight decided to call himself Elton John and Cherilyn Sarkisian became Cher.

Consider Madonna, the pop diva of songs and dance. A USA Today article points out that, since the birth of her daughter, Lourdes, Madonna is seeking serenity. She is newly immersed in spirituality and self-discovery. Her past incarnations as the avaricious material girl or the slutty bride in *Like a Virgin* were just mileposts of her evolution, notes the article. "I am reinventing myself," Madonna says. "I'm going through the layers and revealing myself. I'm on a journey, an adventure that's constantly changing shape. I was trying to fill myself up with wrong things. For years I've been imploring people to express themselves freely and to not be ashamed of who they are. But I was really saying it to myself, because I was raised with so much repression. I used to be so much goal-oriented. This time I am living in the moment and enjoying the journey, and not thinking what I'm going to get out of this." Madonna says she's just growing up, discovering her ownself.

People with coherent thinking judge themselves more by their internal standards than by what other people expect or think of them. They enjoy others, but success doesn't depend upon other people's opinions or even on external circumstances. Their inner values are aligned. This allows them to automatically and unconsciously move toward what is important in life. When your thinking is congruent, it attunes with your life's purpose. Coherence consists of vibrations that are all synchronized, that all add together constructively, and are focused in one direction; toward the dreams, visions and mission in life. Inner standards contribute to fulfillment in life and to be successful, we need to find a way to bridge the gap between our highest values and the way we live our day-to-day life.

All people seem to have a natural desire and capacity to contribute to life. However, each one of us has to have a unique purpose of our own. We can learn but not adopt the purpose of another. We must each discover our own. We must trust our intuition. Until we make peace with our purpose, we will never discover fulfillment in our work or contentment with what we have. Your work must turn you on; it must feel passionate. Then you live like a whole person, integrated in mind, body, and spirit, with the natural curiosity and enthusiasm for life. You are now at a point where you are being yourself, not what other people wanted you to be and the behavior you show to others matches your inside. To find purpose in life, we need to examine potential opportunities that we feel passionate about. If you want to be effective, you've got to find out what your gift is. Don't look at anybody else or else try to act like somebody you are not. Just be yourself and believe in yourself. What is that one thing that represents who you really are? What is your talent, your interest, your gift or your ambition? When you find that, your life will have a new sense of purpose and meaning, and then you can begin to educate those talents and instincts so you can become the best you can be in your chosen field. People who discovered what moved them had to overcome their self-imposed doubts and obstacles to getting started. Meaning comes to those who seek it. Any successful person can attest to the absurdity of waiting to be inspired. First we begin. Then the insight appears. Purpose evolves over our life-time. It is an ongoing process. It's through detours and frustrations that we get back on track. Whatever you are doing today, whatever is frustrating you, there is a clue embedded in the heart of your frustration that can lead you to the next step. Every clue counts, and nothing is for drill, no experience is wasted. Events that seemed random will show themselves to be parts of a coherent whole. Decisions that we were hardly aware of making will reveal themselves as significant choices. In the long run, we do not discover our purpose, it discovers us. Listen inwardly to hear the Voice that gives us direction. When you allow your mind to settle and clear, then you get the response.

Overcome the need to have other people like you. Successful people tend to be equally at home spending the day alone as they are going to a party. We spend too much of our lives trying to get people like us. Because of this we invite people to manipulate us. To become successful, you must surrender the need to have other people like you. When you quit being so concerned about whether people like you or not, you draw people to you. Life is not going to be an adventure if impressing other people concerns you. If you can get past those obstacles, then what you have left in your life is love of doing what you enjoy the most, and that is the true definition of the meaning of life. Our purpose in life is the very act of enjoying and appreciating life itself. If you can eliminate fear from your life you've taken a big step toward learning to appreciate the present moment.

Life's vision is wrapped up tightly with our own identity as persons. Believe in yourself. Don't let anyone, even someone trying to help you, destroy your belief in yourself. Don't ever stop believing in yourself and you will win whatever race you are in. Stay focused, don't let yourself become distracted from your goals. But remember, after all, it's only a game. Enjoy it while you can.

Personal fulfillment is a feeling that you are becoming everything that you are capable of becoming. It is a sure knowledge that you are moving toward the realization of your full potential as a human being. It is the primary characteristic of the healthiest, happiest and most successful men and women in our society.[4]

Maharishi Mahesh Yogi, the apostle of transcendental meditation, puts his thoughts on following your dreams this way: "Keep your desires turning back within and be patient. Allow the fulfillment to come to you. Gently resist the temptation to chase your dreams. Pursue them in your heart until they disappear into the self, and leave them there. Attend to your inner health and happiness. Happiness radiates like the fragrance from a flower and draws all good things toward you."

The process of discovering who we are and what we are here to do is dependent to a great extent on our ability to stay positive and find the silver lining in all events. Staying positive is a dynamic system propelled by nothing less than the constant flow of small miracles. Therefore, stay alert and make the time necessary to explore what is occurring. No matter how chaotic and random life seems at the moment, we also sense that it contains some underlying order. Chance events can offer a clue to some deeper pattern in our lives. When life seems to be the most complicated, a simple order may be just around the corner. Coincidences always seem to be pulling us toward some special destiny. Coincidences can involve the timely arrival of some special information that we want but have no idea how to get, or the sudden realization that our experience with a past interest was actually a preparation for landing us a new opportunity.

The Swiss psychologist Carl Jung was the first modern thinker to define this mysterious phenomenon. He called it "Synchronicity," the perception of meaningful coincidence, a law that operated to move human beings toward greater growth in consciousness. A synchronistic phenomenon occurs when an inwardly perceived event, such as a dream or vision, seems to correspond in a meaningful way to an external reality. Neither the inner nor the outer event can be explained by causality, yet they seem to be connected. Most people have examples of this, such as when you are thinking of someone you haven't talked to in years and suddenly a letter shows up in the mail from that very person or you bump into the person on the street. Once we have opened to the divine energy within and found a truth that inspires us, and kept our questions in mind, the flow of synchronicity accelerates and becomes easier to interpret. Synchronicity appears to the uninitiated to be coincidence or luck, but it is neither. It is simply the operation of natural laws which you have set in motion with your thoughts. Everything that happens in our life is synchronicity because it leads step-by-step to our destiny. Many people who practice meditation of one kind or another have found that deeper and clearer their meditations, the more they experience curious patterns of coincidences. This tends to be particularly so after extended meditation retreats; or returning to regular activity. This relationship between synchronicity and one's state of mind is not a new finding. Twenty-five hundred years ago the Upanishads of ancient India observed that "When the mind rests steady and pure, then whatever you desire, those desires are fulfilled". Spiritual insight comes through paying attention to the movement of one's own soul and not always through outer reliance on teachers and teachings. Our capacity to find meaning in all synchronistic events is what gives our life the quality of a single unified story. What looks on the outside to be simply a series of chances, you are, in fact, doing what you need to be doing, both for your spiritual life and your vocation. When you consciously will something, many seeming coincidences begin to occur to help you move toward the path. And when one step is completed, another sets in motion. It becomes an ongoing process.

Find self-acceptance no matter what you feel or do. "If one can examine oneself inwardly and find nothing blameworthy, what is there to worry about or fear," said Confucius, the great Chinese Scholar. Cultivated people are neither anxious nor fearful. If you can accept that you are who you are, that you feel what you feel, that you have done what you have done – if you can accept it whether you like it or not – then you accept yourself. When you accept all that, you have put yourself on the side of reality.

John F. Kennedy, in his book *Profiles In Courage* states:- "In whatever area of life one may meet the challenge of courage, whatever may be the sacrifices he faces, if he follows his conscience, – each man must decide for himself the course he will follow – each man must look into his own soul."

Here is what other outstanding people have to say about being yourself:

> *"Everybody is the sum of his or her experiences, and*
> *brings to his work that set of values, experiences,*
> *influence of persons, peak moments that make life.*
> *Nobody is me and I am not that person." — Bill Moyer,*
> *America's famous interviewer*

> *"I feel that Harvard Business School has taught me*
> *little that has been useful in my career thus far. I am my*
> *own boss and to large degree control my own destiny.*
> *For the most part, I do what I like to do. For this, I*
> *am compensated generously." — A Harvard MBA,*
> *Investment Banker*

> *"My break in life never came until I got the chance to*
> *be myself, after seventeen years of people telling me*
> *to do it other ways. When I finally got a chance to be*
> *myself, that's when my success track began." — Rush*
> *Limbaugh, TV talk show host*

> *"I learnt from my dad never to give up my dreams,*
> *to believe my myself and follow my instincts." — Jim*
> *Carrey, comic actor*

"It is falsehood to assume that you can be somebody else. You have to make peace with yourself." — Nick Nolte, actor

"Don't try to take on a new personality, it doesn't work. We forfeit three-fourth of ourselves to be like other people." — Arthur Shopenhauer, great German scholar

"Real happiness comes from inside. Nobody can give it to you." — Sharon Stone, Hollywood star - after achieving fame and fortune

"You must face the situation as it comes. You give it your all. You do your very best. That's all you can do. You can't do better than that, and then you should not be bothered about the rest." — Indira Gandhi

"Knowing yourself is probably the only journey in life, actually. Because I like myself very much, I can't make a mistake, I can't be mediocre." — Calvin Klein, designer

"If I have a secret at all, it's that I do just what I want. I think that stops the aging process as much as anything else." – Cary Grant, actor

"I want to explore the light.
I want to know how to get through.
Through to something new.
Something of my own
Move on. Live your dreams." — Stephen Sondheim

"When you accept yourself, the whole world accepts you." — Lao-Tzu

"Break with the past, and become your authentic self. Take a journey inward along the road less traveled, but one that leads to the greatness that is you." — Anonymous

"I shall be telling this with a sigh
Somewhere ages and ages hence:
Two roads diverged in a wood, and I –
I took the one less traveled by.
And that has made all the difference." — Robert Frost

"Be with yourself. Watch yourself in daily life with alert
interest, with the intention to understand rather than
to judge, in full acceptance of whatever may emerge,
because it is there. By doing this you encourage the
deep to come to the surface and enrich yourlife and
consciousness with its captive energies." — Sri Nisarga
Datta Maharaj

"It's being and becoming what you believe in. That's
self-realization." — Swami Vivekananda

"We have all been placed on this earth to discover our
own path, and we will never be happy if we live someone
else's idea of life." — James Van Praag, Reaching to
Heaven

"You must learn to be yourself, you should forget how
to be others. I have lost half my life in my attempt to
emulate other people of virtue and possessions. I wanted
to be what I was not. It has taken a long time to discover
that one can't be and have both." — Hermann Hesse

We have no "self" as such. Our selves are merely the
masks we wear in response to the social situations in
which we find ourselves. — Role theory

"Don't ever compromise "being you" for any damn job
in any institution." Jack Welch, former CEO, GE

CHAPTER NINE- TRUST
YOUR INTUITION

*"Power of intuition can eventually carry us to complete
enlightenment about the world and ourselves." — Hunter Lewis* [1]

In addition to the three dimensions of thinking, sensation, and feelings,
there is a fourth dimension of consciousness which is crucial to personal
growth and self-realization. It is intuition. It seems that when all three
of the first dimensions of consciousness are integrated and balanced, the
mind can readily move into an expanded state of awareness in which linear,
logical thinking is put aside in favor of a more comprehensive functioning.
And in this expanded state of consciousness, intuitive insight happens
instantaneously. It is an effortless phenomenon of the mind, coming to us
when we surrender to it.

Intuition is really the ability to make spontaneous decisions with
incomplete data, take risks, to gamble on calculated vulnerability. Most
fundamental and creative way to tackling a problem is intuitive. Intuition
is highly developed and powerful mode of abstract thinking. One that
synthesizes masses of facts and theories with extraordinary speed. Intuition
sometimes compresses years of experience into instant insight. We rely on
intuition to form some of our most personal beliefs, our values. Intuition
is a springboard to the release of our inner immense potential. Sudden
intuition represents moments in which the greater cosmic meaning of our
life becomes visible. It is different from intelligence which is defined as
the ability to attain goals by means of decisions based on rational rules.
The rational mind takes us a certain distance and no more. It works with
the data derived from the senses and the associative processes of the

intellect. Its limitations are that it cannot handle paradoxical or illogical information. During many breakthroughs in our understanding of the universe, the role of intuition, or some mysterious comprehension, led to the breakthrough rather than any systematic analytic process. Since the process of intuition is thoroughly nonlinear, involving multiple feedback loops, it cannot be fully analyzed with our conventional, linear ways of reasoning, and hence we tend to experience it with a sense of mystery. Intuition has been called our sixth sense. It's a spiritual gift. Wild animals rely on their intuition to stay alive; we need to hone ours to thrive, despite any fear of consequences.

An intuition is an image of an occurrence in the future, a precognition that has been demonstrated to be a human ability. Most real intuitions involve the picture of some future action on our part that would move our lives in an advantageous new direction. Intuition appears to be some ability which permits, for example, an inventor, in a way not yet explained and possibly inexplicable, to tune in like a radio, and to learn, somehow, some facts or laws that are not yet known, or imagine and create a mechanism or part in correct accord with natural laws not yet discovered at the time of invention. The Russian-born Igor I. Sikorsky, a brilliant inventor and aircraft manufacturer, always had a belief, even as a small boy, that he would sometimes build and fly machines. "Consciously, I did not pay much attention to this idea because for many years I considered it simply impossible, but subconsciously the conviction was always there." His fantasy of flying machines turned into reality in 1909, when he was not yet twenty years old, with the construction of a helicopter which he successfully flew on his own.

Intuition works even when one does not recognize it as such. In other cases, it works with a surprising speed and brilliance, when, in a moment, a solution of a difficult and complicated problem comes in with remarkable clarity, and so convincingly that no doubts are left as to its correctness. Quite often it is possible to select one out of a dozen sketches of proposed solutions and state positively that one is the best, when it is still not possible to say why. The reverse also happens once in a while, and it is possible to predict that certain solutions will not be satisfactory even when they appear to be correctly designed and calculated. Intuition may be a form of a fact or information held in the memory for which there is no data or known foundation, but supported by a firm conviction that it is true.

Intuition is an inner awareness and a sense of knowing that is outside the realm of logical thought. Yet it possesses a wonderful flowing logic all its own. A powerful inner guide, intuition manifests itself in the hunches and inspirations that lead to the added insight, new direction, creative breakthrough, or the ability to be at the right place at the right time. Yet, its message can be so subtle that you might not realize you're receiving them. The answers we are seeking are found by letting go of our questions and sinking into deep inner silence with an innate intuitive understanding entirely beyond the scope of words ever to express. Intuition is an inherent trait that we all have. Wisdom comes only through intuition. The proof is the ceaseless strife and contradiction of opinion among those who trust in the mind. Truth is divined long before it is clearly seen, and then begins the long battle of the mind against the real, fighting doggedly for its supremacy. Intuitive power, like intellectual or artistic gifts, may be inborn or, it may be realized through intense exercise of the meditative power of the mind. Early in the twentieth century, there had been an Indian mathematical genius who had grown up without any knowledge of the modern idea of proof but who had, by a strange mixture of pure intuition and experimental enumeration, come up with scores of deep and unproven formulae about numbers which surprised and in some cases defeated the ablest mathematicians of the day. His name was Srinvasa Ramanujan. As a child he was recognized as quite extraordinary, with exceptional powers of memory and calculation. The remarkable contributions he made to the number theory were evidence of Ramanujan's intuition about the properties of numbers. He was a formalist who didn't use logic, thus illustrating the point that our most basic notions regarding "proof" may be subject to question.

Intuition means an intimate penetration of truth. Intuitive consciousness has the characteristics of immediacy and clarity. It is independent of perception and inference. It is inarticulate and can not be readily translated into conceptual terms. Intuition bears toward spirit. Intuitive consciousness is brought into existence by a mental process. When mind, by gradual training, is freed from the influences of the concepts and memory-images of the past, it merges itself in the object and is absorbed and pervaded by it. The nature of the object is then fully revealed. It is different from sense-observation, mathematical and logical reasoning. It comes in a flash as distinct from patient observation or logical analysis. It is creativity. It is an experience which is a blend of wonder, ecstasy, and awe at what is too great to be realized by intellect.

We have abilities that we can tap into by quieting our inside and by learning not to think so much. Of the two witnesses, listen to your conscience. When confronted with different points of view of what is right, use this slogan to remind yourself that your conscience is the main judge of your actions. Neuroscientists estimate that our unconscious database outweighs the conscious on an order exceeding ten million to one. This database is the source of our creative potential. Through the unconscious mind, the soul provides us with answers to all of life's questions. Unconscious contains memories not only from this life but from other lives as well. Our conscious mind has no direct communication with our unconscious mind. To pursue our unconscious mind's vast information, we must use processes that include astrology, dream interpretation, meditation, and various forms of symbology. Unconscious can be defined as all the future things that are taking shape in us and will sometime come to consciousness.

Human brain is divided into two separate but equal hemispheres, each governing a different way of thinking. The left hemisphere houses logical, linear thought and is characterized by objectivity, reason, analysis, criticism, and what is generally accepted as adult behavior. The right hemisphere is the home of intuitive, nonlinear thought and is characterized by subjectivity, inspiration, play, creativity, child like wonder, and psychic ability. Clearly the seat of intuition is the right hemisphere of the brain. Exactly how intuition works is not known, though science has been working hard to find out. No one currently knows what type of neural circuitry is responsible for our inner conscious experiences. If conscious experiences are an emergent property of the nervous system, then we should not expect them to be localized to any one region of the brain. Dreams, drugs, sensory isolation, and hallucination all reveal that input from the external world is really not necessary for conscious experiences to occur, and every attribute of a conscious mind can be altered by lesions, stimulation or chemical modification of the neural circuitry. Science has proven that there is an identifiable field of electromagnetic energy surrounding each of us. Through a special process known as Kirlian photography, this field becomes visible to the naked eye. Kirlian photographs of humans, plants, and certain inanimate objects show an aura emanating from each one. This field of energy, which surrounds us all, stems from a larger universal energy field. We all conduct this energy and to connect with its source, it is necessary to give your left brain a break so that your right brain can generate that powerful, instinctive spontaneity. Connecting with your intuition is the act of turning in to the never-ending flow of energy. For example, the discipline of yoga is based on the art of tuning in to the flow of energy and using it to experience harmony with the self.[2] Cognitive scientists who study how information flows through the brain tell us that only a small fraction of what the mind takes in, less than one percent, ever reaches conscious awareness, yet this bit of information is good enough to stimulate intuitive power.

The intuitive mind seems to have access to an infinite supply of information. It appears to be able to tap into a deep storehouse of knowledge and wisdom.(the universal mind). It is also able to sort out this information and supply us with exactly what we need, when we need it. If we follow this supply of information, the necessary course of action will unfold. As we learn to rely on this guidance, life takes on a flowing, effortless quality.[3] Our inner wisdom is always trying to help us bring balance and true fulfillment into our lives. It is constructive as long as we take the time to listen to it. It must be reinforced through action and decision-making processes. Act, if your heart confirms it, despite feelings of fear, self-doubt, or insecurity that may arise. In the end, our vision must be implemented. That is the key. In May 1997, Ryan Jaroncyk, New York Mets baseball player, shocked the sports world when he announced his retirement. He was only 20 years old when Mets paid him a signing bonus approaching $1 million as a number-one pick in the 1995 amateur draft. Jaroncyk said simply he didn't like playing baseball. He had only played to please his parent, who had pressured him earlier in his career to persevere. In an age of $100 million megadeals, Jaroncyk had the courage to listen to his inner voice, to walk away from the pursuit that in all likelihood would have paid him exponentially more than he will ever make doing anything else. One day soon after making his decision, Jaroncyk reportedly packed all the baseball equipment he had accumulated over the years into a big box and threw the box into a dumpster. He couldn't remember ever being so happy. He had been in conflict for a long time over baseball because of his parents' expectations, but he recognized intuitively that his path lay elsewhere.

To unlock intuitive powers, you must make every effort to attain emotional equilibrium, calm detachment, openness and flexibility. Let your body and mind rest together in an alert but thoroughly relaxed fashion. Relax and fill your mind with faith and expectancy that the correct answers will come to you. Faith and confidence are not only attitudes, but vibrations of energy. These vibrations will attract the appropriate solutions and answers just as a magnet attracts metal filings. You will always know you are receiving intuitive information by the quality of the ideas, and by the feelings they produce within you. The exhilaration, the certainty and the overpowering sense that "this is it!" are what distinguishes intuitive ideas from all the other thoughts occurring in our minds. Clear the mind of anger, impatience and fear to receive innermost intuition. This goal has manifested itself in burgeoning interest in meditation and the exploration of Eastern religions. Yoga, meditation and other right-brain practices accelerate the development of intuitive ability. Perhaps these practices help because of sheer discipline their pursuit requires, a rigorous attentional focus that enhances concentration. Perhaps, these practices clear the mind, leaving practitioner a purer channel for accurate, uncontaminated information to come through. Or may be the neurohormones that these activities produce in the blood stream produce strong psychic effects. We know from research that they actually alter blood chemistry, producing body's natural equivalent of tranquilizers and antidepressants. Studies with EEG machines, electrodes and graphs show that practices like meditation do indeed change the frequencies of people's brain waves and affect their quality of consciousness.[4]

The key to tapping your intuitive energy is to first stop the chattering of mind that goes on all the time. Introspect persistently until you see nothing with any shape or substance or individuality. The mind must be quiet, must empty itself of all knowledge, not only to be free, but to comprehend something that is not of time or thought or of any action. The mind tends to remain always occupied because we are trying to run away from reality; because we are conditioned by our circumstances, by our environment. When mind becomes serene, you see Self through the self. What thought might comprehend has been cancelled out because one has reached a level of consciousness beyond rationality. Whereas several techniques suggested before, such as, yoga, breath-control, meditation, repetition of mantras, restriction on food etc., are aids for rendering the mind quiescent, the one which is claimed to be the most effective is called "Self-inquiry," the term used by the great Indian sage Sri Ramana Maharishi. According to this concept, as each thought arises, one should inquire with diligence "To whom has this thought arisen?" The answer that would emerge would be "To me". Thereupon, if one inquires "Who am I?" the mind will go back to its source. Not letting the mind go out but retaining it in the Heart is what is called "Inwardness"(Antar-Mukha). Thus the mind stays in the Heart, the "I" which is the source of all thoughts will go and the Self, which ever exists, will shine. This luminosity of the mind is called by different names, such as, consciousness, intuition, sixth-sense, awareness or Sat-Chit-Anand (PureBeing-PureConsciousness-PureBliss) depending on your approach. Just as the pure crystal takes color from the object which is nearest to it, so the mind, when it is cleared of thought-waves, achieves sameness or identity with the object of its concentration. It experiences super-sensory knowledge. In Zen Buddhism, if the koan or meditation theme, is "Who am I?," it takes an average of six years for the successful student to have the first profound satori or genuine breakthrough to the True Self, according to Yasutani Roshi. All our thoughts are merely borrowed from the great database of consciousness, and were never really our own. Prevailing thought systems are received, absorbed, identified with, and, in due time, replaced by new ideas. As we place less value on such passing notions, they lose their capacity to dominate us, and we experience progressive freedom of – as well as from – the mind. Pure consciousness is the cessation of the ordinary flow of thoughts. When you are fully engaged in what you are doing, your mind does not wander. In this state, self becomes Self. Everything is now being seen in an awareness that is no longer confined by the conventional dimension (of time and space) and mind set. You enter a dimension beyond conditioning. The basic aim of silencing the thinking mind is to shift awareness from the rational to the intuitive mode of consciousness. By slowing your mind and freeing it from the endless chatter of thoughts competing against other thoughts, you get attuned to the vibrational frequency necessary for getting connected with the universal mind or greater consciousness. This potential remains dormant when you are in ordinary human consciousness. People who want to reach their intellectual zenith have to allow their brains to be free, unlocking all logical associations so new ones can be formed. This is the key to optimum creativity. In theory and practice, you have within you the power to approach the frequency of light and spirit. Information and energy, in the form of electromagnetic waves, continuously span out into space at the speed of light (186,000 miles/sec). Some physicists go so far as to propose that personal information actually travels instantaneously (the technical term is nonlocality). When you let go of your ego and surrender to the power of the divine forces, you free yourself from getting caught in the trap to use the rational mind to understand and dissect the mysteries of life. When you allow ego to get out of the way, your spirit comes through to empower you and change the course of events. When the mind is quiet, solutions emerge spontaneously. A blank mind invites insights that simply can't be heard over the normal everyday noise generated by the brain. The late John Lennon of the 'Beatles' rock group understood that to receive the muse you've got to empty your mind. "You can't paint a picture on a dirty piece of paper," he surmised. The fertile emptiness is the essence of all things. From "nothingness" a very different kind of "something" emerges, as if one gets connected with some type of a comprehensive energy grid akin to Einstein's Universal Energy Field. It is through this channel that our intuitive and psychic abilities come into play. Modern-day scientists define emptiness as phantom particles of energy composed of electromagnetic and electrostatic lines of forces which, by bending, can release tremendous amount of energy. There is enough energy in the vacuum of a solitary light bulb to boil all the earth's seas, according to the Nobel Laureate physicist, Richard Feynman. From neurological point of view, by quieting our conscious mind, we block sensory input to the area of the brain called 'Superior Parital Lobe.' Certain brain circuits must be interrupted when the sense of self disappears. With no information from the senses arriving, this area of the brain cannot find any boundaries between the self and the world. Everything feels timeless and infinite. One is left only with pure consciousness. This rewiring of the brain under mystical conditions has become a favourite subject called 'neurotheology,' the study of the neurobiology of religion and spirituality.

It is said that ninety percent of our energy comes from breathing, yet most people use only ten percent of their full breathing capacity. A normal person breathes about fifteen to eighteen breath-cycles per minute when at rest. With proper posture, it is possible to slow down this cycle to five or few breath-cycles per minute. You really don't need to breathe any more than that. When you settle into a natural rhythm of breathing, it will come from the lower abdomen (not stomach). Belly breathing emphasizes using the abdominal muscles and that can be quite powerful in deepening your concentration. The easier your breathing, the quieter your mind will be. Breathing deeply in and then completely exhaling involves the entire internal mechanism of a diaphragmatic breath. Conscious breathing means to breath deeply and intentionally. It deepens your awareness of this particular moment and brings you directly into contact with the present. It internally messages the major internal organs, relaxing them, and creates a heightened awareness of yourself and, by its very nature, causes you to expand both spiritually and physically. Spirit and breath are from the same root; inspiration means to breathe in. Breathing is inspiring. Some gurus believe the awareness of our breath is the key to enlightenment. Dr. Kenneth Cooper, originator of the concept of aerobics, and many other modern scientists have confirmed that regular moderate exercise has profoundly beneficial effects for the body and mind. Aerobic exercise strengthens our cardiovascular system, improving blood and, therefore, oxygen flow to our body and brain. However, when you push so hard that you breathe-in through your mouth, then your body is producing lactic acid. Instead of helping your body, you are generating toxins. Our brain is, on an average, less than three percent of our body's weight, yet it uses more than thirty percent of our body's oxygen. As we become aerobically fit, we double our capacity to process oxygen. The state of our body influences our mind. Many organizations are introducing message sessions, yoga and aikido classes to help their people discover greater physical and mental flexibility.

The left brain orders and sequences, analyzes and computes, evaluates and stores data. Like a computer, it processes all input in a linear fashion.

But the left brain is not much of a problem solver. It can't come up with new ideas. It is not creative. Where the left brain is absolutist, insistent on only one correct answer, the right brain reflexively furnishes alternatives. To make lightening-fast or life-affecting decisions without seizing up or blanking out, you must use your right brain, the intuitive, instinctive one. By engaging in rituals that are strongly visual, kinesthetic, or auditory(such as chanting, music, yoga, meditation), you shift to the right-brain mode, the nonverbal, non-analytical, intuitive and creative mind. Quite literally, brain waves shift from high frquency, high amplitude, beta waves to flatter, longer alpha waves, causing a lulling effect on the left brain. Once you have made the switch, once you have silenced the mental noise, single-mindedness takes over. You close the gap between intention and accomplishment. You become one with the object of your focus. You actually merge with it; there is no perceptible boundary between your mind and the thing it beholds.

Brain may have extraordinary capacities which are often untapped. It is frequently quoted in psychology that we only use 10 percent of our brains. If this is so, the interesting question is how can we develop the other 90 percent? One method of reaching the right brain resources of creativity, intuition, and sensitivity is by slowing down the frequency of brain waves, as measured by an electrical recording machine called an electro-encephalogram. Our brain is powered by electricity. Every second, trillions of neurons in our brain are firing their electrical impulses. Like most regular, repeated impulses in nature, these neural firings naturally organize themselves into rhythmical patterns, or waves. Like all other waves, brain waves occur at varying speeds, or frequencies. In the waking state the electrical discharge of the brain oscillates at a frequency of 14-20 cycles per second. This speed is associated with logical or linear left-brained thinking and is called beta-rhythm. In the sleeping state, the brain waves oscillate much more slowly, at about 4 cycles per second. In this state there is little logical thought and, at times, much seemingly undirected creativity (as, for instance, in dreams). Between these two states – between sleep and conscious awareness – at about 10 cycles per second, it is possible for left and right brain functions to occur simultaneously. Intuitive and creative faculties can be combined with logical direction to make mental faculties more incisive. This slower rhythm of between 8-13 cycles per second is called alpha rhythm. Techniques for reaching slower brain rhythms to augment mental abilities have been used for thousands of years in many different cultures. Meditation, self-hypnosis, and various trance induction techniques are examples. During meditation, having your spine straight helps the energy flow and makes it easier to get a deep alpha wave pattern. Alpha rhythm occurs spontaneously at times of going to sleep and waking up. Most people have experienced seemingly unsolvable difficulties to which a solution arrives when they wake up in the morning. Under alpha rhythm, intuition and creativity become more available, as the beliefs of the mind are temporarily suspended.[5] Even though our measures of frequency (through EEG) are relatively crude, they seem to provide a window into excitability within the brain. Medical research has amply demonstrated that people in a meditative state display very real and sometimes very dramatic changes in the body's physiology, including everything from blood chemistry to brain-wave patterns. Scientists believe that with the development of new technologies for mapping neural activity in real-time, we may see more clearly how a particular situation, thoughts, and feelings activate specific genes and vice versa. In simpler terms, those neurons that are actively engaged during an experience undergo certain chemical changes that activate genes and thereby initiate the synthesis of proteins inside these active cells. The proteins are then shipped to the active synapses on the active cells, where they alter the ability of those synapses to receive messages from the neurons they are connected with. According to Ken Wilber, author of *The Marriage of Sense and Soul*, this research did more to legitimize the meditative state than all the Upanishads put together. In this state of consciousness, qualities characterized as "spiritual" come increasingly to the fore. It begins to disclose the divine reality.

The intuitive process does not work in vacuum. Using internal (where none is available by other means), sometimes subconscious knowledge of facts, data points and/or sensory impressions, it can provide a coherent picture. Brain's capacity is almost inexhaustible. Estimates range 10-12 billion cells in the brain, each of which has a set of microscopic tendrils that pass electrochemical messages from one cell to another. Millions of these switches go on and off to make it possible for us to assimilate ideas, connect them with past experiences, form pictures, and file the data away. We have more "bits" in our heads than any computer ever built. A computer with the same number of "bits" would be a hundred stories tall and cover the state of Texas. Our brain is the most complex structure, natural or artificial, on earth. It is obviously capable of an imponderably huge variety of activity; the fact that it is often organized and functional is quite an accomplishment. We have over 50,000 thoughts each day, most of which are reruns from the day before. Dr. Ralph W. Gerary, neurophysiologist at the University of Michigan, once estimated that after seventy years of activity, the brain may contain as many as fifteen trillion separate bits of information.[6] To develop a unique capacity for abstract thinking, the billions of neurons in the neocortex have to extend their dendrites to make over a trillion connections with other dendrites. Our journey into higher consciousness is a matter of learning how to properly program this remarkable biocomputer.

Intuitive thought, or the notion of hearing a calling, may take a while to digest. It requires an openness of the heart and, above all, patience. The discovery of our calling often requires an incubation period. The architect, Le Carbusier said that the birth of a project was just like the birth of a child: "There's a long period of gestation—— a lot of work in the subconscious before I make the first sketch. That lasts for months. Then, one fine morning the project has taken form without my knowing it." One aspect of creative thinking definitely can be attributed to nature: intelligence, which is inherited. Scientists say your chances of creating a brilliant invention or work of art are small if you don't have an IQ above 120. But you also need an inborn proclivity to excel in a certain field: in other words, talent. The environment affects the creative process in sometimes surprising ways. For example, literature, philosophy and biology deal with living beings that can't be studied apart from their environments. These fields are so subtle and diffuse that it takes decades to master them, and creative discoveries are not immediately obvious. Whereas, mathematics, physics and music are tightly organized fields that operate according to absolute rules that can be quickly grasped, according to Root-Bernstein.

Intuition has always been important to leaders and remains so, in spite of all the information available today to decision makers. It's a matter of striking a balance between what you know instinctively is right and what you can prove with facts. Many important leaders have made fine decisions intuitively. Ray Kroc decided to spend $2.7 million he didn't have in 1960 to buy out the McDonald brothers in spite of the negative advice he was getting because "My funnybone instinct kept urging me on." Intuition is not uninformed guesswork. "It means knowing your business and bringing to bear on a situation everything you've seen, felt, tasted and experienced in an industry," says Ros Perot. Life is not always logical. It is filled with paradoxes and mystery. That's why it's important to trust our intuition, feelings and hunches. When we do this we are closer to the truth than when we dogmatically remain within the narrow confines of our rational mind. The two modes of consciousness, called 'rational' and 'intuitive' have always been recognized as essential aspects of human nature, They have been associated traditionally with science and religion, respectively. The Chinese Taoist system called these two modes of consciousness, or the two modes of knowledge, the *yang* and the *yin.* They have never seen them as experiences belonging to separate categories, but rather as extreme parts of the single whole. The *yang,* having revealed its climax, retreats in favor of the *yin,* and vice versa. In Hindu Tantrism, there is the idea that these are two interlocked creative principles: *Shiva,* the male rational principle, and *Shakti,* the feminine principle, which represents energy, change and dynamism. *Shiva* and *Shakti* are not separate, they're pictured together in an orgasmic embrace, in a state of union.

Among the great teachers of wisdom in this century, J. Krishnamurti has been one of the most outspoken in advocating that individuals attend to their own inner directives. In a 1928 lecture he stated, "That time has come when you must no longer subject yourself to anything – I hope you will not listen to anyone, but will listen only to your own intuition, your own understanding, and give a public refusal to those who would be your interpreters – Do not quote me afterwards as an authority. I refuse to be your crutch. I am not going to be brought into a cage for your worship." The intuition of a genius is sometimes beyond the scope of rational thinking. There is a story told about a sufi mystic by the name of Mulla Nasruddin, who was confronted by a gang of rascals who wanted the shoes he was wearing. Trying to deceive the Mulla, one of the rascals said, "Mulla, nobody can climb that tree." "Of course one can. Here I will show you," said the Mulla, taking the bait. Initially the Mulla was going to leave his shoes on the ground while he climbed the tree, but on second thought, he tied them together and hung them from his belt. Then he started to climb. The boys were discouraged. "Why are you taking your shoes with you?" shouted one. "Oh, I don't know, there may be a road up there, and I may need them!" called down the Mulla. The Mulla's intuition told him that the rascals might attempt to steal his shoes.

Today, artificial intelligence(AI) seems years, possibly decades, away from achieving human-equivalent computer vision or natural language processing, for these are complex abilities that rely on intuitive reasoning and common sense. Computers excel at logical reasoning and mathematical computation, however, which is why the IBM computer Deep Blue won its first game against world chess champion Gary Kasparov in February 1996. It was, however, Kasparov's very human ability to intuit patterns of flow on the board, and to select from those patterns, that allowed him to take the match. Kasparov, like any human, relies on the brain's ability to parallel-process information – to distribute the calculations necessary to solve any problem among a number of relatively independent processors (or, in the brain, neural configurations). Through parallel processing, the average human brain, which contains more than 100 billion neurons and trillions of interconnections, can make perhaps 20 billion calculations a second, generating an ability to select and to evaluate sufficient to defeat Deep

Blue's astonishing, if simpler, search abilities.[7] Human brain has been described as its on-board computer. It does not work in the same way as an electronic computer. It is made of very different components. These are individually much slower, but they work in huge parallel networks so that, by some means still only partly understood, their numbers compensate for their slower speed; and brain can, in certain respects, outperform digital computers. The evolution of human brain over the last million years or so is perhaps the fastest advance recorded for any complex organ in the entire history of life. Something a bit similar seems to have happened in the growth of the computer.

Creative ideas are not consciously thought out – but come out automatically, spontaneously, and sometimes like a bolt from the blue. Implement the idea after securing the necessary information. Then additional struggling, fretting and worrying over it does not help, but seems to hinder the solution.[8] First intuition, without giving much time to play around with ideas, often tends to be true and logical. The most consistently creative people have given much time and thought to developing their inner senses. Entering the inner realms gives our minds a kind of map to follow that,with practice, can be used to travel quickly to our interior spaces. It is wrong to trust only those answers that come from facts and statistics, and to ridicule solutions that arise from imagination and intuition. Once you recognize the omnipotent power that exists in the subconscious mind, you will never want for answers. You will merely adjust your consciousness and direct your intention to bring you the required information.

Thousands of decision-makers in all types of businesses acknowledge that their victories came when they trusted their guts. Often, ignorance, determination and enthusiasm will create a very positive result based on intuition than pile of data created through years of experience and projections. Media mogul Barry Diller shocked all his peers in the entertainment industry when he took the helm at QVC, the home shopping net work. He expressed his excitement at coming into a new industry and environment with a clean slate where you get to screw things up a lot and act on instincts.

In science and technology, intuition is widely recognized as an essential source of innovation and discovery. That is the most common denominator amongst great scientists and inventors. The philosopher, Bertrand Russell maintained that science needs both, intuition and logic, the first to generate and appreciate ideas and the second to evaluate their truth. Japanese government's Science & Technology Agency, since 1987, has initiated a program to study man's spiritual activities in its creative science & technology promotion department. According to Tadshiro

Sakimoto, president of NEC corporation, the study of the sixth sense and telepathy will certainly prove a cornerstone of future modes of communication. "We can make wonderful communication equipment if we build it on theories of electric wave engineering," he says. Using a technology-enhanced telepathic communication system to "call" a friend in a distant spacecraft, or someone in a deeply submerged submarine, does make sense, and these are the applications likely to show up first. As more scientists become aware of the evidence, innovative corporations will increasingly pour resources into psi applications. There is no doubt that whoever develops psi-based practical applications first will become the leaders of twenty-first century high technology.

Our feelings come to us before our thoughts. As many smart investors, marketers, and designers will attest, stock market killings, media blitzes, and new product development often depend on hunches. There isn't always time for methodical gathering of data. Nor is there always a need. Your hunches, after all, are the product of instantaneously gathered and sorted emotional information that tells you what matters most to you in any situation, what might be wrong based on your previous experiences, and when something is not what it seems to be. Heeding them is not taking a crazy risk. It's often the smartest, most responsible move you can make. You may get a lot of opposition, but stand firm and follow your hunches. Without them you lose the ability to switch gears, grab opportunities, and respond to emergencies. Part of the process of becoming intuitive is learning to trust 'gut feeling.' When you are faced with a difficult decision, as you weigh each alternative, simply notice how your body feels. If you have some misgivings or uncertainty, you will feel some discomfort in the body. Listen to what is going on around and within you as an indication of which direction you should go. Bob Baffert, who was trying to become the first horse-trainer in 125 years of Kentucky Derby race to win for three consecutive years, has the following to say when asked about the secret of his success: "I never set any goals. Twenty years ago I was happy training horses at Rilito, Ruidoso and Los Alamitos. I never thought I would be where I am. All I do is get my thorough-breds in position where they can win. After that, fate, karma, whatever takes over. I live day by day and just try to stay calm, cool, and enjoy the moment." Trainer Bob Baffert failed to become the first person to win three straight Derbys. His three horses ran out of the money-prime in the 1999 Kentucky Derby race, the last of this millennium. "We don't know how to act. We didn't have any luck," Baffert said. "Now I don't have to worry about the Triple-Crown."

Under high stakes and intense time-pressure, experienced people make brilliant decisions they often attribute to the mysteries of intuition. But psychologist Dr. Gary Klein says in his book *Sources of Power* that there is nothing mysterious about it. Intuition, he says, is recognizing complex patterns without knowing how we do the recognizing. Professionals react to trends and patterns of experience. A fire chief senses danger in the living room of a house and orders his crew to withdraw, even though the flames are small. A moment later, the floor collapses. How did he know disaster was imminent? Dr. Klein says the fire fighter was reaching into personal experience, racing through patterns and contexts for a match with the problem of the moment – so rapidly he could not see doing it. He withdrew from the house fire because he was troubled by the combination of an intense heat, small flames and quiet. Only later did it become obvious that a fire was raging beneath the floorboards. After decades of demystifying how experts make decisions, Dr. Klein is working to marshal the powers of intuition in the workplace, at a time of constant surprise in business.

Once you become conscious of the questions active in your mind, you always get some kind of intuitive direction of what to do, of where to go. Sooner or later, coincidences will occur to move you in the direction indicated by the intuition. Stay alert to every coincidence, every answer the universe provides for you. You are constantly in the process of consciously evolving yourself.[9] When your subconscious gives you a plan, start immediately to work the plan. Inspiration is precious and must be used at once.

Most creative discoveries are intuitively derived, and only later 'dressed-up by logic, observation or some other conscious technique. "After struggling with this problem all day, I went to bed confused and exhausted. The next morning, as I awakened, the solution came to me in a flash, and I just knew it was true." [That is intuition at work]. Mitch Kapor, founder of Lotus, once a leading producer of computer software in the USA, and thus a company specializing in logical applications, said about himself:- "Intuitive style of decision-making lets the entrepreneur make a creative leap."

Intuition does not surface by accident. It is the evolution of years of learning and experience into an instantaneous flash. Answers to the tough problems can leap fully conceived into an awareness. This ill-defined instinct known as intuition has to be understood, nurtured and trusted if it is to be turned into a powerful tool. Logic and analysis can lead a person only part-way down the path to a profitable decision. The last step to success frequently requires a daring intuitive leap. Many chief executives who control the destinies of America's biggest corporations will reluctantly concede to this fact. There is a success mechanism deep down in the subconscious that will intuitively steer an individual to a desired objective – provided the individual has a vivid mental picture of his ultimate victory - and does not jam the mechanism with fear and doubt.[10]

One of the most powerful methods to enhance clarity of thinking and to put yourself into a more mentally coherent state is by relaxation and stress reduction. As the mental activity lowers and reaches a certain critical level, the brain waves get synchronized in frequency between the left and right. Proper exercise can provide leverage for energetic, empowering states. It activates the endorphins in the brain which help thinking process to sharpen. A major key to how we make life meaningful is how we feel physically and emotionally. Exercise strengthens the heart and lungs, protects against high blood pressure, lowers the cholesterol and the risk of cancer. Not exercising causes widespread damage to the body, including reduced vital capacity, reduced oxygen availability to cells and organs, elevated triglycerides and loss of muscle mass. Meditation, Yoga, Zen, chanting, fasting, dancing, running and many other techniques have been used to propel intuitive power. [Things which improve circulation and provide the brain with bio-chemical nutrients, called brain waves]. Scans of people in a self-induced state of 'passive attention' have been shown to turn off areas of the brain normally associated with seeking stimuli, including the parietal, anterior and premotor cortexes. Fasting is a traditional spiritual practice that purifies the body and strengthens the mind by requiring you to resist the overwhelming compulsion to eat. While fasting, the body clears itself of toxins. Fasting quiets the mind, producing deepest form of concentration, called Samadhi. Sitting cross-legged during meditation, or fasting long enough trains the mind to overcome the deprivation and distraction, thus bringing in a higher state of clarity and vision. At the same time, stress, pain, exhaustion and boredom have the opposite effect, agitating the mind and blocking the pathway to intuition. Over millennia, various human cultures have developed a series of specific practices to control these conditions, but these have been thoroughly systematized in the eight steps of classical yoga: tolerance, self-restraint, physical exercise, breathing, detachment, concentration (prayer), meditation and trance (deep meditation). When an athlete is totally focused on a task with a positive frame of mind, his physical energy is increased and is in sync with his mental vibrations. The energy of the universe interacts with that of the body through the brain-waves (typically 8cycles/sec) during these moments of concentration. This cumulative energy carries him to another level of performance. It is noticeable in some ace athletes and super-star performers. Carol Vinolia, author of *Healing Environment*, stresses the importance of rising with the sun. By doing so, we are in balance with the nature. The gradual increase in light and warmth of the sun allows the body to complete its brain-wave cycle, thereby giving us a natural energy boost.

How can we stimulate our ability to use all our mind that controls conscious thought? The secret seems to lie in not trying too hard. Happy ideas come unexpectedly without effort like an inspiration. On the other hand, some kind of preparation is required. You must give your problems to your subconscious mind in the form of definite assignments, after assembling all the essential facts, figures and arguments. The cooking process must first be started by focusing our minds on this material long and intently enough to get it thoroughly heated with our best conscious thinking. Then – go fishing – golfing or motoring, or if it is night, go peacefully to bed. Thomas Edison, for example, took self-induced 'cat naps' to solve the complex problems that perplexed him, resulting in many inventions that we all still use daily. According to Ester Buchholz, the psychologist, solitude brings forth our longing to explore, our curiosity about the unknown. Alonetime is fuel for life. Life's creative solutions require alonetime. Solitude is required for the unconscious to process and unravel problems. We need quiet time to figure things out, to emerge with discoveries, to unearth the original answers. Both, creativity and curiosity, are bred through contemplation. The natural creativity in all of us – the sudden and slow insights, bursts and gentle bubbles of imagination – is found as a result of alonetime. Tidal pools, empty fields, mountains, trees, and ocean evoke peace and contentment. Sleep is nature's way of ensuring solitude. 'Time out' has been heralded as a coping strategy, as an emotional breather.

Famous British scientist Fred Hoyle was trying to solve a complex mathematical problem on cosmological theory of electromagnetism. Along with his student from India, Jayant Narlikar, in 1960, they were struggling over a particularly complicated integral. Hoyle decided to take a vacation from Cambridge to join some colleagues hiking in the Scottish highlands. Then something suddenly happened. He writes: "As the miles slipped by, I turned the quantum mechanical problem over in my mind in a lazy way I normally have in thinking mathematics in my head. My awareness of the mathematics clarified, as if a huge brilliant light had suddenly been switched on. The problem was solved in less than five seconds."[11] Hoyle believes that cosmos is controlled by 'Super Intelligence' which can implant thoughts or ideas from the future, ready-made, into the human brain. Prayer, meditation, or mindful walks along a lonely stretch of beach are not indolent times. These etch reality into awareness, enable us seeing ourselves clearly, as in a mirror. They restore and renew our vigor.

Dreams are your ongoing flow experience. You are quite likely to be at your most creative right after you wake up from dreaming because that's when you are closest to the natural flow state. Look for clues, messages, and ideas in your dreams. Pay special attention when you wake up in the morning or in the middle of the night. Sting, for example, wrote the song "Every Breath You Take" in a single stroke upon waking up with an inspiration in the middle of the night.

Intuitive action is embodied with superior problem-solving capabilities, particularly in situations where a single impression or mental image is worth a thousand carefully crafted words. Use intuition where high degree of risk or uncertainty is involved, and problems with little precedent.

Some experts believe that intuition is a mental process that absorbs and integrates information unconsciously. A good intuitive decision-maker is able to sort and classify information, distinguish among the valuable, the worthless and the redundant, assign values and priorities: and integrate the whole into an accurate picture of the decision situation. Get in touch with your mind at the level that produces spontaneous judgments. Ask yourself at appropriate times, such as, when you face a decision, "What is my gut feeling about the situation?" Don't hesitate to act on intuitive feelings. Those who trust their intuitions tend to be among the most successful. People with their salt play hunches, and their mistakes are minor compared to their successes.[12] Scientific breakthroughs, great musical compositions, inspiring books, and all other ideas for original accomplishments are born within the subconscious mind. It's the source of hunches, intuitions, and flashes of brilliance. It's 'the still small voice' within. We are conscious of something within that is deathless, something immortal, divine. This silent messenger accompanies us through life, directing our moves, advising us, warning us, protecting us, no matter where we go. There is something within that tells us we are at one with the power that made all things. Many great people have called it by different names, (spirit, infinite-intelligence). Believe in it. The epiphany is not a masterstroke but a tweaking of a passionate pursuit of one's ideal, sometimes lasting as long as ten years, says Steven Pinker, the psychologist and cognitive neuroscientist at MIT, in *How The Mind Works*.

Entrepreneurs, who get into new ventures tend to be experimentalists – trying this, trying that, feeling around in the dark, unsure of what they are looking for, but quite certain they will know it when they find it (by intuition). Our subconscious minds suggest a course of action. Follow each step leading eventually to the goals that underlie the minor daily decisions. All the answers are within yourself, only look. Let your thoughts flow, and follow them. Even if you don't feel totally committed to your mission, the energy of setting it in motion can help convince you of its viability. If you are headed in the right direction, you will feel it. The only help you need comes from within. For example, following publication of his autobiography, Iacocca, which sold seven million copies, Lee Iacocca, the charismatic auto executive flirted briefly with making a run for the presidency. In the end, he decided against it, realizing he would never have the patience required to deal with the congress. Compromising to achieve consensus wasn't his long suit. In 1997, he founded EV Global Motors, the electric car company.

Purpose of life is to trust your instincts and act accordingly, because that is our destiny. When you are guided by the instincts from within you, you discover your purpose. Success comes when you connect with your feelings. You have to make that emotional connection between what you do and what your heart desires. You know where you are going because you have a compelling image inside. An inner force compels behavior, it comes from within, not from any external circumstances. What counts is not what you accomplish or what you have, but what you are. To know what you are, you must unlock and develop your intuitive powers by learning to be calm, peaceful, immune to the storms of life. Listen to your inner voice, and follow it with all the strength and willpower to resist any thoughts of failure or temporary setbacks.

Everything that happens to you depends to a great degree on what is happening inside you. You can achieve your full potential only by finding your area of excellence and then throwing your whole heart into developing your talents in that area. You will never be happy or satisfied until you find your heart's desire and commit your life to it. Your area of excellence may change as your career evolves, but all truly successful men and women are those who have found it. It is doing what you most enjoy and doing it well.[13] Learn to confront change, rather than simply react to it, to shape the rest of your life. People who dread and fear change have little hope for the future. Change is clarifying, like getting a new pair of glasses with a better prescription. Fuzzy things become clearer, perspectives sharpen; the focus changes. After a while, what you feel is different from what you felt. You've rearranged yourself. According to Jack Welch, former chairman of the General Electric Company, "Any time there is change, there is opportunity. So it is paramount that an organization or the individual get energized rather than paralyzed." In reporting a proposed acquisition of Honeywell for 45 billion dollars by GE, The Wall Street Journal commended Welch as an unparalleled CEO, with a unique gift for unflinchingly assessing the realities and fearlessly charging toward the opportunities. Everything that happens to you, everything you become or accomplish is determined by the way you think, by the way you use your mind. As you begin changing your mind, you begin changing your life. Act according to your deepest beliefs – and your ideas will follow. Strong beliefs will help you focus what could otherwise be too general creativity. Without a strong conviction, your heart and your head will always be at odds. We need to follow what we feel in our guts. We need to be asking what it is that enlivens, empowers, excites us, turns us on, make us genuinely feel satisfied and fulfilled. That is what actually heals us, and heals the world. Be guided first and foremost by your internal compass, not the standards, conventions, trends of the outer world. Your own ideology should guide all your dealings. If done right, you will likely astonish competitors, business experts and other strategists.

Whatever you do to earn a living has to come from yourself. Never follow other people's dreams. Instead, fulfill your own. Learn to listen carefully and respond aptly to inner guidance. To become aware of this magnificent, living presence in our daily events and to let it lead us to fulfillment is worth whatever the cost. The seat of our power resides in our heart. It takes patience to move through the months or even the years of uncertainty with faith. It is a difficult road, but the results are well worth it. We must learn to live in harmony with our hearts. We must always go within to our highest wisdom to chart our path in life. The destiny we intuit in our hearts will become a reality. Now, listen to this:

> *"Time and again, contrary to all wise counsels, I have allowed myself to be guided by the inner voice – often with spectacular success." — Mahatma Gandhi*

> *"I have seen lots of disappointments in life, and successes too; but have learnt one thing that when you trust your instincts, you follow your heart." — Michael Bolton, singer and song-writer*

> *"The bigger question is not what intuition is or how it works, but whether or not we are willing to trust it ourselves. I have survived on trusting my intuition and going with my instincts, but it is still so easy to allow a lot of external garbage to get in the way, to look out for outside validation, to reassure and comfort ourselves that we are doing the right thing, instead of going inward to find whatever answer we are seeking.*

166

*As always, it is in the doing that we really make a
difference in our lives, and the more I trusted my
instincts and intuition, the more I started to believe in
myself."* — Demi Moore

*"I have considered myself to be very fortunate in that
I have been able to do mostly only that which my inner
self told me to do."* – Einstein

"Why do I always get my best ideas in the shower?"
— *Einstein*

*"Scientific truth is revealed first through intuition, and
only later verified by logic."* —Einstein

*"There comes a time when the mind takes a higher
plane of knowledge but can never prove how it got
there. All great discoveries have involved such a step."*
— *Einstein*

"All exists within." — *Upanishads*

"There is only one journey. Going inside yourself."
— *Rainer Maria Rilke*

*"The creation of something new is not accomplished by
the intellect but by the play instinct acting from inner
necessity. The creative mind plays with the object it
loves."* – C.G. Jung

"Follow your bliss." — *Joseph Campbell*

*"There is nothing more powerful than an idea whose
time has come."* – unknown

"The more we pray and meditate, the more we develop a divinely inspired intuition to find our higher purpose." — *Gandhi*

"Faith is not complacent; faith is action. When you have faith, you move." — *Anne Wilson Shaef*

"A new idea surfaces—-from whence, I don't know, I am aware that sparks fly, and I capture them." — *Jonas Salk, discoverer of polio vaccine*

"Within every person lies the Divine spark. By focusing powers of concentration and imagination on a single idea or emotion, one has the ability to absorb the universal impulses and bend them to his will." — *Late John Lennon, of the Beatles rock group*

"I obey only my instincts and intuition. I know nothing in advance. Often I put down things which I do not understand myself, secure in the knowledge that later they will become clear and meaningful to me. I have faith in the man who is writing, who is myself, the writer." — *Henry Miller, writer, 1941*

"I just write a song and know it's going to be all right. I don't even know what it's going to say." — *Bob Dylan, song writer, 1965*

"Only when the mind is tranquil – through self-knowledge and not through imposed self-discipline – only then, in that tranquillity, in that silence, can reality come into being. It is only then that there can be creative action." — *J. Krishnamurti*

"Let go and trust what lays ahead for you, even though you don't know exactly what it is." — *unknown*

"I didn't arrive at my understanding of the fundamental laws of the universe through my rational mind." — A. Einstein

"Act as thou thinkest best." — The Bhagavad Gita

"When I face a situation, the solution comes to me. I react to situations intuitively. Logic comes afterwards, it does not precede the event." — Gandhi

"If you meet the Buddha on the road, kill him." — Old Zen saying, implying that creation and inspiration come from deep inside, not from an external source.

"Knowledge is not gained by any process of reasoning. It is a direct perception and, therefore, its nature is akin to what we call faith. It is a metaphysical belief." — Max Planck, Nobel Laureate in physics, and father of modern quantum theory

"We are not fair when we ask for a material proof where matter does not exist. If we want spiritual proof, then we must awaken that part in us which transcends matter." — Swami Parmananda

"Don't rush to your book
Looking for knowledge
Pick up the flute instead
And let your heart play." – Rumi, poet

CHAPTER TEN - GO WITH THE FLOW

"Stop worrying where you're going move on.
If you can know where you're going you have gone.
Just keep moving on...." — *Stephen Sondheim*

Life is just fine the way it is, especially when we consider it one day at a time. You might think you are lonely, but accepting is a bliss. There is a time and purpose for every matter under heaven. How dull and meaningless and hopeless life can seem – only to become exciting, vibrant and filled with hope the next day. Daily, we redeem ourselves in unspoken rituals of renewal, building, repairing and remodeling our lives.[1] It is an audacious notion to put forth in this age of science and willful determination that one's existence is somehow inspired, guided, and even managed by unseen forces outside our control. Whether called fate, destiny, or the hand of God, mysterious forces are at work bringing coherence and continuity to our lives.

Rational consciousness cannot determine all things. For some of us the thought of trusting a power outside ourselves to help make our dreams come true is definitely a threatening concept, especially if we are used to the illusion of being in control. Instead, we are better off to suspend disbelief and be willing to believe that a companion spirit is leading us every step of the way, and knows the next step. We know in our bones what we are meant to be. There are lines of intention guiding all our human experience. These become more apparent as we grow sensitive to life's messages and vibrations. We can only follow their lead and yield to their unfoldment. Natural impulses are pathways to enlightenment. The messages are always coming. Life is taking us on a mighty journey, if we will only go.

If you can accept the flow of life and give in to it, you will be accepting what is real. Only when you accept what is real can you live with it in peace and happiness. The alternative is struggle that will never end. Going with the flow means holding onto your goals lightly and being willing to change them if something more appropriate and satisfying comes along. In short, it means being firm, yet flexible. Despite the fact that our ego hates unpredictability, think for a moment the unexpected opportunities that have come our way, offers of help we never anticipated, sudden brainstorms and inspirations, impulsive decisions to move or talk to a stranger that opened new horizons. This is the natural way to live. Trust in each stage or event, celebrate it, and allow the next one to come to you effortlessly.[2]

Love your life and have the faith that it's unfolding exactly the way that's perfect for you. Everything happens for a purpose and it serves the master plan of the universe. Everything that shows up in your life is supposed to be. What seems to be happening at the moment is never the full story of what is really going on. Things are constantly unfolding on different levels. No matter what situation you are in right now, there is a purpose to that situation. You may not want to stay in that situation for long, but a meaningful purpose has brought you to this place. By working with the specific conditions in front of you, you will begin to discover things about yourself that will give you clues to the next step. It is for us to learn to follow our own threads through the tapestry of life with authenticity and resolve. Surrender to the fact that you don't always know what is best for you. When you learn to surrender, you have mastered the first step in finding fulfillment in life. When you surrender yourself to the almighty power of nature, devoid of any intellectual play or emotional twist, you place your consciousness on the level of the natural flow of evolution. As long as the individual is on a thinking level, he maintains his identity. As long as the individuality is maintained, the state of surrender cannot be. "I'll be washing dishes and get this flash – the word and music come together. I have to sit down and write. I know what it's like to experience epiphany," says the country Western star Naomi Judd.

Ever since turning pro in 1989, Deion Sanders has been known as "Prime Time," the hottest defensive back in the National Football League and a base-stealing sensation in Major League Baseball. By the age of twenty-five, Deion was already at the top of his game, but he was desperate for something more. He discovered after arriving at the pinnacle of success that meaning and purpose lay in another direction. He felt emptiness inside. His life was out of control. He found peace eventually by having faith in God and a new vision and purpose for his life. He let Him take control of his life. He just surrendered.

Suze Orman, a certified financial planner, and author of New York Times #1 best seller, *9 Steps to Financial Freedom*, worked as a waitress for seven years after college. Then she found a position as an accounts executive at Merrill Lynch and went on to become vice president of investment at Prudential-Bache before founding her own firm in 1987. She writes in her book, *The Courage to Be Rich*, "How scared I was to enter each new realm. How terrifying each of these moves into unknown arenas of life was for me. Never mind the idea of writing books! If anything, entering the publishing world was more intimidating to me than Wall Street had been, because working with money, numbers, I always felt at home. For the longest time, every expansive act I took made me feel not richer but smaller, poorer, afraid of what I might lose. So many times I felt like retreating, going back to who I had been – but I didn't. I kept going as if I were propelled by some force far greater than me."

No matter how carefully we tailor our action to fit our goals and objectives, random events do conspire to turn situations around. That's what navigating through life is all about. Living each day continually affords the possibility of knowing that there is so much more to life than five-year plan. The events in our lives happen in a sequence in time, but in their significance to ourselves they find their own order, confides the writer Eudora Welty. With patience and quiet observation, these events will provide the seeker in you with a continuous thread of revelation. Life is not an exercise that can be fully planned. Serendipity plays a large role. One never knows when certain skills that seem minor or insignificant can be pressed into service when one requires them the most. Learn to detach the effort from result. Of the former you are in complete control. The latter is governed by forces you cannot control, and learning to accept that fact is the essence of happy life. Buddha found enlightenment only when he stopped seeking it – when he let it come to him. But who can doubt that enlightenment came to him precisely because he had devoted at least sixteen years of his life to seeking it, sixteen years in preparation. He had both to seek it and not seek it.

Great ideas come almost by the 'eureka' effect; sitting quietly and suddenly you see it. Great discoveries, real intellectual conceptional breakthroughs, do have that moment of clarity. Yet most of the advances do not occur that way. When asked about how he arrived at the theory of gravity, Newton said, "By thinking about it continually." The cry of 'eureka' conceals the enormous amount of work that has to precede it.

Sometimes it takes a very dramatic event to change someone's course in life. Sometimes you feel as though nothing was happening, in spite of your best efforts. You begin questioning everything, lose focus and motivation. But, remember, you have to go through darkness to truly know the light. Often the greatest doubts occur just before a breakthrough. Trust your inquisitive, skeptical inquiring mind and find out for yourself the answers for all your questions. Relax a little and go easier on yourself. As time goes on, one moves from blind faith to self-knowledge, and finally to unshakable inner conviction.

Jacques Cousteau, the French oceanographer, inventor and documentary film-maker had a near fatal car crash at the age of 26 while he was with the French Naval Aviation School. The accident denied him his wings and he was transferred to sea duty, where he swam vigorously to strengthen weakened arms. The water therapy had unintended consequences as Cousteau wrote in his 1953 book, *The Silent World*, which sold five million copies in more than twenty languages:

> *"Sometimes we are lucky enough to know that our lives*
> *have been changed, to discard the old, embrace the*
> *new and run headlong down an immutable course", he*
> *wrote. "It happened to me on that summer's day when*
> *my eyes were opened to the sea."*

Cousteau died June 25, 1997 of a heart attack at age 87. He was the coinventor of SCUBA (Self-Contained Underwater Breathing Apparatus). Scuba diving has now become the world's fastest growing sports.

Just go with the flow of your own nature. If you consciously try to be something you are not, you will feel uncomfortable. You never know what is around the corner. Consider your current physical, emotional and mental strengths. Make list of characteristics you like most about yourself. Clues to where you are headed can be found in who you are now. After looking within for answers, look without. There is much we can learn from those who are going before us. Reappraise yourself throughout life. Review the past, and decide how you want the future to go.[3]

When the calling is strong, there is no use trying to hide from it just for the promise of material comfort. Surrender and trust in the wisdom that created you. Terminate the intellect's domination. The mind must surrender its role as full-time judge and allow the heart to contribute its wisdom. Trust the natural process and you begin to trust the nature of all things. When we insist on controlling nature, we are interfering with nature. You need this trust to attract to yourself all that belongs to you in the universe. Everything that shows up in your life is supposed to. This includes the falls in your life, which provide you with the energy to propel yourself to a higher state of awareness. Accept whatever arrives without passing judgment. Your mind will attempt to use logic, employ negativity, but refuse to accept anything that contradicts the unlimited power that is within you and move on with your goal. Never think that it is the end of all experience and awareness. Supersede your mind's limitations. Meditation and intuitive feelings are two ways to achieve that. Both bring harmony between the inner, spiritual and outer material glories of the life.

The material life of man is brightened by the light of the inner self. That's why the emphasis of all the scriptures of religions and of the whole field of metaphysics is that the state of self-realization or God-realization is the goal of man. Success of the divine quest brings the height of success in the world in a most natural way and the individual life is fulfilled. Individual mind, however intelligent it may be on the superficial conscious level, can be overcome by its failure to understand and encompass a situation which obviously lies beyond its control, unless it is in tune with the unlimited cosmic mind. The universal intelligence works at its own perfect pace. It will deliver when you are in alignment with it. The delivery is guaranteed by the absence of doubt that you cultivate, and total trust in the presence of this energy. Relax, trust, do not push. Transcend your mind's preoccupation with results and trust in something that your mind cannot see. Let your inner most feelings become your guides in your life and trust those guides. You absolutely know when you have reached the purpose of your life. No one has to tell you. You know because you no longer question the meaning of your life. You know that all you do is synchronized with God's work, because you are at harmony and every single activity of your life is involved in the fulfillment of your purpose.

Stephen Hawking, Lucasian professor of theoretical physics at Cambridge University, an illustrious position once held by sir Isaac Newton, was afflicted with Lou Gehrig disease since early twenties. The progress of the disease has been slow, but by the time he became Lucasian professor, he could no longer walk, write, feed himself, or raise his head if it tipped forward. He lived with increasing disability and the promise of an early death. Work in theoretical physics was one of the few careers he might have chosen in which physical disability wouldn't be a serious handicap. It would have been courageous and required tremendous will power to have chosen such a difficult course as cosmology deliberately, but that wasn't how it happened. He simply did the only thing possible. Now, in his fifties, he is active, brilliant mathematician and physicist, whom some have called the most brilliant since Einstein. He says,

> *"One has to be grown up enough to realize that life
> is not fair. You just have to do the best you can in the
> situation you are in."*

His book, *A Brief History of Time*, became a best seller, It has brought to millions all over the world not only his keen excitement about the work but also the important truth that there is health that transcends the boundaries of any illness. For a quarter of a century Stephen Hawking has kept up the spirit of optimism and determination. His survival and success depends on his doing so.

In 1928, an Indian student, Subrahmanyan Chandrasekhar, set sail for England to study at Cambridge with the British astronomer Sir Arthur Eddington, an expert on general relativity. During his voyage from India, Chandrasekhar worked out how big a star could be and still support itself against its own gravity after it had used up all its fuel. This mass is known as Chandrasekhar limit. His finding is now considered as a breakthrough in our better understanding of the galaxy. Even though Chandrasekhar was known to be one of the few scientists in the world who understood theory of relativity clearly, Eddington refused to believe his results. He thought it was simply not possible that a star could collapse to a point. This was the view of most scientists. Einstein himself wrote a paper in which he claimed that stars would not shrink to zero size. The hostility of other scientists, particularly Eddington's, his former teacher and the leading authority on the structure of stars, persuaded Chandrasekhar to abandon this line of work and turn instead to other problems of astronomy. However, it was more than fifty years later that Chandrasekhar was awarded Nobel prize in 1983 for his work on limiting mass of cold stars. On July 23rd, 1999, NASA launched an advanced X-ray facility aboard the space shuttle Columbia commanded by astronaut Eileen Collins. It was named "Chandra," a shortened version of Chandrasekhar's name. It will help astronomers world-wide better understand the structure and evolution of the universe. Chandrasekhar is now widely regarded as one of the foremost astrophysicists of the 20th century. He served on the faculty of the University of Chicago until his death in 1995.

Just play the hand you are dealt with, and not what you wished to have. There is a sense of constantly accepting the world as it is, realizing there are certain things you can or can't have an impact on. The secret in search for meaning, in whatever we do, is to find your passion and pursue it. When the passion is there, and you refuse to allow any interference from any external sources, nothing will stop you. Change your expectations and goals as you age. Shape a new self that calls for qualities that were dormant earlier. Our attitude toward change should be as if we were sky looking at the clouds passing by. That is, let go, let it happen, accepting the impermanence of the previous stage while preparing to relish the new life to come.[4] You can never foresee what future has in store for you. Jimmy Carter in his book, *The Virtues of Aging,* reflects on his second term loss in the presidential election to Ronald Reagan, and then returning to glory by pursuing a different course in life as a writer, preacher, and goodwill ambassador. He says, "Our legitimate human ambitions often cause us the anger, envy, suffering, pain, frustration, and a sense of inadequacy that deprives us of inner peace and joy. The prospect of failure always exists, and it is painful and often embarrassing when we do fail. It is a sign of maturity when we can accept honestly and courageously that frustrated dreams are a normal facet of a person's existence – and that despite these, we can still continue to learn, grow and adopt challenging goals. We need to explore the maximum capabilities we have. With faith, either in God or in ourselves, it may be surprising where it leads. Obviously, my life has been quite different from what I anticipated," says Jimmy Carter.

For decades, Western psychology has promised fulfillment through building and strengthening the ego. None can deny the existence of ego; it is impossible to dismiss out of hand its power and obstinacy; and it is particularly troubling for One who desires to make progress on the spiritual path. And yet, according to the testimony of many mystics, this ego is said to dissolve into nothing at the very moment of enlightenment, just as if it had never existed. Our most sought after attributes are self-esteem, self-awareness and self-development. Most of us have developed our egos enough; what we suffer from is the accumulated tension of that development. In Buddhism, self is more of the problem than the solution. Happiness does not come from any kind of acquisitiveness, be it material or psychological. Happiness comes from surrendering our egos and let go. Enlightenment is generally taken to be something that we will someday achieve if we adopt the right spiritual practices and work diligently toward becoming enlightened. Enlightenment is not an attainment. It is realization. It's an attitude toward everything that you do. Inside or outside yourself you never have to change what you see, only the way you see it. That's enlightenment.

John Briggs and David Peate in their book, *Seven Life Lessons of Chaos,* suggest that instead of resisting life's uncertainties, we should embrace them. Ancient and indigenous cultures handled their uncertainties through dialogues with the Gods and unseen forces of nature. Western industrial society has taken a different route, they surmise. We dream of eliminating uncertainty by conquering and controlling nature, but such a

177

dream is an illusion. Chaos is central to the creation of universe. Chaos is nature's creativity.

Many researchers have noted that when people felt under pressure to perform or to be accurate or to make something happen, their accuracy declined. All of this supports the importance of staying in the non striving, passively receptive mode. This attitude of surrender, while staying in the open receptive state of mind, almost all the time brings in a continual flux of ideas or intuition to foresee things. Sometimes the greatest acts of commitment involve doing nothing but sitting and waiting until you just know what to do next. When we believe in this approach, there is a flow around us. Things just seem to happen. A state of stillness is achieved when the activity of the nervous system is brought to a state of restful alertness, when even the activity of mind is reduced to nil. At this point, perception remains in the state of absolute consciousness and the state of enlightenment is gained.

To find your mission in life, know God and enjoy Him forever, and see His hand in all His work. Do what you can, moment by moment, day by day, step by step, to make the world a better place, following the guidance of God's spirit within you. And, once you have begun doing above in a serious way, your third mission on earth is the one uniquely yours, and that is:- exercise your talent which God has caused to appeal to you the most. Your hunt will end with being able to say: "Life has deep meaning to me, now. I have found my mission, and the reason why I am here on earth."[5]

Learn to accept whatever is happening around you, most importantly, whatever is happening with you and within you. In essence, you must accept and say yes to everything you find. Life is uncertain: therefore, living with uncertainty is part of living in the so-called real world. Become more comfortable with joy and satisfaction. After all, that's what you want, isn't it? Each day is a mixed bag of experience and feelings of good and not-so-good encounters and events. No matter what the circumstances, you can always choose to live each day as a creative act and be willing to be surprised by joy.[6] The true joy of life is to relish the moment, rejoice and be glad in it. It isn't the burdens of today that drive people mad. It is the regrets over yesterday and the fear of tomorrow. Life must be lived as we go along. Stop waiting for things to happen. Let everything be as it is. Through doing this, you will find a place where there is freedom from time and thought, from the desire for pleasure and the fear of pain. In that place there is a mystery that mind cannot comprehend. That's enlightenment: seeing beyond the mind and knowing beyond memory.

Let go your expectations and preconceived outcomes. Remain calm when everything around you is in confusion. You need to develop skills to remain centered. Simply observe and appreciate what is going on. Doubt, worry and attachment will only interfere with success. Let go of the desire. Live in the present for it is the only moment you have. Relinquish your need for external approval. You alone are the judge of your worth, and your goal is to discover infinite worth in yourself, no matter what anyone else thinks. There is great freedom in this realization. Listen to your body's wisdom, which expresses itself through signals. Pay attention to your inner life so that you can be guided by intuition rather than externally imposed interpretation of what is or isn't good for you.[7]

When you play a game with the feeling that you have nothing to lose, you relish those moments. Therefore, adopt a nonchalant attitude, while doing the very best your mind and body can do. Simply play with the unconscious knowledge, unconcerned with surroundings. Conscious effort interferes with the natural flow of events. Give life your best shot and be at peace with yourself and with the results. The best example was set by Tiger Woods in the 2000 British Open Golf Tournament played at St. Andrews, Scotland. Responding to a question with a twenty under-par and a nine shot-lead at hole sixteen, he said, "I know what it takes to play in a final round of any tournament. You can't let yourself look ahead to the final outcome, because if you don't take care of the present, the final outcome may not be what you want." At age twenty-four, he went on to become the youngest player to win the British Open with a record-breaking score of nineteen under-par at 269, and only the fifth player in the world to win all four majors. Tiger's phenomenal success in golf is not only because of his physical strength, but also due to mental toughness that he was not born with. It took time to develop under the expert supervision of trainers in meditation, mind-body-spirit connection and clinical psychology. His mental supremacy allows him to stay focused on the target. A calm mind and the ability to stay in control under pressure are two of his greatest assets. Losing never enters his mental equation.

Chance encounters often have a deeper meaning. That begins to happen when you become alert and connected with the energy. If one can connect and build up enough energy, then coincidental events begin to happen consistently. The findings of physics, psychology, mysticism and religion are coming together into a new syntheses based on a perception of coincidences. Everything that occurs in nature does so according to some natural law. Each event has a direct physical and understandable cause. There is some unfinished business between the two parties which needs to be addressed.[8]

179

We should not worry and seek to shape the future by interfering in things before the time is ripe. Instead, enhance your powers and abilities through inner development. "Fate comes when it will, and thus we are ready." [*I. Ching*] Don't try too hard to make something happen. Simply allow it to happen in its own time frame. It can't be forced or rushed, since it is all part of your unfolding journey. Allow yourself to be with questions, without demanding answers. When answers do come, they may come in surprising ways and unexpected moments. During your consciousness, work will automatically bring your higher purpose into focus. Keep the channel open. The important thing is not to focus on the destination, being at peace with the fact that there isn't any final end point. We need to become fascinated with the journey itself, so that every moment in the process of learning, growth and expansion becomes its' own rich reward.[9]

Among dozens of books that famed psychotherapist, Dr. Viktor Frankl has authored, *Man's Search for Meaning*, a personal narrative of Nazi death camp, was intended to be published anonymously so that it could never build up any reputation on the part of the author. However, it did become a best-seller and is considered as the origin of logotherapy, a treatment to find meaning in life in spite of distressed existence. He, therefore, admonished his students worldwide with the following:

> *"Don't aim at success – the more you aim at it and make it a target, the more you are going to miss it. For success, like happiness, cannot be pursued; it must ensue, and it only does so as the unintended side- effect of one's personal dedication to a cause greater than oneself. Happiness must happen, and the same holds for success: you have to let it happen by not caring about it. I want you to listen to what your conscience commands you to do and go on to carry it out to the best of your knowledge. Then you will live to see that in the long run – in the long run, I say! – success will follow you precisely because you had forgotten to think of it."*

Luck is a reality that makes itself felt in every aspect of daily life. It is-a fact of life. Luck and circumstances always play a role in our lives. This is inevitable, and actually makes the game more interesting. Yet it is intriguing to explain the destabilizing influence of luck on merit. There are times when we have to make decisions in the light of incomplete information, and thus are inevitably at the mercy of luck. When matters do turn out as we design, then it is good luck rather than rationally determined planning and execution. And if things go badly, then it is by bad luck rather than sheer incompetence. The role of chance in human affairs is such that no matter what we yearn for – money, power, prestige, or whatever – we will be at the mercy of luck. The element of chance is as important as that of choice. For example, everybody in book publishing knows that if Macmillan's editor had not been overcome by a cold while visiting Atlanta, he wouldn't have stayed in bed and read the huge manuscript a lady had given him in the hotel lobby, which was to become, after much editing and renaming *Gone With The Wind.* Hollywood's legend, Gregory Peck, has had a lifelong back problem due to a ruptured disk and displaced vertebra. It was caused during his days as a young student while practicing for a movement in the New York Play House. This condition made him ineligible for the draft and which, with a number of leading-man types fighting overseas, arguably helped launch his film career. He went on to make 50 plus films besides Broadway shows.

Miracles do happen. On the other hand, our best-laid plans go awry for reasons entirely beyond our knowledge and control. The fact is that most human enterprises are, to some extent, chancy. Effort alone is seldom sufficient because of all the things that could possibly go wrong: a mixture of effort and luck is often needed to achieve success. Since luck involves unforeseeable situations, people have to be accounted lucky when they succeed in life beyond the level of reasonable expectation that their inherited endowment and acquired condition would indicate. There is nothing we can do to explain or rationalize luck. Luck prevents life from being too rational or too predictable. It mixes things up and adds to "the spice of life". No matter how carefully we plot our journey, an unexpected squall can always blow us off course. Therefore, be realistic—accept luck for what it is, the offspring of unpredictability. Chance, while in one way random, yet in another way favors the prepared—those who are so situated as to be in a position to seize opportunities. A person who is actually on the lookout for unanticipated openings can best take full advantage of them when they occur. People of persistence and determination can often overcome bad luck. Meeting life's upsets with an energetic and positive response, they treat bad luck as a challenge to the achievement of greater goods.[10] Bad luck helps you develop survival instincts and skills that you did not have before. It also forces you to experiment, leading you to discover aspects of yourself that you never knew existed. But to view misfortune as an opportunity, you must first believe that you are eventually going to succeed.

Trusting that larger forces than yourself are at work in your life, you will give up the demand for the outcome you think you want. Learn to make room for surprise. Never is the outcome of a major expenditure of energy all-or-nothing proposition. You will have new connections, deeper understanding, expanded knowledge as a result of your efforts. Follow your heart, giving everything you have got (and sometimes more) to achieve your goals. Always trust your heart. If you attempt to obtain by force something for which the time is not yet ripe, you will harm your project - by expending your strength prematurely. This is not and never was your show. You can hold on to a positive attitude and still not be heading anywhere: and you can be depressed now and get an offer beyond wildest dreams in five minutes from now. It is neither your positive attitudes nor your fearful ones that create your reality. There are forces at work in your life far greater than your moods and emotions. The most you can hope for is to positively influence the circumstances that fate hands you by walking the path of correct conduct. This you can do - happy or sad - anxious or full of faith. Persist in doing the everyday work regardless of your mood at the time. You will pile up small advances. Everyday adds to your reservoir. When you have piled up enough, you will tumble over the top, flowing effortlessly into what is next for you.[11]

Kirk Douglas, the legendary actor, after being rejected in 1993 for a perfect role in a movie, *Wrestling Ernest Hemingway*, says that one should be grateful for unanswered prayers. God has a sense of humor. Sometimes he looks down as we pray, and he laughs, "How can I tell this guy that the movie is going to be a flop? How can I tell this guy that the nicest thing I am doing for him is not to answer his prayers?" It was the story of a growing friendship between two old men dealing with the twilight of their lives. "The script spoke directly to me and I loved it," he says. It was the part of Frank, the vulnerable drifter who pretended to be a macho. Robert Duvall was slated to play the other part. After auditioning Kirk, the director decided to give the role of Frank to Richard Harris in stead. Kirk was devastated and almost cried. The movie, however, turned out to be dull and slow instead of light and bouncy as Kirk had imagined, and it flopped in the box office[12] After a recovery from the stroke at the age of eighty, Kirk writes in *My Stroke of Luck* published in 2002: "Learn to live with uncertainty, to know that in life there are no guarantees. We all have a handicap – big or small. But we must overcome our hardships to become better people. We must try."

Go with the flow. Structuring our experience toward the attainment of reasonably challenging goals and attending to the feedback we receive as we strive to work toward those goals can provide the most reliable conditions for the optimal enjoyment of our experience. For every choice that is made, many more must be denied. For every door that closed, many more open up. No matter what is lost through circumstance or poor judgment, new possibilities always arise. It is a fascinating and truly inexhaustible process. Human values always migrate. New possibilities always arise.

Enjoy and appreciate the way things already are. Remind yourself that life is okay the way it is, right now. When you have inner peace, you are less distracted by your wants, needs, desires and concerns. It's thus easier to concentrate, focus, and achieve your goals. Learn to live in the present moment, irrespective of what happened yesterday or last year, and what may or may not happen tomorrow, the present moment is where you are – always. "Be patient. You'll know when it's time for you to wake up and move ahead," says the renowned scholar Ram Dass. When you go with the flow, you connect with your soul. Your conscious mind doesn't know the plan but you trust your inner self. That is a big part of the journey for many of us – trust. There is always hope, purpose, and a new magical lesson.

Let go of a goal alltogether. This attitude does not make you less ambitious. Instead, it saves you from chronic dissatisfaction of not achieving lofty goals on account of their limitations or realities of a given situation. Tone down your expectations that are unrealistic, unreasonable and, therefore, you will actually get better results by aiming for a little less. Maury Povich, TV talk-show host, worked at five different TV stations during the year 1977-1983 without achieving national success. He says, "I finally went back home to Washington to work for a local TV station. I was not going to grab the brass ring, I was not going to be the headliner on a national marquee, and that, I should better suck up. It was only when I settled for less that things started to turn around for me." Media baron Rupert Murdoch bought the chain for which he worked, in 1985, and used it as the basis for his Fox Broadcasting Network. And Fox started *A current Affair* with Povich as host in 1986. Once he got into the tabloid TV genre (instead of straight TV news), he achieved national success almost overnight.

> *"Everyday is a miracle. Savor them. Everyday the play*
> *begins anew. Strategies rarely unfold as we imagined.*
> *Intended consequences are rare."* — *Tom Peters*

> *"Don't wait to be happy. There is only one right time to*
> *make your move to happiness: now. Don't put it on hold*
> *for better times to come. It will continue to elude you."*
> — *Bobbe Sommer*

> *"Here is your plan, and there's God's plan. Your plan doesn't matter. Just keep working for a cause." — David Geffin, Movie mogul*

> *"Enjoy the present. There is more to life than increasing its speed." — Gandhi*

After forty years in parliament, at the age of 64, Churchill was at last in power as prime minister of England. He took over from Neville Chamberlain after a vote of no-confidence during World War II. He then wrote:

> *"As I went to bed at 3 a.m., I was conscious of a profound sense of relief. At last, I had the authority to give directions over the whole scene. I felt as if I were walking with destiny, and that all my past life had been but a preparation for this hour and for this trial. I slept soundly and had no need for cheering dreams. Facts are better than dream." Winston had, at last, found his destiny.*

> *"In not wanting to think of what tomorrow will bring for me, I feel free as a bird. I don't want to foresee the future. I am concerned with taking care of the present. God has given me no control over the moment following." — Gandhi*

> *"Every time I come up with a philosophy of life, I find that my circumstances in life change and I have to come up with a new philosophy. Therefore, I have decided to drop the philosophy and to continue with my life." — Neil Simon*

> *"I think to be open to whatever happens to you in life is the best possible way to be." — Lauren Bacall*

> *"Celebrate your successes. Find some humor in your failures. Don't take yourself so seriously. Loosen up, and everybody around you will loosen up. Have fun. Show enthusiasm – always. When all else fails, put on*

a costume and sing a silly song. Then make everybody else sing with you." — Sam Walton

"Live in the present
Do all the things that need to be done
Do all the good you can each day
The future will unfold." — Peace Pilgrim

"If we really know how to live, what better way to start the day than with a smile. Our smile affirms our awareness and determination to live in peace and joy. The source of a true smile is an awakened mind. Each step we make should be joy. If we are determined, we can do it. We don't need the future. We can smile and relax. Everything we want is right here in the present moment." — Thich Nhat Hanh, Zen Master

"Expect nothing; live frugally on surprise." — Alice Walker

"The man who, casting off all desires, lives free from attachment – obtains tranquillity." — The Bhagavat Gita

"We must be willing to get rid of the life we've planned, so as to have the life that's waiting for us." — Joseph Campbell

"Life is what happens while we're busy doing something else." — unknown

"The very purpose of our existence is to seek happiness. That is clear. The method, the daily practice, involves gradually increasing our awareness and understanding of what truly leads to happiness and what doesn't." — His Holiness, the Dalai Lama

"Do you have the patience to wait till your mud settles and the water is clear? Can you remain unmoving till the right action arises by itself?" — *Lao-Tzu*

"If by eternity is understood not endless temporal duration but timelessness, then he lives eternally who lives in the present." — *Ludwig Wittgenstein*

"Watch, wait. Time will unfold and reveal its purpose." — *Marianne Williamson*

"And yet if every desire were satisfied as soon as it arose, how would men occupy their lives, how would they pass the time?" — *Arthur Schopenhauer*

"The purpose of life is to believe, to hope, and to strive." — *Indira Gandhi*

"Let go of the desire and accept whatever life brings you in the faith that it will further your spiritual aspirations. When we stop resisting and surrender to the situation as it is, things begin to change." — *unknown*

"I never planned for 'Linux' to have life outside my own computer. It just happened by default." — *Linus Torvalds, creator of 'Linux' operating system*

"I didn't dissect beetles or anything when I was a boy. There was no great event that made me go into medicine. When my elder brother failed two years of his studies in engineering, he told me medicine was a better choice. So I did, even though I was interested in engineering." — *Dr. Christiaan Bernard, world's first heart-transplant surgeon*

"Just when I discovered the meaning of life, it changed" — *George Carlin, Stand-Up Comedian, in Napalm & Silly Putty*

"Quiescence, a kind of philosophical inaction, a refusal to interfere with the natural courses of things, is the mark of the wise man in every field." — Lao-tze, in Tao-Te-Ching

"When action is needed, it will appear. When effortlessness becomes essential, it will assert itself. You need not push life about. Just flow with it and give yourself completely to the task of the present moment. The role of destiny unfolds itself. You can not change the course of events." — Sri Nisargadatta Maharaj

EPILOGUE

As mentioned in the prologue, I migrated to the United States in 1973 along with my wife Saroj and two children, Mona and Mickey, age nine and five respectively. I was thirty-eight years old then. It was that first job interview in the U.S. which led to my quest to know who I really am, and whether we all have one life to live, as the interviewer had exclaimed. This takes me back to the year 1934 when I was born in Quetta, now a part of the North-West frontier of Pakistan. It is located near the border with Afghanistan and was occupied in 1876 from the Afghans by the British colonial forces. It became a thriving, prosperous market-center with a spectacular, natural amphitheater of the surrounding mountains when the British established an Imperial Staff College for military officers there. My father was employed in the district high-court under tutelage of the English high command, as India was a part of the British Empire at that time. As luck would have it, our family, including my two older brothers and a sister, were on vacation when a cataclysmic earthquake destroyed the entire city of Quetta in 1935 while killing about twenty thousand people. Our house was gutted to a rubble burying my maternal uncle alive. That was the first brush with destiny that I experienced personally, even though this realization came to me later as I grew older and heard this episode time and again from my folks. Quetta was rebuilt and the clean, wide boulevards and pleasant weather make it one of the most popular holiday resorts in Northern Pakistan.

In the year 1942, my father retired from service and we moved back to his home town, Mithan Kote, in the Multan subdivision of Punjab, now a part of Pakistan. It's a small town known as the confluence (Punj-Nad) where five rivers of Punjab merge with the river Indus. We owned farming land there and my father set up a grain merchandising business to be run by my older brother Joti. Because of his intellect and integrity, my father was revered by the local community. By popular demand, they elected him unanimously as president of the municipal corporation, the office he held until the partition of India in 1947. As a result of the partition, the country got divided in two: the Hindu-majority Republic of India and the Islamic State of Pakistan. We became a part of the Pakistani territory and, being Hindus, had to evacuate to the Indian side of the border, leaving behind all of our material possessions. Ten million refugees crossed lines that were hastily drawn on maps through the Punjab and Bengal provinces as international borders between the newly formed nations. I was age thirteen then and witnessed a massacre on both sides of the Punjab border in the name of religion. About one million innocent Hindus and Muslims became victims to this political maneuvering and lust for power. Trains loaded up to roof tops with refugees were ordered to a halt at gun point and victims butchered mercilessly. One of these victims was my older sister Shanti, married at that time, and with a son Harish, four years old. They lived in another city. Her entire family was massacred while boarding a train to migrate to the Indian side. Her son was spared out of the desire of a Muslim friend present on the seen who wanted to adopt him. Later on, however, Harish was contacted and brought back to India with the help of rescue mission. He now lives in the U.S.

On the other hand, my parents, younger sister, a brother and myself, were at the mercy of the destiny as to where we end up on the Indian side, if we arrived safe at all. Fortunately, we made it to free India, but did not know what lay in the future. One of my older brothers, Pratap, was sent to New Delhi to pursue medical education just before the partition of India. When he got the news of our safe arrival, he contacted us, and later made arrangements to move us to New Delhi to live with him at the boarding house where he resided. Later on, that campus became a refugee camp. Pratap gave up his medical education and took job with a government agency in order to support us. We had arrived in India almost penniless. In spite of financial hardship, my father allowed me to pursue my education, with bare minimum subsistence. I completed high school graduation with honors in the year 1951. It was at this point that my father wanted me to go into a business of my own, instead of going to college. However, I persisted and got a commitment from my father that as long as I performed well, he would not stand in my way, and would support me financially. This is how I went on to complete a master's degree in chemistry from the university of New Delhi, later to be followed by a Ph.D. in materials science and another master's degree in metallurgy from the University of Sheffield in England on a scholarship program.

While in India, I was fortunate to progress steadily to the executive rank and file in the private and public sector jobs. However, the desire to be the best one can be and attain a measure of fame and recognition across the border was still burning in me. This led to a break from my Indian past and I ended up as an immigrant in the land of opportunity in the year 1973. I feel blessed that here again destiny played its role and I moved on to hold supervisory as well as management positions in such top organizations as Westinghouse, General Electric, and Bendix, what is now known as Honeywell. To put my ego at rest, I must state that during my professional career, I published more than thirty research and technical articles in journals of international repute, and won several awards for invention disclosures. Even though I did not achieve the level of fame and recognition that I aspired for prior to arriving in the United States, yet it was during this period that I inculcated in me the characteristics that inspire thoughts about the purpose of life, and what is all this evolutionary process about. As the basic material needs got fulfilled, my focus steadily shifted inward. I spent years probing into questions: " Who am I? What is the purpose of life? Can I be what I want to be?" That took me into an extensive study of literature pertaining to psychology, metaphysics, spirituality, religion, consciousness, and philosophy.

Over all these years, in spite of concerted efforts and several training programs, some of the traits in me remain unchanged. For example, I burn the midnight oil, but can never get up early in the morning, as wise people advise. I love solitude and perform best when left alone. This may have caused me some set backs in the pursuit of higher ladders in the corporate world where networking and communication skills are emphasized to be the key ingredients for success. I have always followed my conscience, and was never reluctant to defy orders against my will. I may have paid a price for that too, but have no regrets in listening to my inner voice. I have always been my own person and feel at ease being so. Are these traits a part of my nature or nurture? Perhaps both. Suffice to say, that while some of the traits are deep rooted in my genes, the circumstances of our family before and after partition of India had a great bearing on my personality. In this connection, it is worth mentioning here that my mother was much younger in age than my father. She was beautiful, fair-complexioned, and a graceful lady. However, she spent her life as a housewife, rearing children. My oldest brother, Moti, got adopted early on by my aunt who did not bear children of her own. My second brother, Joti, became a grain merchant, and the third, Pratap, gave up medical school education in order to support us after partition of India. As mentioned before, my older sister, Shanti, became victim to the communal riots. My younger sister, whom I carried on my shoulders during evacuation from Pakistan, had contracted polio soon after birth in 1940, and became disabled permanently. Doctors who examined her at that time claimed that she wouldn't survive longer than few months. None the less, she lived to be sixty-two before expiring in December 2002. My younger brother, born in 1943, died in an accident while a student in college. Due to grief and ill health, my mother passed away prematurely in 1960.

This twist of fate raises the pertinent question as to who controls our life? Did I, Pritam (or Peter as they call me here), accomplish all what I did on my own, or was the hand of destiny playing a pivotal role in molding my career? Another point of interest is the part played by my father in my thought process toward spirituality. Right from my childhood, I witnessed my father getting up early in the morning and reciting prayers loudly. I resented that because I was in the habit of studying till late at night and getting up leisurely in the morning. However, what happened over the course of time was that I ended up remembering all his prayers by heart, even though I did not understand what he was saying. At one point during my studies, he had advised me that after I was all done with my academic education, I should focus on the knowledge of 'self'. I didn't pay much attention to him then thinking that it was typical of people when they get old that they take on to religion and the pursuit of spiritual aspects of life. It is now that I understand what he said, and what it means to purify our life in order to achieve some measure of enlightened consciousness. For example, he would recite:

> *"God is truth; the world is an illusion.*
> *Individual soul and the universal spirit are the same.*
> *Everything that happens in the world is the will of the Lord.*
> *It's not 'I' who is doing the deeds, it's Your will.*
> *I am merely a tool in Your hands; use me as You wish.*
> *O'Lord, liberate me from this cycle of life and death."*

Attraction to karma is the main cause of our bodily existence. Dissolution of karma is the path to liberation. Any passionate desire only affirms that a certain theme of life has not yet been concluded. If we desire a fundamental conclusion of this theme, we need consciously to confront it to a positive conclusion, or follow a different positive line of thought or action. Our emotional attachment to matter blocks the immense inherent capabilities of our consciousness. Once liberated, thinking and intuition merge into one leading to a precise grasp of reality.

The purpose of life is to attain liberation, which is the gaining of original status of the soul whose karma has brought bondage. The mind causes desires; desires cause karma; and karma binds the soul. Liberation could mean freedom from bondage; letting things be just as they are, without wishing they were different; detachment from the outcome of one's actions; letting go of the individual ego or total renunciation. My father believed that one cannot achieve liberation merely by elimination of karma. The cessation of bondage is to be obtained only through freedom from the physical state, because life always has in it the element of unfulfillment which causes suffering. We will always be drawn to further embodiments as long as unfulfilled aspirations still exist. If the mind is merged in the Supermind, the desires of the mind will be destroyed and the soul will be released from the clutches of maya, or illusion. Having no desires left, the soul will not take rebirth, and that is mukti, or liberation. Union with 'Brahman' (Cosmos) is the real aim of all accomplishments. The ultimate goal of life is to enter this non-dual Self domain. When the soul of an individual 'Atma' realizes its true identity as being a part of the Divine, it strives toward perfection and freedom by dissociating itself from false personalities; in other words, body and mind. Actions are to be performed only as long as the soul is not awakened to this inner Reality. Once awakened, it goes beyond the operation of the laws of karma; it becomes free from the cycles of life and death. When the ego which comes into existence between the body and the Self merges in its source and loses its form, then there is no 'I', and, therefore, no karma. Ego is the agent upon which karma depends. The function of the body thus becomes redundant. This Self is a mere experience; it's the knowing faculty, and, therefore, it cannot be produced from matter. And since it cannot arise from a material cause, it must come from a ceaseless continuum. Also, it cannot arise from nowhere and without a cause. It is from this premise that one is led to believe in the existence of former lives.

My father was a pious person and led a life of discipline, hard work and self-reliance. He believed in the dignity of labor. He breathed his last on January 17, 1970 at the age of ninety. He left an indelible impression on me. At this stage in my life, I feel as if I have my father in me. He is directing me to fulfill a mission that he left behind unfinished.

In their book, 'The Living Energy Universe', Dr. Gary Schwartz and Dr. Linda Russek of the Human Energy Systems Laboratory at the University of Arizona have come up with a hypothesis that our loved one's energy and information, their spirits and souls, literally continue beyond physical death, and that their wishes and our wishes can continue to co-create and evolve. Perhaps, that's the quest which drove me to write this book. The search for the answers to questions, "Do we have one life to live?" or "Can we be what we want to be?" has continued to challenge me all my life. If I have succeeded in solving at least a part of the puzzle, I shall feel that I have fulfilled a wish left behind by my father. Destinies shaped individually merge and interact with the collective destinies of families, groups of like-minded people, nations and the world at large. This is how we grow. May be, at a future date, you will hear more on this subject from me, or someone who will carry on this divine mission as a part of the karmic cycle which has to go on until the day of salvation of the soul.

REFERENCES

PART I – Introduction

(1) Marshall Sylver, "Passion, Profit & Power", 1995, Simon & Schuster.

(2) Rush H. Limbaugh III, "See I Told You," 1993, Pocket Books.

(3) Nehru, Congress Presidential Address, 1929 (Purna Swaraj).

(4) Forbes Magazine, November 1992.

(5) Jerome Tuccilla, "Rupert Murdoch," 1989, D. I. Fine.

(6) Donald Trump, "Surviving at the Top," 1990, Random House.

(7) Brock Yates, "Enzo Ferrari," 1991, Doubleday.

(8) Randall E. Stross, "Steve Jobs and the Next Big Thing," 1993, Atheneum.

(9) Napoleon Hill, "Think and Grow Rich," 1966, Wilshire.

(10) Hugh Downs, "On Camera," 1986, Thorndike.

(11) 'Inc.' Magazine, December 1991.

(12) Diane Hailparn, "Fear No More," 1989, St. Martins.

(13) Richard D. Logan, "Alone," 1993 Stackpole Books.

CHAPTER 1 - PASSION

(1) Zig Ziglar, "Over the Top," 1994, Nashville & Lou Holtz, "Winning Every Day", 1998, Harper Business.

(2) James M. Kouzes & Z. Posner, "Credibility," 1993, Jossey-Bass.

(3) Carol Osborn, "How Would Confucius Ask for a Raise?" 1994, W. Morrow.

(4) Robert J. Ringer, "Million Dollar Habits," 1990, Wynwood Press.

(5) Harry Wulforst, "The Rocket Makers", 1990, Orion Books.

(6) Marsha Sinetar, "Developing a 21st Century Mind", 1991, Villard Books.

(7) Peter M. Sengo, "The Fifth Dimension", 1991, Doubleday.

CHAPTER TWO - PERSISTENCE

(1) Tom Peters, "Liberation Management," 1992, A. A. Knopf.
(2) Vic Braden, "Mental Tennis," 1993, Little, Brown & Co.
(3) Alan Lakein, "How to Get Control of Your Time and Life," 1993, P. H. Wyden.
(4) Zig Ziglar, "Something to Smile About", 1997, Thomas Nelson.
(5) Michael Gershman, "Getting it Right, the Second Time," 1991, Addison-Wesley Publishing.

CHAPTER THREE - ATTITUDE

(1) Bobbe Sommer, "Psycho-Cybernetics —-2000," 1993, Prentice Hall.
(2) Richard Gaylord Briley, "Are You Positive?" 1987, Acropolis.
(3) Robert L. Dilenshneider, "A Briefing for Leaders," 1992, Harper Business.
(4) Brian Tracy, "Maximum Achievement," 1993, Simon & Schuster.
(5) Bernard Haldane, "How to Make a Habit of Success," 1960, Prentice Hall.

CHAPTER FOUR - DECISIVENESS

(1) Napoleon Hill, "Think and Grow Rich," 1966, Wilshire Books.
(2) Roy Rowan, "The Intuitive Manager," 1986, Little Brown and Company.
(3) Al Ries, "Focus," 1996, Harper Business.
(4) Harry S. Dent, "Job Shock," 1995, Martin's Press.
(5) Harvey Mackay, "Shark Proof," 1993, Harper Business.
(6) William Safire & Leonard Safir, "Leadership," 1990, Simon & Schuster.
(7) John Rogers & Peter McWilliams, "Do It," 1991, Prelude Press.
(8) Barbara Sher, "Wishcraft",1983, Ballantine Books.

PART II - INTRODUCTION

(1) Melvyn Kinder, "Mastering your Moods", 1994, Simon & Schuster.
(2) Dean Hamer & Peter Copeland, "Living With Our Genes", 1998, Double Day.
(3) Keith Harary et al, "Who Do You Think You Are?", 1994, Harper San Fran.
(4) Robert Frager editor, "Who Am I?", 1994, Putnam
(5) Time Magazine, "In Search of the Real Bill Gates", Jan 13, 1997.
(6) Joel Wells, "Who Do You Think You Are?", 1989, Thomas Moore
(7) Viktor E. Frankl, "Man's Search for Meaning", 1962, Beacon Press.

CHAPTER FIVE - ONE LIFE TO LIVE

(1) Hunter Lewis, "A Question of Values," 1990, Harper and Rowe.
(2) Roberta Jean Bryant, "Stop Improving Yourself and Start Living," 1991, New World Library.

[3] Joel Garreau, "Edge City (Life on the New Frontier)," 1994, Doubleday.

[4] Priscilla Donovan and Jacquelyn Wonder, "The Forever Mind," 1994, W. Morrow and Company.

[5] Vic Braden, "Mental Tennis," 1993, Little Brown and Company.

[6] Frederick G Harmon, "The Executive Odyssey," 1989, Wiley.

[7] Richard Gaylord Briley, "Are You Positive?", 1987, Acropolis.

[8] Robert J. Kriegel, "If it Ain't Broke, Break it," 1991, Warner Books.

CHAPTER SIX - KARMIC CYCLE

[1] Ram Dass, "The Only Dance There Is", 1974, Anchor Press.

[2] Kewal K. Anand, "Indian Philosophy", 1982, Bharatia Vidia Prakasam.

[3] Parmahansa Yogananda, "Autobiography of a Yogi," 1987, SRF.

[4] Ram Dass, "Be Here Now", 1994, Lama Foundation

[5] Mary Ann Woodward, "Edgar Cayce's Story of Karma", 1971, Coward-McCann

[6] Rene Querido, "A Western Approach to Reincarnation and Karma", 1997, Anthroposophic Press.

[7] V.Hanson et al, "Karma", Rhythmic Return to Harmony, 1990, Quest Books

[8] James Redfield and Caroline Adrienne, "Celestine Philosophy, An Experimental Guide," 1995, Warner Press.

[9] Genevieve Lewis Paulson, "Reincarnation", 1997, Llewellyn Publications.

[10] Carol Osborn, "Inner Excellence," 1992, New World Library.

[11] Paul Z. Pilzer, "God Wants You To Be Rich," 1995, Simon and Schuster.

[12] James Redfield, "The Celestine Prophecy," 1993, Wheeler Publishing.

[13] Alcyone, "At the Feet of the Master", 1910, Theosophical Publishing House

[14] Jim Marrs, "Alien Agenda", 1997, Harper Collins

[15] Shirley MacLaine, "Out on a Limb," 1984, Thorndike Press.

CHAPTER SEVEN - SELF AND SPIRITUALITY

[1] Gail Sheehy, "New Passages," 1995, Random House.

[2] Deepak Chopra, "Ageless Body, Timeless Mind," 1993, Harmony Books.

[3] Michael Sullivan Trainor, "Detour", 1994, IDG Books Worldwide.

[4] Parmahansa Yoga Nanda, "Autobiography of a Yogi," 1987, SRF.

[5] Ram Dass, "The Only Dance There is," 1974, Anchor Press.

[6] Deepak Chopra, "Boundless Energy," 1995, Harmony Books.

[7] Timothy Ferris, "The Mind's Sky," 1992, Bantam.

[8] Shakti Gawain, "The Path of Transformation," 1993, Natraj Publications.

[9] David Darling, "Soul Search" 1995, Villard Books

[10] Swami Prabhupada, "Bhagvad-Gita" 1996, The Bhakti-Vedanta Book Trust

[11] Bruce Goldberg, "Soul Healing" 1997, Llewellyn Publications

[12] Nick Herbert, "Elemental Mind", 1993, Dutton Books

[13] Paul Davies, "The Fifth Miracle." 1999, Simon & Schus(14) Walter Truett Anderson, " The Future Of The Self", 1997, Putnam

(15) Frank Tipler, "The Physics of Immortality", 1994, Doubleday
(16) Francis Crick, "The Astonishing Hypothesis", 1993, Charles Scibner's Sons
(17) Michael J. Denton, "Nature's Destiny", 1998, The Free Press
(18) Jeremy Rifkin, "The Biotech Century", 1998, Jeremy P. Tarcher
(19) Winifred Gallagher, "Working on God", 1999, Random Press
(20) Charles Lindholm, "Charisma", 1990, Blackwell
(21) Deepak Chopra, "Unconditional Life", 1991, Bantam Books

PART III - INTRODUCTION

(1) Oliver North, "Under Fire," 1991, Harper Collins.
(2) Stephen R. Covey et al, "First Things First," 1994, Covey Leadership Center.
(3) Dr. Viktor Frankl, "Man's Search for Meaning," 1962, Beacon Press.
(4) Betty Friedan, "The Fountain of Age," 1994, Simon and Schuster.
(5) Wayne W. Dyer, "Real Magic", 1992, Harper Collins
(6) Marsha Sinetar, "Do What You Have, the Money Will Follow," 1987, Dell
(7) Michael Murphy, "The Future of the Body", 1992, Jeremy P. Tarcher
(8) Sian Griffith, "Predictions", 1999, Oxford university Press.
(9) Stuart H. Walker, "Winning (The Psychology of Competition)," 1980, Norton
(10) Stan Davis and Bill Davidson, "20-20 Vision," 1991, Simon and Schuster.
(11) Napoleon Hill, "Think and Grow Rich," 1966, Wilshire Books.
(12) Edward O-Wilson, "Consilience", 1998, Alfred A. Knopf.

CHAPTER EIGHT - JUST BE YOURSELF

(1) Steven Lee Weinberg, "Ramtha," 1986, Sovereignty Incorporated.
(2) Marsha Sinetar, "Developing a 21st. Century Mind," 1991, Willard Books.
(3) Barbara Sher, "I Could Do Anything, If Only I Knew What It Was," 1994, Delaconte Press.
(4) Brian Tracy, "Maximum Achievement," 1993, Simon and Schuster.

CHAPTER NINE - TRUST YOUR INTUITION

(1) Hunter Lewis, "A Question of Values," 1990 Harper and Rowe.
(2) Patricia Einstein, "Intuition", 1997, Element.
(3) Michael Sullivan Trainor, "Detour (The Truth About Information Highway)1994, IDG Books Worldwide.
(4) Belleruth Naparstek, "Your Sixth Sense", 1997, Harper, San Fran.
(5) Richard Gillet, "Change Your Mind, Change Your World", 1992, Putnam
(6) Dr. Alan Loy McGinnis, "The Power of Optimism," 1990, Harper and Rowe.
(7) Jeff Zaleski, "The Soul of Cyberspace", 1997, Harper Edge.
(8) Maxwell Maltz, "Psycho-Cybernetics," 1960, Simon and Schuster.
(9) James Redfield, "The Celestine Prophecy, (An Adventure)," 1993, Wheeler Publishing.
(10) Roy Rowan, "The Intuitive Manager" 1986, Little Brown & Co.

[11] Paul Davies, "The Mind of God", 1992, Simon & Schuster.

[12] Auren Uris, "The Executive Deskbook" 1988, Van Nostrand Reinhold Co.

[13] Brian Tracy, "Maximum Achievement" 1993, Simon & Schuster

CHAPTER TEN - GO WITH THE FLOW

[1] Robert Fulgham, "From Beginning to End (The Rituals of our Lives)," 1995, Willard Books.

[2] Deepak Chopra, "The Way of the Wizard," 1995, Harmony Books.

[3] Priscilla Donovan and Jacquelyn Wonder, "The Forever Mind," 1994, W. Morrow and Company.

[4] Gail Sheehy, "New Passages," 1995, Random House.

[5] Richard Nelson Bollas, "What Color is Your Parachute?", 1990, Ten Speed Press.

[6] Roberta Jean Bryant, "Stop Improving Yourself and Start Living," 1991, New World Library.

[7] Deepak Chopra, "Ageless Body, Timeless Mind," 1993, Harmony Books.

[8] James Redfield, "The Celestine Prophecy," 1993, Wheeler Publishing.

[9] Shakti Gawain, "Path of Transformation," 1993, Natraj Publications.

[10] Nicholas Rescher, "Luck", 1995, Harper Collins

[11] Carol Osborn, "How Would Confucius Ask for a Raise?", 1994, W. Morrow

[12] Kirk Douglas, "The Perfect Part", Dec 1997, Readers Digest.

APPENDIX:

SOME PRACTICAL STEPS TO NURTURE BODY, MIND, AND SOUL.

1: BREATHING

There is a close relationship between the breath and body's subtle energies. Breathing is the vehicle that directs mind to the object of our concentration. Breath not only gives life, it also creates a bridge between the subconscious and conscious. Ninety percent of our energy should come from breathing, yet most people use only ten percent of their full breathing capacity. Deep breathing increases the blood's oxygen level. Clearing the opening in the nostrils using yoga exercise helps link the inner channels with the infinite source of energy. Some gurus believe that the awareness of our breath is the key to enlightenment.

When you settle into a natural rhythm of breathing, it will come from the lower abdomen. Belly-breathing using the abdominal muscles can be quite powerful in deepening your concentration. Expand your belly (not your chest) when you inhale, increasing the amount of air available to your lungs and body. Pull your belly in when you exhale, causing the diaphragm to push the air out of your lungs. Take a deep breath, hold it for five seconds, and then slowly blow it out. Repeat this about ten times while counting each breath cycle. Start all over again if you make a mistake in counting. The principle involved is that when you are totally focused on counting your breath, there is no distraction of thought. Years of practice allows mindfulness to develop and ultimately merge with the Whole.

2: EXERCISE

Brisk walking primes the pump physically and mentally. The blood begins to circulate through every part of the body, surging into the cells and gently washing away the waste they no longer need. In addition to burning calories and revving metabolism, perspiration-prompting exercise heightens the effect of a brain chemical called 'dopamine' which produces sensation of satisfaction.

Maintaining a schedule of activity that can burn upto 2,000 calories/ week for an average person of about 150 pounds weight increases the level of cardiovascular fitness. Depending upon your specific situation, you can, for example, pick any of the following options to stay healthy:

Activity	Calories burned/hour
Golf (walk, carry bags)	345
Tennis (single)	435
Badminton	390
Lawn Mowing (Push type)	300
Gardening	300
Jogging (6mph)	600
Walking (3.5mph)	400
Walking (2.0—2.5mph)	300

Thirty minutes of brisk walking each day can often yield the same benefit as a far more demanding regimen.

3: FOOD

Chemicals in our body form a dynamic information network, linking mind and body. Eating healthy food containing a rainbow of colors generates a combination of antioxidants, phytochemicals and fibers that work together to confer health benefits.

Generally, foods that leave acid waste in our body are heavy, overcooked, overprocessed, and sweet, such as, meat, flours, pasteries, alcohol, coffee, and the sweeter fruits. Alkaline foods are greener, fresher, and more alive, such as fresh vegetables and their juices, leafy greens, sprouts, and fruits. Alkaline residues can be quickly extracted from our bodies with little energy. However, if these waste products are acids, thay are very hard for the blood and lymph systems to eliminate. They get stored in our organs and tissues as solids, ready to be attacked by microbes of some sort or another, thus causing disease.

At the conclusion of a meal, our stomach should be half-full of food, one-quarter full of water, and one-quarter full of air. Drink eight glasses of unchlorinated water every day. Avoid consuming white sugar as it changes the profile of peptides released from the pancreas which result in fat-storing mode.

4: FASTING

Fasting is a traditional spiritual practice that purifies the body and strengthens the mind by requiring you to resist the overwhelming compulsion to eat. While fasting, your body clears itself of toxins. Controlled fasting is a quick and dramatic method of restoring damaged bodily functions which. in turn, produce pronounced emotional and psycho-spiritual benefits.

During fasting, none of the energy in our body has to go into digestion. It's all channeled into healing. Fasting cleanses the body and detoxifies it of medications, drugs, pollutants, and junk foods. When we fast, our body repairs and regenerates diseased or injured organs. It strives to achieve balance.

5: PRAYER AND MEDITATION

Prayer and meditation teach us to focus and quiet our minds. They encourage mindful discipline, consistency, and repetition. It is likely that daily prayer and meditation solidify new neural circuits. Prolonged meditation reveals distinct changes in brain activity as the mind goes through a meditative state. Using sophisticated brain-imaging techniques, medical scientists have observed that during prayer and meditation, there is a change in blood flow in particular regions of the brain leading to lower blood pressure, slower heart-rate, decreased anxiety and enhanced sense of being. Specifically, it is believed, that the activity decreases in the parts of the brain involved in generating a sense of three-dimensional orientation in space. Losing one's sense of physical place could account for the spiritual feeling of transcendence, beyond space and time.

To calm your mind and break your identification with your own thoughts is to achieve inner freedom. Thought and action are two separate forms of consciousness, two separate lives we lead. Our completeness as human beings begins when the mind and body are in harmony, and one does not interfere with the other. That requires liberation of the mind. Some 'mantras' (Chantings) resonate within in such a way as to open one of your 'chakras' (energy-centers). My favourite mantra is 'Om Tat Sat' (God is the Absolute truth). By repeating a mantra, you are continually meeting and merging into perfection. And that, of course, needs years of dedicated practice.

ABOUT THE AUTHOR

Born in India, Pritam migrated to the United States in 1973. He holds a master's degree in Chemistry and a Ph.D. in Materials Science. He has authored over thirty articles of topical interest published in international journals.

Having worked with major U.S. Corporations in technical and management positions, Pritam is presently a consultant and free-lance writer. His poem, 'Karma' was published in '2000 Anthology' by the International Library of Poetry. The dissertation, 'Can You Be What You Want To Be?' is based upon many years of his personal research and exploration of various approaches to being who one wants to be.

Pritam is well-traveled. His hobbies include playing bridge, tennis, and jogging. He now lives in Cincinnati, Ohio, with his wife Saroj and children.

Printed in the United States
39113LVS00004B/199-201